THE

INSIGHT-DRIV

LEADE

JENNY **DEARBORN** KELLY **RIDER**

THE
INSIGHT-DRIVEN
LEADER

HOW HIGH-PERFORMING
COMPANIES ARE USING ANALYTICS
TO UNLOCK BUSINESS VALUE

WILEY

Published by John Wiley & Sons, Inc., Hoboken, New Jersey.
Published simultaneously in Canada.

For general information on our other products and services or for technical support, please contact our Customer Care Department within the United States at (800) 762-2974, outside the United States at (317) 572-3993 or fax (317) 572-4002.

Wiley also publishes its books in a variety of electronic formats. Some content that appears in print may not be available in electronic formats. For more information about Wiley products, visit our website at www.wiley.com.

Library of Congress Cataloging-in-Publication Data is Available:

ISBN: 978-1-394-30888-0 (cloth)
ISBN: 978-1-394-30889-7 (ePub)
ISBN: 978-1-394-30890-3 (ePDF)

Cover Design: Paul McCarthy
Cover Image: © Getty Images | Sergey Ryumin
SKY10104358_042525

For my parents, for their unconditional love and support.
For my boys, who inspire me daily.

– Kelly

The best part about working hard is that it's so fun to be part of a great team. This is for everyone—across the world, in the past 30+ years, from different companies—that I've met at work and is now an indispensable part of my life. My friends, you are too many to list, I love you. Of course, I couldn't do this without the support of my husband and our kids. A thousand thanks.

– Jenny

Contents

Acknowledgments

THANKFUL FOR THE amazing team who supported this project:

- **Deb Arnold**—Project Manager. Jenny never saw a tangent she didn't like, but you kept us on task, gave us tough love, demanded excellence, and never gave up on us. Our undying gratitude, respect, and love. Need a content extractor and logic checker? Contact www.debarnoldink.com.
- **Hallie Bregman**—Technical Expert. Thank you for your clarity of purpose and No-BS style.
- **Lori Fraser**—Case Study Re-Writer. Thank you for taking our wonderfully long narratives and making them structured and succinct.
- **Joel Freedman**—Research Consultant. Thanks for dotting every I and crossing every T!
- **Cameron Hunt**—Research Intern. Thanks Cam, we appreciate all you did for us!
- **Filipe Muffoletto**—Graphics. The GGGOAT! Greatest Graphics Guy of all time!

This book was informed in part from conversations with more than 100 Workforce Analytics practitioners, senior HR professionals, business executives, consultants, academics, researchers, and thought leaders (please *see* Appendix). We are grateful for their wisdom, perspectives, stories, and the great gift of their time.

In addition, we are thankful for the hundreds of experts and leaders we interviewed unofficially, the executives globally who completed our research survey, and the many more HR practitioners and business leaders with whom we test-drove some of the concepts and models for the book.

Deep thanks as well to **Karie Willyerd**, **Steve Hunt,** and **David Swanson** for reviewing our work and giving thoughtful feedback. Our book is better thanks to your wisdom (and thanks to all we learned from you long before this book was even an idea).

Finally, we are deeply indebted to a few individuals for their inspiration. **John Boudreau**, your wise scholarship on all things HR + People + Leadership has been instrumental in the success of our careers. Thank you. **Max Blumberg**, thank you for your generous contributions of time and thought leadership to our endeavors. **Ram Charan**, your work has been a constant north star of thought leadership. From *Execution* to *The Leadership Pipeline* to *Blowing Up HR*—thank you for challenging us.

Foreword
By John Boudreau

YOU'VE STARTED READING *The Insight-Driven Leader*. Congratulations! If you had any doubt that the time is right for you, your leadership team, and your entire organization to start using Workforce Insights to make better decisions about your talent and organization, this book will dispel those doubts. It will motivate you to shift your thinking about your workforce, the partnership between HR and other leadership functions, and the role of leaders outside HR in improving your ability to harness the untapped potential of the workforce to better achieve your goals.

For me, reading this book stimulated my thinking and recollection of some pivotal experiences in my career, and some principles that I'd like to highlight as you read the book.

For 40 years, I had the privilege to teach at Cornell University's School of Industrial and Labor Relations and the University of Southern California's Marshall School of Business. I often introduced my classes on HR Analytics and Competitive Advantage Through People with this exercise: I would write the header, "Human Resources" over one column on the whiteboard, and then "Financial Resources" over a second column. I asked the students to call out the words associated with each column. Inevitably, the words beneath "Human Resources" were things like "compliance," "administrative," "cost center," "soft," "unpredictable," etc.; and the words beneath "Financial Resources" were things like "strategic," "analytical," "rigorous," etc. To be sure, in each class there were those who also paired "Human Resources" with words like "essential," "impactful," etc., but this was far rarer for "Human Resources" than "Financial Resources."

Then, I would ask the students to recall the lessons from their courses in Competitive Strategy, about the characteristics of resources that are deemed "strategic" according to theories such as the Resource-Based view of organizations. Students were quick to list the four standard characteristics of strategic resources:

1. **VALUABLE** resources aid in improving the organization's effectiveness and efficiency while neutralizing the opportunities and threats of competitors.
2. **RARE** resources are those held by few or no other competitors.
3. **DIFFICULT-TO-IMITATE** resources often involve legally protected intellectual property such as trademarks, patents, or copyrights. Other difficult-to-imitate resources, such as brand names, usually need time to develop fully.
4. **NONSUBSTITUTABLE** when the resource combinations of other firms cannot duplicate the strategy provided by the resource bundle of a particular firm.

With that in mind, I asked the students to consider how Financial and Human Resources would stack up against these characteristics. Students realized that while decisions about Financial Resources were certainly Valuable, the Financial Resources were less Rare, Difficult-to-Imitate, and Non-substitutable. I would then ask the students, "If you look ahead to your career as a leader, do you think you will create more strategic value through your decisions about money or through your decisions about people, talent, teams, and how they are organized?" The students realized that the science of people decisions was obscure to most business leaders, the talent resources of the organization are often hard to understand—let alone to imitate—and the people in organizations often act in combinations that make their collective capability difficult to substitute with other assets. They felt that there was a great "mystery" about how to engage, develop, motivate, acquire, and retain people, and how to build collective organizational elements such as culture and teams. Indeed, it was precisely that "mystery" that made decisions about human resources so potentially valuable and strategic.

Jenny Dearborn and Kelly Rider will masterfully demonstrate through their many frameworks and examples how Workforce Analytics can provide Workforce Insights that pierce the veil of mystery about how talent decisions and their outcomes affect organizational success. This will motivate you to pursue better analytics and insights. That pursuit is important, but it must be in the context of two fundamental ideas that underlie the Dearborn and Rider book, and may be less obvious than the vivid examples of analytics and insights. I first wrote about these two principles with my colleague, Pete Ramstad, about 20 years ago, and featured them in our 2007 book, *Beyond HR*. They are fundamental to many subsequent books and articles with colleagues such as Ravin Jesuthasan, Wayne Cascio, Alexis Fink, Ian Ziskin, Alec Levenson, and Edward Lawler III.

The two principles are as follows.

First, the most important decisions for achieving value through talent and organization do not occur within the HR function, but with the organization leaders, employees, executives, Board, and investors that are *outside the HR function*. So, leaders outside the HR function must be held accountable for their decisions about talent and organization, just as they are for their decisions about resources such as money, technology, and customers. Line leaders should report the people outcomes (engagement, recruitment, turnover/ retention, development, performance, etc.) of their units in the same way that they report their financial results, as a regular part of their quarterly or other regular unit reviews. Dearborn and Rider offer many examples of such reporting. Leaders are not permitted to say, "I don't know why I'm hemorrhaging cash, I just do what Finance tells me to do." Yet, all too often, those same leaders are allowed to say, "I have no idea why my unit can't attract and retain people, I just do what HR tells me." The talent-related outcomes of the unit then become "HR's problem."

Second, HR must shift its concept of its value from a sole focus on how the HR organization functions, delivers its services, and insures compliance, to embrace the value proposition of *teaching* key decision-makers how to use rigorous mental models and logical frameworks in their decisions about talent and organization. Too often, leaders rely upon naïve and simplistic mental models about things like motivation, development, attraction, retention, culture, and teams. We can't hold leaders accountable for good decisions unless those leaders hold HR accountable for teaching them the frameworks needed for great people decisions. As you read Dearborn and Rider's vivid comparisons between HR and Finance that illustrate how Workforce Analytics can aspire to the power of financial analytics, keep in mind how these comparisons also offer templates for enhancing non-HR leader decisions about talent.

I know you will enjoy and be deeply moved by this book!

Preface

Who This Book Is For

This book is for CEOs, business leaders, and those who aspire to unlock the full potential of their workforce data and HR organization. If you're a leader who has dismissed HR as "soft" or overlooked its strategic importance, this book will challenge your assumptions. For CHROs, it's a call to action to embrace business-first thinking, build stronger relationships with CEOs, and use data-driven storytelling to lead change.

How It Came to Be

In 2015, I published *Data Driven*, a fictionalized account of my experience at SuccessFactors, where we achieved remarkable improvements in sales productivity through the power of data. Later, I co-wrote *The Data Driven Leader* with David Swanson in 2017, capturing our journey to apply those same principles to leadership productivity at SAP. The lessons we learned were clear: data-driven insights can unlock untapped potential across an organization. But something was missing.

As I moved deeper into the world of HR leadership, I noticed a troubling pattern: business leaders often dismissed or overlooked the potential of HR. While every other function—sales, marketing, operations—was held accountable to metrics and outcomes, HR was largely exempt from this scrutiny. This indifference was both bewildering and infuriating. Why didn't leaders demand more from HR, the function responsible for hiring, developing, and retaining the very people who drive every aspect of the business?

Why I'm Passionate About This Topic

I know in my bones that people are the most important asset in any company, and HR—when done well—is the most foundational function supporting them. But here's the problem: too many CEOs don't understand HR's value, don't know what great HR looks like, and inadvertently undermine their CHROs. When this misalignment happens, even the most talented CHROs are driven away, leaving organizations with a critical leadership void.

The HR function at many companies is broken—but it's fixable. I've seen it done. With the right leadership, a growth mindset, and a commitment to first principles thinking, HR can become a driving force for business success. This book aims to demystify that process and provide a road map for CEOs and CHROs to build a strategic partnership that delivers results.

A huge THANK YOU to Kelly Rider who accepted my challenge to work with me on this research and book process. Kelly is the perfect balance of amazing strategic thinker and practical doer, she's a natural researcher, writer, deeply curious, and an execution machine. I'm grateful she agreed to be my co-author. [Note from Kelly: Thank you, Jenny, for inviting me on this journey. It was an honor to be part of this experience.]

What You'll Learn

There are countless resources on Workforce Analytics (sometimes called people analytics), but most are written for HR professionals who are already believers. This book takes a different approach. It's written specifically for business leaders—especially CEOs—who may not yet understand the transformative power of HR data to help uncover Workforce Insights (WFI). Through real-world insights and practical strategies, you'll discover how aligning with your CHRO and leveraging WFA can unlock not only WFI but also growth, innovation, and a thriving workforce.

A Call to Action

The insights in this book come from years of experience as a business-first, HR-second leader who has seen what works—and what doesn't—in organizations big and small. If you're ready to break down silos, rethink old assumptions, and build a data-driven, people-first culture, then let's get started. Together, we can transform HR from a misunderstood function into the strategic engine it's meant to be.

Jenny Dearborn and Kelly Rider

Introduction

Water, water, every where,
Nor any drop to drink.[1]

The thirsty sailors stranded on a windless sea in this 1834 poem by Samuel Tayler Coleridge bemoan their fate, surrounded by an ocean of salty water. If you're a business leader, you are undoubtedly in a predicament akin to "The Rime of the Ancient Mariner" (hopefully minus the fever dream-like magical realism): surrounded by data— data *everywhere*.

Operational data, sales data, customer data, employee data, and on and on. But at most companies, that data is as useless as vast sea water to beleaguered sailors, unless you can extract insights from it.

It's no easy task. For years, companies have declared themselves "data-driven" with much fanfare but little to show for it. So, *insight-driven*? All the harder. But can you really afford not to try?

Businesses worldwide face storms of increased competition, economic uncertainty, rapid technological developments, severe talent shortages, global instability, cybersecurity threats, and complexities from social and political shifts. And a "workforce" doesn't even mean what it used to: now employees, gig workers, outsourced labor, robots, and AI bots, with all the attendant potential for extraordinary advancement by getting it right or crushing value destruction from getting it wrong. You need every possible tool at your disposal to understand how your organization functions—and more importantly, where, when, and why it *fails* to function. And you need it RIGHT NOW.

Fortunately, a mere 200 years after Coleridge penned his magnum opus, technology is poised to make transforming data into insights a daily reality. Artificial intelligence, especially Generative Artificial Intelligence (GenAI), is transforming not just work but also data and analytics, making it easier (even for those with little data science training), more affordable, and more realistic than ever to generate **Workforce Insights (WFI)**, the powerful revelations that come from **Workforce Analytics (WFA)**: combining, studying, and maximizing the value of data about your workforce (human+machine) and data about your business.

Becoming Insight-Driven

Workforce Analytics is like having the cheat codes to understand what makes your business tick. Imagine spotting exactly why some teams are firing on all cylinders while others lag. Or uncovering which behaviors lead to high sales, customer loyalty, or top-notch service. Businesses are using Workforce Insights right now to solve real problems—from slumping sales to digital transformations.

In fact, research published in November 2024 by The Josh Bersin Company, a highly respected source of human capital management insights, found that companies excelling at Workforce Analytics[i] are more likely to experience a range of benefits (*see* Figure I.1). These include exceeding financial targets (3 times), delighting customers (3 times), and effectively adapting to change (9 times).

---

[i]The study's term is "systemic business analytics," a different name for the same game-changing approach.

Companies that excel at systemic business analytics are:

3x
more likely
to exceed
financial
targets

8x
more likely
to have high
workforce
productivity

4x
more likely
to engage
& retain
employees

9x
more likely
to adapt
well to
change

3x
more likely
to delight
customers

8x
more likely
to be highly
diverse & inclusive

7x
more likely
to innovate
effectively

**Business
Outcomes**

**People
Outcomes**

**Innovation
Outcomes**

Figure I.1   The Impact of Systemic Business Analytics

Source: Josh Bersin, Stella Ioannidou, and Kathi Enderes, "The Definitive Guide to People Analytics: The Journey to Systemic Business Analytics," 2024, 5, https:// joshbersin.com/definitive-guide-to-people-analytics/. Reproduced with permission from Josh Bersin Company.

The Albatross

Yes, we're going to carry the metaphor a bit further, because honestly, it's pretty perfect. In Coleridge's tale, the eponymous Mariner is burdened by an enormous white bird he's carrying around his neck, having shot it for no good reason (only the start of his troubles). While it's unlikely that you've shot an albatross recently, the imagery is useful. Think of that fetid fowl as the untapped potential of your data becoming a drag on your productivity, innovation, highest-visibility project, and competitive advantage. Or your own inability to make sense of the staggering quantities of data within your remit (you'd be in good company on that front). Whatever the case, Workforce Insights is powerful enough to free you from those burdens.

There's just one catch. Workforce Analytics requires workforce data from, and deep partnership with, Human Resources. Yes, HR—the function so many love to hate.

Are We Any Smarter?

In July 2015, *Harvard Business Review*'s cover boldly declared, "It's Time to Blow Up HR and Build Something New." The articles inside laid out a revolutionary vision for HR, courtesy of thought leaders like Ram Charan, John Boudreau, and Peter Cappelli. They presented clear, brilliant ideas on how to evolve HR from process-focused to driving measurable business outcomes.[2]

Yet here we are, exactly 10 years later, still grappling with many of the same issues. The problem wasn't the vision; it was the follow-through on the part of business leaders. That's what we hope to change with this modest volume. Because an evolved, insight-driven HR function isn't a nice-to-have anymore. If you want the competitive advantages of Workforce Analytics and AI, the time for hesitation has passed.

It's (Mostly) Not HR's Fault

If you're a business leader—especially a CEO—and something that's not working optimally at your company never gets fixed, wouldn't that be . . . on you?

Sure, some of HR's bad rap is merited. HR *can* be slow and out of touch, too focused on operations and rules. That's not good for business—yours. But some of HR's baggage just comes with the territory. The function has many unenviable roles—interpersonal relations referee and policy enforcer are just two. And HR impacts every employee in ways that no other function does, including extremely sensitive issues like hiring, firing, and pay. It's messy. And often really not fun.

And yet, is an entire field truly doomed to *never* grow into its potential? With business leaders paying the ultimate price in the form of problems that go unsolved, productivity that remains weak, workers that are un-engaged, paying sky-high costs to rehire and retrain employees headed for greener pastures, and lost opportunities to innovate and gain (or keep) a competitive edge?

We've Seen This Movie Before

So, what if your HR department was . . . great? What if it was staffed with strategic, efficient, business-minded, analytical problem-solvers? Professionals who reliably helped you maximize productivity and create the conditions (operational and cultural) where employees would go the extra mile to achieve your most important goals?

It's not so crazy a notion, even if many business leaders have never seen great HR in action. Once upon a time, Finance was a bunch of paper-pushers focused on bookkeeping. IT was the nerds who kept the computers running. Marketing printed ads and threw parties. These functions all grew into strategic powerhouses because shifting realities meant companies couldn't stay competitive otherwise. And they became high-performing when leaders saw it was in their own best interest to make it happen: they raised expectations and accountability, elevated those functions' leaders to the C-suite and made them active participants in Board of Directors meetings, aligned their strategies, drove cross-functional collaboration, and invested in the right people and technology.

HR is on the brink of that same transformation, especially now that automation is removing so much of the function's administrative load. We wrote this book to show how you can help HR evolve into an essential value creator, too. This isn't about doing HR a favor—it's about making sure you have the strategic support you need. If you want HR to deliver insights that align with your goals, you've got to let them do more than process paperwork. The highest performing companies already have top-notch HR functions (you'll read about them in case studies and through descriptions of "next-generation" HR teams). So why not you, too?

And the time is RIGHT NOW: as AI and automation free HR professionals from operational tasks and enable them to embrace advanced analytics, they can become the strategic partners you need them to be. But they can't do it alone.

Like it or not, if you want to become an insight-driven leader imbued with superpowers by Workforce Insights, we know a two-way street you can take to get there. HR transformation happens when leaders like you see HR as an asset, not an afterthought. The companies that get this are miles ahead. This book will show you how to unleash HR's potential and leverage it as the strategic asset it truly can be.

What's Ahead?

This book is designed to inform, inspire, and motivate you to become a true insight-driven leader (who also happens to make HR history). Each of the five sections concludes with key takeaways:

- **Section 1 – Change What You Measure, Transform What You Can Manage:** Changing how you think about metrics, analytics, and insights to transform what you can manage, and gain guidance on exactly how to start expecting more from HR.
- **Section 2 – Enabling Workforce Analytics:** Start positioning WFA to take hold at your company by understanding its components and the coordination, governance, and professionalization required to make it a reality. And if you ever wondered how human-machine collaboration gets measured, you'll have your answers.
- **Section 3 – Moving the Goalpost:** Increase your expectations of HR by appreciating how other functions have made the journey to a high performing strategic partner, and by reading about what good HR (outstanding, actually) can look like. Plus, some sojourning down that two-way street with KPIs in tow.
- **Section 4 – Become Truly Insight-Driven:** Did we mention that to make WFI your new BFF, you'll also want to help your entire company become insight-driven? You will. It includes upleveling HR. And it's hard. You'll need to have guts and patience. But the payoff is astonishing.
- **Section 5 – Higher Math—Workforce Analytics at the C-level:** Truly evolving HR will require executive authority and commitment, including ensuring alignment between the CEO and the head of HR and giving that leader a seat at the elusive

strategic table. If you're not a CEO but don't want to remain a downcast sailor staring across the horizon at an ocean of water you can't drink, this section will show you how you can help things along.

Along the way, you'll read plenty of case studies and cautionary tales, and gain wisdom and insights from our more than 100 interviewees and the results of our CEO/CHRO survey. Also awaiting you is a boatload of secondary research, revealing statistics, pithy quotes, and hopefully enough humor and gentle poking to make you forget you're reading a business book about data and HR.

Invitation to Redemption

Back to our poem. The Mariner's redemption begins when he acknowledges the beauty and value of the natural world. Realizing the strategic value of your workforce and business data and HR's potential to drive your success can be your turning point, when you deftly shift from being burdened by data, data everywhere to thriving because of it.

Case Studies

THROUGHOUT THE BOOK, we have provided stories to help inspire you to meaningful action and avoid serious pitfalls. Most have Workforce Insights at their core. They come from our interviews as well as secondary research. We hope you find them enlightening and memorable, but most of all we hope they spur you to act.

Title	Industry	Challenge	Location
Forecasting Retention: How Experian Data Secured Its Talent	Information Services	Retention	Section 1, Commit to Insights, Not Metrics (p. 14)
No More Guesswork: Forecasting a Future of Workforce Stability	Healthcare	Profitability	Section 1, Embrace Workforce Insights (p. 22)
Revving Up Sales: How Workforce Analytics Drove the 24-Hour Follow-Up Advantage	Automotive	Sales	Section 1, Embrace Workforce Insights (p. 27)

Title	Industry	Challenge	Location
Bridging the Experience Gap to Deliver on a High-Stakes Project	Technology	Product Development	Section 1, Embrace Workforce Insights (p. 29)
Penny Wise, Pound Foolish: Save Money by Asking HR	Financial Services	Restructuring	Section 1, Let HR (Get Better) at Help(ing) You (p. 40)
Acting on Insights: One Sales Executive's Insistence on Success	Shipping and Mailing	Business Transformation	Section 1, Act on the Insights (p. 44)
The High Price of Data Privacy without Partnership	Technology	Digital Transformation	Section 2, Support Data Integration (p. 56)
Integrating for Impact: How Data-Driven Insights Transformed Sales Success	Technology	Sales	Section 2, Support Data Integration (p. 57)
Unpacking the Guest Experience: How Software and Regulations Undermined Loyalty	Hospitality	Customer Loyalty	Section 3, Take Your Preference (p. 107)
The Innovation Illusion: A CEO's Pricey Pitfall	Hospitality	Leadership	Section 3, Take Your Preference (p. 107)
Engineering Alone Can't Steer the Ship: The Human Solution to Maritime Risks	Maritime Shipping	Safety	Section 3, Take Your Preference (p. 110)
Data vs. Preference: A Location Strategy Gone Wrong	Technology	Office Expansion	Section 3, Take Your Preference (p. 111)

Title	Industry	Challenge	Location
Overcoming a Resistant Culture to Achieve Business Transformation	Technology	Business Transformation	Section 4, Making Culture Your #1 Strategic Asset (p. 126)
IBM: Achieve More with AI-Driven Talent Strategies	Technology	Retention	Section 4, Upleveling HR (p. 135)
Striking Oil: How Digging into Data Uncovered the Real Safety Issue	Oil and Gas	Safety	Section 4, Upleveling HR (p. 142)
Salesforce: Embedding a Culture of Security and Trust	Technology	Cybersecurity	Section 4, Creating Your Insight-Driven Culture (p. 147)
Beyond the Dashboard at Protective Life: A CEO's Data-Driven Moment	Insurance	Insight-Driven Culture	Section 4, Creating Your Insight-Driven Culture (p. 149)
Lloyds Banking Group: Modeling Data Culture Change	Financial Services	Insight-Driven Culture	Section 4, Creating Your Insight-Driven Culture (p. 159)
Vision vs. Reality: Lessons from a Stalled Transformation	Technology	CEO/CHRO Alignment	Section 5, CEO: Be a True Partner, Get a True Partner (p. 180)
The Powerful CEO/CHRO Partnership That Helped Transform Microsoft	Technology	CEO/CHRO Alignment	Section 5, CEO: Be a True Partner, Get a True Partner (p. 181)

SECTION

1

Change What You Measure, Transform What You Can Manage

As THE SAYING goes, you can't manage what you can't measure. There's no better sentiment to accompany you as you launch into the book. After all, like charity, change begins at home (or perhaps your home office).

So much of what you'll read in these pages is about mindset shifts: for you, other business leaders, HR professionals. Evolving one's thinking is the key first step to transforming one's actions. We're starting with our attitudes toward numbers.

Numbers on their own have little meaning. Or value. That's true whether it's one number on a page, tens of thousands on a massive spreadsheet, or gigs of data in the cloud.

The meaning comes from the *stories* those numbers tell. The *mysteries* one can unravel with them. The incredible satisfaction of figuring out WHAT in the devil is going on with your most important project. That's what we're after: combining data about your workforce with data about your business and deeply exploring them through the mechanics of **Workforce Analytics (WFA)** to yield **Workforce Insights (WFI)**.

1

You'll learn things you never could before: why things are happening, or not happening, in your business and what you can do about it. You will, quite literally, transform what you can manage.

It begins with thinking differently about every number you see. Soon enough, you'll do it automatically. And then the magic will really begin. Let's dive in.

A Note on Language: We're taking a bit of a different approach to concepts you may read about. Instead of the more common People Analytics, we've chosen Workforce Analytics, as today's workforce, which encompasses human-machine collaboration (HMC), is broader than just people. We know, though, that in general, the intent of the term is the same. Also, we use "insight-driven" as we feel it emphasizes, advances, and makes explicit the aspiration behind the customary term, "data-driven": seeking out information to broaden understanding and make better decisions. Research and stories we cite mentioning People Analytics and data-driven initiatives and concepts, therefore, align with our definitions and meaning.

1.1 Commit to Insights, Not Metrics

As a business leader, a key item on your WFA transformation to-do list is moving your focus away from just numbers and toward insights. Not only you, of course. HR, too.

HR has traditionally been asked to report operational data versus evaluate business outcomes. And many (if not most) stakeholders, maybe even you, have typically nodded and gone on with their day. These same executives also tend to accept standalone numbers on critical metrics like engagement and retention, not expecting context or explanation as they would from Finance, Operations or, frankly, any other business unit. When it comes to HR data, leaders somehow do not ask colleagues to reveal trends, flag risks, or offer a deeper understanding of the factors impacting the workforce.

These often deeply engrained habits—both among the givers and receivers of HR data—can and must be unlearned, with your support. To help you achieve your goals, HR must change what it measures and why, and how it uses data to reveal the general and specific health markers of the corporate organism. To do so, they will need to integrate HR data with operational and financial data from across the company to create a holistic view of organizational performance (discussed further in the pages ahead). You can and must help create the conditions for that to happen, starting with your own metrics mindset.

Stop Looking Only in the Rear-View Mirror

Basic operational data tells simple stories: what happened. It looks in the rear-view mirror and reports the facts. Yet looking *only* at WHAT happened and not WHY? or NOW WHAT? will do very little to help you analyze or accomplish your goals. Without ALSO keeping your eyes on the road to navigate to where you want to go, you won't get far.

All too common in HR, rear-view mirror metrics wouldn't be allowed from any other function. This is just one way that business leaders hold HR back: they simply don't ask for much, especially when it comes to data. As a result, HR professionals remain in reactive mode, versus proactively seeking to measure efficiency, effectiveness, and impact—and to find ways to improve them all.

As Jenny shared in her book *The Data Driven Leader: A Powerful Approach to Delivering Measurable Business Impact Through People Analytics* (*see* Figure 1.1):

> Too much HR reporting uses only *descriptive analytics*, which capture what has happened: number of people hired, time to fill requisitions, and employee engagement scores are all examples of these "rear view mirror" metrics. We need to move toward diagnosing the "why" behind these metrics, using *diagnostic analytics*, or, in the case of *predictive analytics*, what might happen. Once we quantify these metrics, we can act, guided by *prescriptive analytics*.
>
> Moving from simple reports to predicting the future is a crucial journey we all must take, and the time to start is now."[1]

That book was published in 2017. Years after, the time to start is somehow still now.

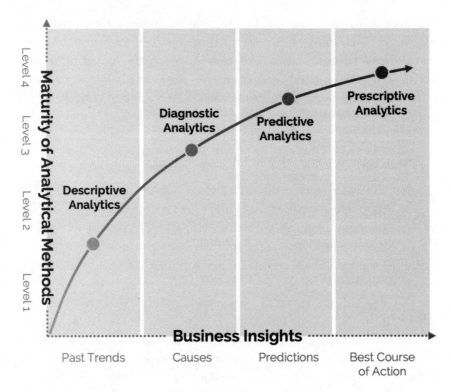

Figure 1.1   Four Stages of Analytics

Source: Jenny Dearborn and David Swanson, *The Data Driven Leader: A Powerful Approach to Delivering Measurable Business Impact Through People Analytics* (Hoboken, NJ: Wiley, 2018), 75. Reproduced with permission.

To briefly link Figure 1.1 with what you care about as a business leader, predictive analytics can, for example, help you identify the job candidates most likely to succeed in their role. Wouldn't THAT be nice?

The best example of predictive work I've seen was at Teach For America, where they developed a predictive model to assess candidates for their teacher corps. They measured academic achievement and persistence, among other factors, to predict success in the classroom.

—Brandon Sammut, Chief People Officer, Zapier

Business leaders and especially CEOs: ask for more. Convey that HR must separate quantifying administrative tasks from capturing insights about strategic impact.

And while we're on the subject of stages of analytics, a fifth level is coming into play. **Cognitive analytics** leverages artificial intelligence (AI) technologies to simulate human thought processes. Integrating machine learning, natural language processing, and deep learning, cognitive analytics enables systems to interpret and analyze complex data, even unstructured data like text, images, and videos. This can enable organizations to more quickly uncover hidden patterns, generate insights, and make informed decisions by processing vast amounts of diverse information.[2]

The cognitive analytics market globally was valued at $3.95 billion in 2023, forecasted to increase to $44.51 billion by 2032, driven by growing demand for personalized customer experiences.[3] We anticipate growth of cognitive analytics for WFI, too.

Measure Impact Versus Activity

Avoiding a rear-view-mirror-only view of the world allows a critical shift in focus from activity to impact. One brief example can help paint the picture. Let's say your company has a call center that is struggling to meet its key performance indicators (KPIs), and underperforming agents have been assigned mentors to help boost their results. Comparing the two types of data paints a fairly clear picture of the distinctions, and the advantages, of impact metrics.

Activity (rear-view mirror) metrics might include:

- Total number of underperforming call center agents who were assigned a mentor
- Total number of mentors
- Average number of agents each mentor worked with
- Average amount of time each mentor/agent pair spent together
- KPIs mentors focused on (example: one-call resolutions)

These figures would describe what happened. And that's it.

Impact metrics would entail data such as:

- KPI improvements among mentored agents, like an increase in one-call resolutions
- Comparing KPIs of agents who trained with different mentors, to identify mentoring best practices
- Resulting improvements such as customer satisfaction survey results
- Increased engagement and/or retention among mentored agents whose KPIs improved, to uncover links between job performance and employment satisfaction

Now you can see WHETHER the mentors made a difference, if any, HOW they did it, and exactly WHAT those differences were. That kind of data yields actionable insights, enabling you to make informed decisions about whether to continue or even expand the mentor program, enhancing it based on the impact data.

Activity metrics aren't irrelevant, they're simply insufficient. Below are several additional examples of how you can improve results for your workforce by shifting from activity to impact measurement.

See Learning & Development in a Whole New Light

Our role is really workforce enablement—translating corporate strategy into meaningful learning experiences that drive change and build culture. It's not about learning, it's about what learning enables, and that's what the business wants from us.

—Barrett Evans, Chief Learning Officer, Ford Motor Company

Both of us spent most of our careers in Learning & Development (L&D). We've seen a lot. And we know that if business leaders want to actually gain measurable benefits from L&D programs, here are more habits to unlearn.

- **STOP relying on volume of training completions or courses created:** They offer no information on training *impact*.
- **STOP seeing as gospel learner evaluation scores:** These "smile sheets" are historically poor predictors of learning-driven *outcomes*. While at SuccessFactors in 2015, we conducted rigorous research and found the three strongest drivers of learner evaluation scores were (1) room temperature, (2) quality of catering, and (3) instructor likeability.
- **START building training around *specific tasks* to be accomplished:** Tasks offer concrete measurements of quality and output and are much easier to compare against targets or other benchmarks than the very nebulous knowledge gain.
- **(We beg you to) START defining *specific business goals* to be achieved:** We have seen far too many business leaders giving L&D professionals vague goals—if they provide goals at all. Yet creating L&D programs that don't drive toward specific targets is a huge waste of time and resources. We are, frankly, astonished that the logic of this continues to escape so many highly intelligent, experienced businesspeople.

These new habits will require more work from both those *requesting* the training and those *designing* it. Neither may be accustomed to being held accountable for measurable outcomes. But the return on investment should more than compensate for the extra effort.

Imagine being able to accurately assess, as in the call center agent mentoring example above, the EXACT impact of a training initiative, instead of hoping for a modicum of success and wondering whether you achieved it.

Better Understand Talent Acquisition Here, over-emphasizing rear-view mirror metrics can seriously impede quality outcomes. Making the RIGHT hires in the RIGHT sections of the business at the RIGHT time should be the guiding objectives, yet measuring activity often wins the day. That is a disservice to your business unit, the company, and the job candidates as well as to HR.

For example, prioritizing "time to fill" at the cost of all other outcomes can (and often does) lead to poor hiring choices, especially for managers and other strategic hires. Ask—and incent—HR professionals to hire the RIGHT people, not just to quickly fill open slots, assessing hire quality through factors you likely care much more about than filling the spot a few days sooner, like:

- Time to competency vs. target (Appropriate skills and levels?)
- Three-, six-, and 12-month retention (Good cultural fit?)
- Performance reviews (Delivering to expectation?)

"Time to Fill" is important, it's just not (usually) all-important. We get it: open positions come with a price tag. In fact, a recent study found one standard deviation increase in the length of [job] vacancies is associated with 5–6% lower quarterly return on assets.[4]

And of course, if hiring a high volume of workers quickly meets critical business needs, then "time to fill" is the correct strategic priority. In most circumstances, however, speed of hire should not be the *only* priority.

For more meaningful metrics and how to use them to answer important business questions, please *see* the Appendix.

Ask for the WHY and the SO WHAT

Data is telling me the company is at X percent. OK, thank you, but so what? But if we're at 40 percent and we're trying to get to 50 percent, and you can tell me what we need to do to get there and where in the business we need to focus, now that is actually helpful.

—Pamay Bassey, Chief Learning and Diversity Officer, The Kraft-Heinz Company

Now we are getting to the heart of the matter: the insights that can reveal WHY something is happening and the significance behind it, both necessary to understand WHAT TO DO about it. It starts with business leaders asking for better data and asking better questions overall.

Ask for Numbers in Context   A single figure isn't typically meaningful unless you happen to already have the backstory enabling you to put it in context. Yet so much corporate reporting will focus on just one number, with no context provided. This happens across functions, and not just in HR, but if you want to derive benefit from WFA, then HR is where you need to ask for more.

Let HR know you expect them to always provide comparison data to give numbers meaning, for example, vs. target, vs. previous fiscal year, vs. benchmark, vs. competitor, or compared with another meaningful data point.

Ask for Aggregate Trends   Data trends are perhaps the ultimate context. Data is rarely perfect, but aggregate trends are directionally correct and infinitely more valuable than a single number. While Jenny was at SAP, the Chief of Staff to CEO Bill McDermott, Alex Atzberger, now CEO of Optimizely, when coaching her on preparing a presentation for the Board of Directors, advised that she show an eight-quarter view of business metrics. A single data snapshot might show a disastrous decline or unusual spike, but data over time (a one-week, one-month or one-year view) could tell a completely different story.

It's a given that Sales will show eight quarters with percentage of target achieved for revenue and other financials. HR can and should adopt the same approach for a range of metrics. Time doesn't stand still, and neither should HR data.

Ask for Revelations   After progressing from rear-view mirror/activity metrics to impact metrics, and from single digits to trends and comparisons, the next milestone is true, deep, revealing insights. Your ultimate goal as a business leader should be that your HR professionals—with the help of Workforce Analytics—can explain to you and fellow leaders the root causes of business challenges and how to address them.

This won't always happen. Far from it. Cole Napper, Principal Owner of Directionally Correct, has seen a lot of "performative" reporting. As he described to it us, "It's when the Workforce Analytics team goes to a meeting, shares static metrics, and the leaders go 'Ooh' and then nothing changes, because it's just data theater, as if they had shared a book on anthropology."

Ben Putterman, Vice President of Learning and Talent Development at HubSpot, emphasized going beyond traditional HR reporting. "I have a healthy, healthy disdain for just looking at engagement data, but engagement data over time . . . can be very telling," he shared. He told us about an engagement survey he'd once used that asked employees how likely they were to still be at the company a year later. Since the questions were anonymous, it was hard to take any action on the data. To get actionable insights, he and his team looked at trending data over time by job category. They found that Engineering was "the one function we really should listen to when they say they don't plan on working at the company in a year." The analysis gave his team enough insight to pinpoint a specific problem vs. launching a companywide initiative.

Revelations Should Be Your CHRO's Specialty

Your company's CHRO should be a workforce data rockstar, able to walk any leader—CEO, C-suite, Board of Directors—through an HR dashboard and explain what the numbers reveal about issues and opportunities at your company.

Top CHROs deeply understand business and their company: how it makes money, strengths and weaknesses across business units, and, if it's public, the stock price, what causes its rise and fall, pressures from Wall Street, shareholder issues, and more. As a result, great CHROs can also direct their Workforce Analytics as needed to uncover what is not yet known.

Think Accounting

Meg Langan, Founder of ML Consulting & Advisory, drew a parallel with an accountant's ability to derive insights from financial statements. Langan, who had a lengthy career in investment banking and financial services before being tapped as Chief People Officer of Turbonomic, observed that more experienced accountants will ask more sophisticated questions. While getting her MBA at Harvard Business School, a professor insisted her entire class learn to read between the lines of any financial statement. Great CHROs, she said, do the same: they can look at a page of metrics and tell a deeper, more meaningful, nuanced business story.

Requesting these kinds of insights is one of six questions that Peter Burnham, Director of Peoplelytics, advises CEOs to ask of their CHROs. "Stretch them to connect workforce and line of business data together so you can see actual correlations between people capability and business outcome data," Burnham counsels. "Ask them to set hypotheses and test these with data to find evidence-based outcomes."[5]

More on top-performing CHROs in Section 5, All About the CHRO.

Take a Deep Dive into Attrition Attrition may be the most widely reported, misunderstood, and underappreciated HR metric. It is also one of the most expensive problems any company could have. Indeed, in the words of Peter Cappelli, George W. Taylor Professor of Management at the Wharton School and Director of its Center for Human Resources, "If leaders realized that the true cost of turnover is often a multiple of an employee's annual salary, they would immediately demand changes."[6]

Like so many workforce costs considered operating expenses and not investments, turnover costs, as Cappelli and his co-author Ranya Nehmeh point out, "don't show up in any single financial accounting category, they have to be pulled out and highlighted for the C-suite."[7]

NOTE: *Like "attrition," "turnover" also refers to employee departures. Proving our point about human capital metrics lacking standardization (see Section 2, "Get with the (Workforce Data) Program"), definitions of turnover and attrition can vary. To avoid confusion, we are using only attrition in the book (in our work, we use the two terms interchangeably).*

How Should One Examine Attrition? First, know the types of attrition. It can be **voluntary** (*I quit*) or **involuntary** (*You're fired*), **regrettable**—losing good talent (*I'm so sorry to see you go*)—or

non-regrettable (*Good riddance*). Thus, attrition should, always and forever, be reported as four numbers, which, despite their importance to understanding workforce dynamics, are typically buried deep within a single digit glaring on a dashboard, unseen, unmeasured and, therefore, unmanaged. The quadrant chart in Figure 1.2 illustrates this key point.

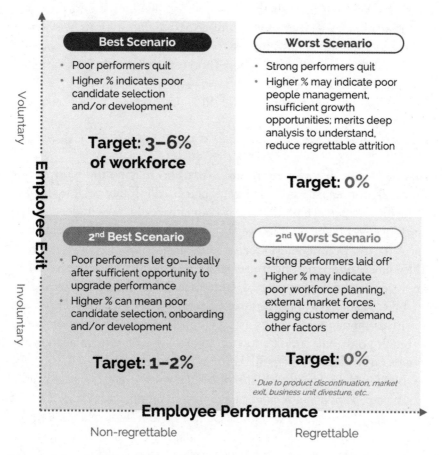

Targets based on mid-size tech firm with Austin HQ

Best Scenario
- Poor performers quit
- Higher % indicates poor candidate selection and/or development

Target: 3–6% of workforce

Worst Scenario
- Strong performers quit
- Higher % may indicate poor people management, insufficient growth opportunities; merits deep analysis to understand, reduce regrettable attrition

Target: 0%

2ⁿᵈ Best Scenario
- Poor performers let go—ideally after sufficient opportunity to upgrade performance
- Higher % can mean poor candidate selection, onboarding and/or development

Target: 1–2%

2ⁿᵈ Worst Scenario
- Strong performers laid off*
- Higher % may indicate poor workforce planning, external market forces, lagging customer demand, other factors

Target: 0%

Due to product discontinuation, market exit, business unit divesture, etc.

Voluntary — Involuntary

Employee Exit

Employee Performance

Non-regrettable   Regrettable

Figure 1.2   Attrition Through Four Lenses
Credit: Actionable Analytics Group.

Other attrition data to pay attention to, so you can manage what you measure, can include:

- **Key employee populations:** Track critical talent groups especially closely, like recently promoted managers, sales reps for a new product line, engineers with rare, in-demand skills, a division that's doing poorly (critical that key talent stay and low-performing talent go), or a division that's doing very well (spikes in voluntary regrettable attrition could spell disaster for you, and a boon for your competitors).
- **Internal comparisons:** Comparing groups can reveal insights invisible in a single companywide (or even division-wide) digit. Examples: frontline employees vs. staff at headquarters; experienced vs. new store managers; call center agents in Country A vs. Country B; groups extensively piloting a new process vs. peers using the legacy process.
- **Trends:** As advised above, plotting attrition trends over time can help identify root causes of peaks and/or valleys. Additionally, you may be able to notice trends in certain geographies, reporting lines, or demographics that can give insight into attrition issues.
- **Industry benchmarks:** Look not only at the one industry average but drill down into key populations wherever available. Industry benchmarks are especially critical given how wildly average attrition rates can vary. The average turnover rate across all sectors in the United States in 2023 was 41%, but was 79% in leisure and hospitality, 37% in manufacturing, and 18% in government.[8]

To get a truly well-rounded picture of employment health, Professor Cappelli also advises that an attrition dashboard include metrics like jobs filled internally and reasons for employee departures, complemented by well-being data like absenteeism, illness, and disability, utilization of wellness and other benefits, and engagement. And, of course, turnover costs—estimated at 50–200% of an employee's salary, according to Gallup and others.[9]

This case study from Experian illustrates successfully using WFA to predict and prevent attrition.

Case Study | Forecasting Retention: How Experian Data Secured Its Talent

Experian, a global leader in information services, was faced with rising employee turnover. Senior executives immediately turned to their People Analytics team, which was regularly relied upon by leaders throughout the company due to their strong record of problem-solving.

The Problem

Experian's global resignation rates, which surpassed industry norms, posed both financial and cultural risks. Each 1% rise in attrition added $3 million in costs and threatened to damage morale and the company's vision for a collaborative, productive work environment.

The Solution

Experian's People Analytics team developed a sophisticated predictive attrition model utilizing the same rigorous methodologies applied to credit risk assessments. The Attrition Risk Model (ARM) used up to 200 attributes to assign a "risk score" to employees and identify those at-risk for departure. With ARM, HR and leadership could see the factors influencing attrition, visualize attrition risk at multiple levels—macro, team, and individual—and model scenarios to proactively launch retention measures. Equipped with insight-led retention practices, decision-makers could proactively address potential turnover.

The Results

- Achieved a 4% reduction in global attrition rates.
- Realized more than $14 million in cost savings.

- Enhanced the People Analytics team's strategic influence.
- HR team began advising outside companies on Experian's proven approach to tackling attrition.

Cutting to the Chase

Experian leveraged a sophisticated predictive analytics model to transform its approach to retention, saving millions in attrition-related costs.

Source: Adapted from Stacia Garr and Priyanka Mehrotra, "Unlocking the Hidden C-Suite Superpower: People Analytics," (RedThread Research & Visier, 2024), https://www.visier.com/lp/dm-redthread-research-report-unlocking-hidden-csuite-superpower/.

For a vignette on how IBM used analytics to better retain top talent (in other words, reduce regrettable voluntary attrition), see Section 4, "Upleveling HR."

Ask for Different Reporting   Now that you're asking for different data, what form should that take? While there is no one right way of reporting data, the two examples below can help spark your thinking.

Balanced Scorecard   The scorecard in Figure 1.3 represents a potential approach to a customized dashboard—or an analog/manual version of one. Across four areas—Customer, Financial, Internal Processes, and People—the starting point is business goals, which cascade down to team goals and are then linked to specific metrics. Ideally such a dashboard would include specific numerical targets for each HR Team Goal. Further drilldowns could include trend data on the metrics for each line item.

This approach helpfully ties corporate priorities with HR initiatives and with metrics by business area, clearly demonstrating how HR is a support partner that responds to the needs of the business. Notice that for each functional area, the HR metrics are owned by the leaders of the business and not HR.[10]

CUSTOMER

Business Goals
- Improve customer satisfaction
- Create more cross-selling opportunities for customers
- Expand customer service quality to drive retention

Team Goals
- Improve employee engagement by 5%
- Improve product knowledge of employees to be able to drive cross-selling
- Train employees on retention skills

HR Metrics
- Employee engagement score
- Product knowledge assessments scores
- Retention metrics
- eNPS scores

FINANCIAL

Business Goals
- Increase profitability
- Increase revenue
- Drive business growth in new markets

Team Goals
- Improve the price of HR services per employee
- Reduce cost per hire while delivering workforce plans
- Scale HR services to support new business expansion

HR Metrics
- HR price point per employee
- Cost of hire
- HR employee ration
- HR budget reporting

INTERNAL PROCESSES

Business Goals
- Improve customer service response times and reporting
- Implement customer relationship management systems
- Improve business insights and reporting

Team Goals
- Improve customer service team lead managerial skills to drive productivity
- Improve system skills in CRM systems
- Build a business intelligence talent pool

HR Metrics
- Leadership 360 satisfaction scores
- System skills proficiency pass rates
- Talent pool health

PEOPLE

Business Goals
- Drive continuity in our sales force
- Reward performance

Team Goals
- Retain sales employees
- Implement a robust performance management process and incentive structure

HR Metrics
- Sales employee retention
- Performance scores

Figure 1.3   Balanced Scorecard (HR Example)

Source: Reproduced with permission from Academy to Innovate HR (AIHR).

Multidimensional Dashboards As a business leader, you recognize the importance of setting goals and tracking progress toward targets. One way to implement this in HR is with KPI scorecards that align back to organizational goals. The recruitment strategy dashboard shown in Figure 1.4 combines information and metrics in ways that tell a complete story versus simply providing data points. The integration of survey data (which generates the manager satisfaction score), financial data (recruitment cost), and recruiting data (such as time to hire), reflects progress against the business goals on the left and offers an entire narrative in one place.[11]

RECRUITMENT STRATEGY MAP		HR SCORECARD KPI	Current score	Target
Strategic	Most innovative organization in the sector	Position in the sector-wide innovation benchmark	5	Top 3
		Time to market of last 5 new products	121 days	95 days
Employee Growth	Hire more qualified professionals	Satisfaction score of manager after 1 year (quality of hire)	0.70	0.85
Financial	Decrease of recruitment cost	Recruitment cost in dollars	4 MM	3.5 MM
Process	• Decrease of lead time • More attractive employer	Time to hire in days	38	25
		Acceptance ratio %	70%	90%
		Top employer benchmark	Top 40%	Top 20%

Figure 1.4 Recruitment Strategy Map

Source: Reproduced with permission from Academy to Innovate HR (AIHR).

Remember, too: Not all reporting is strictly numerical. It's okay to use insightful narratives to convey findings—the bottom line is that reporting should share INSIGHTS and not just numbers.

Expect Better Storytelling

HR leaders must know how to decode and encode. The most impactful HR leaders understand what's important to the business and decode that into the people, processes, and programs needed in response. Further, they need to encode everything happening in HR to what the business cares about.

—Liz Wiseman, Author and CEO, The Wiseman Group

Good stories are memorable, create emotional connection, and convey deep meaning. Yet HR is notorious for not speaking the language of the business, framing their conversations, emails, reporting, and other interactions using HR jargon, concepts, and an HR-centric mindset.

So, while shifting from metrics to insights is a critical part of the equation, your HR partners may also need to upgrade their communications, with your insistence and the aid of the new collegial relationships discussed in Section 5, Evolve the Power Structure. HR will also need to take plenty of initiative and be prepared to do the work—once you set the expectation, gently but firmly.

Know That Data Storytelling Is a Skill   "Data storytelling"—effectively deploying data to convey Workforce Insights—requires multiple competencies. For Jonathan Ferrar and David Green, authors of *Excellence in People Analytics: How to Use Workforce Data to Create Business Value*, three in particular are needed: data literacy, creativity, and an "ability to connect different pieces of information into a single coherent story that resonates with stakeholders and is tailored for each audience."[12]

Good data storytellers analyze complex data, extract key insights, and identify patterns that drive business decisions, then distill all that into simple, understandable takeaways. They link stories to strategic priorities and make data stories relatable and engaging to inspire action and buy-in. And they create clear, impactful visuals (charts, graphs, infographics) that enhance understanding and retention of data insights. After all, a picture is still worth a thousand words. In a recent HR.com report, 80% of respondents named interactive visualization the #1 most effective way to communicate WFA data; graphical representations of data was #2 (72%).[13]

Connect HR with Expert Help   Fortunately, your company has plenty of expert skills who can help HR uplevel their communications.

Deploy Marketing Communications: Your company no doubt has in-house experts to help frame narratives, polish language, and promote success stories.

Dispatch Finance: Adopting the language of finance when presenting WFI will help ensure that the data stories resonate with business leaders. This involves framing findings in the context of financial metrics and business outcomes, making it easier for executives to understand and value the insights.

Forging this new partnership may take some effort when it comes to aligning your WFA team with Finance directly. According to Insight222, only 24% of 271 companies surveyed in their People Analytics Trends 2023 report had established strong relationships between their People Analytics (PA) and Finance teams, but of that group, 99% had delivered measurable outcomes in the past 12 months and 54% had improved business performance leveraging PA work.[14]

Enlist sales: Who else can better position and persuade than your sales leaders? HR can work with Sales to apply a customer-centric view and "sell" their services as products.

Assign "translators": Many WFA teams have at least one member adept at explaining complex topics simply and can "translate" data and insights into plain English for business leaders. Translators can also interpret what stakeholders need. According to McKinsey, leading teams have such "specialized integrators," and some develop cadres of translators.[15] *For more on WFA team members, see Section 2, "Understand Workforce Analytics Capabilities."*

Ask Better Questions

Yes, you have plenty to request from HR. But as a business leader who wants to get more from HR and from WFA, you need to do your part. At the risk of sounding simplistic, asking better questions should yield better answers. Think of formulating questions for HR as prompt engineering.

For example, if you take our attrition deep dive to heart, you won't ask your HR Business Partner, "What's the overall attrition rate for my business unit this quarter?" You'll start by asking for eight-quarter trends for the four attrition combinations: regrettable/non-regrettable, voluntary/involuntary. You'll ask for insights into those trends, explanations for any sudden increases or decreases, and a detailed drill-down into any regrettable voluntary turnover—who left, what influenced their departure, whether those factors make other top talent flight risks.

Similarly, you won't ask, "What's my overall employee engagement rate?" You'll ask about engagement scores for top performers in critical roles, those who work with the most important clients. Inquire about the biggest factors impacting engagement so you can work to improve them. Request regular progress reports on how your unit is responding to findings in last year's engagement survey scores (and if those don't exist—either the progress reports or the responses—ask for that to change).

And finally, if you are having safety issues, you won't ask how many people have completed the safety training. You'll request insights into the factors that contribute to safety incidents and what can be done to mitigate them. Two memorable stories tell this tale—*see* Section 3, "Take Your Preference" and Section 4, "Upleveling HR."

1.2 Embrace Workforce Insights

Investing in WFI can transform your business. As emphasized in the Introduction, research shows companies that are more advanced in using workforce data to inform decisions see better overall performance. And this book is replete with both positive case studies and cautionary tales underscoring the point.

The essential concepts and guidelines below are designed to inform, inspire, and motivate you to make WFA a new standard for your organization: business strategy and decisions informed by a deep understanding of all the factors impacting, and impacted by, your workforce—employees and the AI-driven machines that help them.

Get to Know (and Love) Workforce Insights

I have been in the business of data analytics and HR for more than 30 years, and there's never been a more exciting or promising time for HR professionals or the businesses they serve. Workforce Insights are already well within reach, and we are about to round an historic corner into an era where the stunning transformational power of Generative AI will seem tame. I can't wait.

—**Josh Bersin, Founder and CEO,**
The Josh Bersin Company

What's in a Name?   WFA sometimes goes by other monikers: HR Analytics, People Analytics, Talent Analytics. Exact definitions of each vary depending on who you ask. We are using them interchangeably, with sincere apologies to those for whom this may be tantamount to blasphemy.

Here are key terms as we define them. *See also* Figure 1.5.

Figure 1.5   The Workforce Insights Equation
Credit: Actionable Analytics Group.

Workforce Data: All data about the workforce (people and AI-driven machines) that **lives in HR** and **outside of HR**

+ Business Data: All data on a company's operations, finances, customers, markets, products, services, sales, etc.

× Workforce Analytics (WFA): The combined analysis of workforce data and business data to yield WFI

= Workforce Insights (WFI): Meaningful conclusions about factors impacting workforce performance, derived from advanced data analysis and used to improve critical talent and business outcomes. Savvy leaders use WFI to identify, understand, and address a broad range of challenges and achieve strategic priorities.

The case study below begins to reveal what is possible with WFI.

Case Study | No More Guesswork: Re a Future of Workforce Stability

A U.S.-based healthcare technology company was in crisis. Despite growing revenues exceeding $200 billion, they were grappling with major profitability issues. Escalating workforce costs threatened margins, driven by persistent overstaffing and costly layoffs.

The Problem

This cycle of hiring and firing drained resources, hurt employee morale, and hindered productivity, while severance and recruitment costs climbed, and profits faltered. Company leadership, who had once accepted staffing expansion and contraction as unavoidable, decided it was time for change.

The Solution

The company hired its first VP of Talent Management Operations to break the pattern and to lead a global **Workforce**

Analytics team. In partnership with Finance, they co-developed (and co-funded) a model that looked at both direct and indirect workforce costs. This cross-functional team, led by the new VP, produced the company's **first enterprise-wide workforce planning system** to forecast headcount, hiring, and budget targets more precisely. By using predictive models based on business demand, attrition, and external labor data, the new system stabilized workforce needs and smoothed out the cycle of overstaffing and layoffs.

Beyond workforce planning, the VP drove **data-led strategies** across other key areas, providing analytics support for major culture shifts, diversity and inclusion efforts, talent acquisition strategies, and leadership development. Tools like consolidated People Analytics dashboards, employee surveys, and network analysis equipped leaders and HR with critical insights for actionable change.

The Results

- **$25 million annual savings** by eliminating unnecessary hiring and layoffs.
- **Stabilized workforce**, reducing time-to-productivity losses.
- **Enhanced profitability** and responsiveness to market demands.
- **Improved morale** with reduced disruption from frequent layoffs.

Cutting to the Chase

This healthcare technology company finally broke free from a costly, cyclical staffing model and improved profitability with data-driven workforce planning. With predictive analytics at its core, the organization now aligns staffing to demand, drives efficiency, and supports sustainable growth—all without sacrificing employee morale or profitability.

What Do Business Leaders Need to Know?

Overall Trends   The first key finding highlighted in Deloitte's 2023 High-Impact People Analytics Research, published in June 2024, is that it has become "an organizational imperative." We obviously agree, and were pleased to see other key findings that could be chapter headers in this book: the "single biggest predictor" of success is having a strong data culture; "Tech investments mean nothing without human capability (and vice versa)"; contemporary business challenges necessitate pulling data from additional sources; and "People data is business data—treat it as such."[16] We cover these in depth in the sections ahead.

Key Uses   HR.com's 2024–25 State of People Analytics study, reflecting survey results collected from HR professionals across industries, reported the five most common areas People Analytics (PA) positively impacts (three tied at #2). Data from 2023 reflects shifting priorities:[17]

Area of People Analytics	2024–25 Report Rank	2024–25 Report Percent	2023 Report Rank	2023 Report Percent
Employee experience/engagement	#1	55%	#4	42%
Retention	#2	49%	#2	49%
Performance management	#2	49%	#5	40%
Compensation and benefits	#2	49%	#7	30%
Recruitment and selection	#3	47%	#1	49%

Analytics teams are also busy upleveling HR data literacy (79% of PA leaders) and procuring the tech solutions to scale and streamline PA efforts (80% of PA professionals).[18]

Growth and Opportunity   The WFA and WFI landscape has been steadily changing. From mid-2020 to mid-2023, these functions have grown on average by 43%, and 85% of CHROs said in a 2023 survey that data is an essential part of their HR strategy.[19]

In the HR.com report mentioned earlier, 98% of PA "leaders"—who said their organization was extremely or very effective at maximizing PA value—believe PA leads to better business outcomes versus only 21% of "laggards," which rated their organization's ability as somewhat effective or not effective at all. Unfortunately, only 22% of respondents were "leaders," suggesting that this area has significant room for growth.[20]

Killer Combos Solve Problems The essence of WFA is powerfully combining workforce and business data: creating killer data combos to provide a full picture of organizational performance and get to the heart of, and determine solutions to, your company's challenges. You'll hopefully see in the combinations and following case studies plenty of reasons for optimism and driving change.

The simple examples below are designed to illustrate the killer combo principle.

Workforce Data + Finance Data A *company is closing one business unit and opening another. What should they do with the employees in the unit that's closing?*

Workforce data: Skills, tenure, performance reviews

+ Financial data: Payroll, severance estimates, hiring costs

= Workforce Insights: Because they have transferable skills, current employees can be moved into the new unit at a far lower cost than laying them off and hiring new workers. Such a move also avoids hard-to-calculate layoff impacts like lost productivity and damaged morale.

Workforce Data + IT Data A *company has issued a return-to-office (RTO) policy requiring four days a week in the office. How might they assess the impact?*

Workforce data: Absenteeism rates, engagement survey results

+ IT data: Badge swipes, login/logoff times

= **Workforce Insights:** If people are NOT badging in despite guidelines telling them to, not working their usual hours, engagement is down and absenteeism is up, leadership should revisit the policy.

Workforce Data + Sales Data   Sales of a new product line are not meeting targets. What's going on?

Workforce data: Rep tenure, training completions, performance reviews, retention

+ **Sales data:** Pipeline, deals, revenue

= **Workforce Insights:** Newer reps are taking twice as long as experienced reps to hit quota, and while more than half quit within two months, 90% of new reps who do not complete new hire training quit. It's time to assess onboarding processes and evaluate what additional support new reps may need.

Observational to Aspirational: Distinct Data Types
Observational Data

Some data on employee activity can only be captured through observation, human or otherwise. Understanding some problems may require an individual physically going to see what's happening (*see* the following case study). Where permissible by law, video can track employee movements, for example on a plant floor or in a retail environment; AI can then be used to analyze patterns to identify process improvements, improve safety procedures and/or better train workers (and, yes, find slackers).

Organizational Network Analysis (ONA)

As of this writing, ONA is still an aspirational "killer combo" for most companies. ONA uses advanced analytics across multiple data sources to help leaders understand how employees are collaborating and identify key influencers, critical individuals who connect teams and/or serve as go-to experts.

"We're huge fans of companies that use ONA," Kevin Oakes, CEO and Founder of the Institute for Corporate Productivity (i4cp), told us. "It uncovers the energizers and de-energizers in your organization. That's what most companies who have successfully enabled change initiatives have done."

Vignette | Revving Up Sales: How Workforce Analytics Drove the 24-Hour Follow-Up Advantage

A leading global electric car manufacturer was facing a conundrum: despite high interest during test drives, customers left showrooms without making purchases. Leadership initially suspected the issue was related to marketing, pricing, or product appeal, but could not find a definitive cause. Eventually, they turned to their WFA team for help.

The WFA team analyzed available data on the workforce and in the Customer Relationship Management system (CRM), but no obvious answers surfaced. So, team members hit the road, visiting both high- and low-performing showrooms to shadow sales reps. They discovered a simple yet crucial difference: at dealerships with higher conversion rates, sales reps consistently called potential customers within 24 hours of a test drive to ask how they felt about the experience, address lingering questions, and offer further assistance. Locations with this follow-up practice saw conversion rates 3.5 times higher than those without it.

Visiting the showrooms also helped the team identify key reasons for the differences in approach: a glaring lack of formal training or even a documented sales process. Without structured steps, some reps missed the opportunity to maintain a connection

(continued)

(continued)

with customers, leading to lost sales. With these findings, leadership introduced new guidelines emphasizing timely, personalized follow-up calls, and enhanced training to equip sales reps to succeed.

The solution was not about marketing or even the cars themselves, but about empowering sales reps to connect meaningfully with customers. Thanks to the WFA team's insights, the company transformed showroom enthusiasm into completed sales, creating a powerful new strategy for success.

Workforce Data + Customer Support Data   Let's recall the example above of a call center struggling to meet its KPIs. Did the mentors successfully help underperforming reps boost their results?

Workforce data: Agent tenure, training completed, shifts worked, mentor assigned, total mentoring time

+ Customer Support data: One-call resolutions, escalations, customer satisfaction scores, customer loyalty

= Workforce Insights: Leadership can track impact on metrics including mentored agent KPIs, satisfaction survey results from customers who spoke with mentored agents, engagement and/or retention among mentored agents whose KPIs improved, to assess links between job performance and job satisfaction.

Workforce Data + Engineering Data   In the following case study a tech company is experiencing inexplicable delays on a high-stakes product release. What's the root cause?

Workforce data: Skills, experience, education, location, performance reviews

+ Engineering data: Productivity indicators including work units completed per sprint, team and team member

= **Workforce Insights:** As you'll read in the case study below, the analytics team needed to dig deep and complement system data with team member interviews to single out from among many potential root causes the true culprit.

Case Study | Bridging the Experience Gap to Deliver on a High-Stakes Project

A leading global technology firm headquartered in California faced a critical challenge: delays in product development on a high-stakes project. Despite having more than 400 expert engineers in multiple regions working on it, progress lagged inexplicably.

The Problem

The VP of Engineering grew increasingly alarmed as key milestones continued to slip. Analyzing engineering productivity indicators—including work units completed per sprint, team and team member—revealed that the North America team was making significantly less progress than their counterparts. But why?

The Solution

The analysis involved **probing questions that targeted possible people-centered issues**: Was decision-making slow? Were communication channels across regions effective? Was leadership providing adequate support? Could teamwork and training gaps be impacting timelines? Their investigation included data analysis, interviews with more than 20 engineers, and reviewing past performance. They discovered that the North America engineers, while highly skilled, had significantly less experience

(continued)

(*continued*)

than other teams, which affected their efficiency in critical A/B testing phases, slowing them down substantially.

To address this, the company implemented multiple solutions: team restructuring that integrated newer engineers with more experienced counterparts, peer mentoring with tenured engineers, and short online best practices webinars. Within weeks, productivity increased, and the project was back on track.

The Results

- **20% YoY revenue increase** post-release.
- **On-time delivery** of the product to clients.
- **Higher revenue per employee** driven by increased productivity.
- **Improved team productivity** across all regions.

Cutting to the Chase

Through detailed analytics combining productivity and people metrics, this global tech giant was able to pinpoint the cause of product development delays and develop an effective solution: restructuring teams and setting up mentorship to guide a highly skilled but less-experienced engineering team through some rough patches. The company delivered a high-stakes product on time, securing significant revenue growth.

Integrate Human-Machine Collaboration (HMC)

In the spirit of Generative Artificial Intelligence, we used GenAI throughout the creation of this book. While often highly unreliable as a research assistant, it was a champion at restating research findings, synthesizing ideas, summarizing content, and producing helpful insights.

Most of this HMC content was developed with GenAI. We asked two questions (as follows), the tool "thought" for 11 seconds to answer each, then we discussed and refined. HMC personified, if you'll excuse the expression.*

*A favorite piece of tech nerd humor: Don't anthropomorphize machines. They hate that.

How Would You Define Human-Machine Collaboration? HMC refers to the synergistic partnership between humans and machines—especially advanced technologies like artificial intelligence (AI) and robotics—where both parties actively contribute their unique strengths to achieve common goals or complete tasks more effectively. In this collaborative dynamic, humans bring creativity, critical thinking, emotional intelligence, and contextual understanding; while machines offer computational power, data processing capabilities, precision, and the ability to manage repetitive or complex tasks rapidly.

This collaboration is not about machines replacing humans but augmenting human capabilities. As Jenny points out, human + machine collaboration is really an extension of what it means to BE human: from the beginning of recorded history humans have made and used tools, and today, those tools are machines. What's unique is the interactive communication and real-time feedback between humans and machines, allowing for dynamic decision-making and problem-solving. For example:

- **Healthcare:** Doctors use AI-powered diagnostic tools to analyze medical images, improving accuracy and speed in detecting diseases.
- **Manufacturing:** Workers operate alongside collaborative robots (cobots) that handle heavy lifting or precision tasks, enhancing efficiency and safety.
- **Creative Industries:** Artists and designers use AI software to generate ideas or patterns, pushing the boundaries of creativity.

The ultimate goal of HMC is to combine the best of both worlds: leveraging machine efficiency and human ingenuity to achieve outcomes neither could accomplish alone. This leads to increased productivity, innovation, and the ability to more efficiently tackle complex challenges across various fields.

How Should Workforce Analytics Take into Account Increasing Human-Machine Collaboration?   As HMC becomes increasingly integral to modern workplaces, WFA must adapt to this evolving dynamic. Organizations need a holistic approach that considers both human and machine contributions, as well as their interactions. Incorporating HMC into WFA enables better decision-making, optimizes productivity, and prepares the organization for future challenges. Here are a few ways WFA can be applied to HMC.

Skill Gap Analysis and Training

- **Competency Mapping:** Identify new skills required for effective collaboration with machines. Provide hyper-personalized learning and development recommendations.
- **Training Impact:** Measure the effectiveness of training programs on improving employee performance.
- **Learning Curve Analytics:** Analyze how quickly employees adapt to new technologies over time.

Task Allocation Optimization

- **Task Suitability Analysis:** Use data to determine which tasks are best handled by humans, machines, or collaboratively.
- **Workflow Efficiency:** Optimize processes by reallocating tasks based on performance analytics.
- **Resource Utilization:** Ensure both human and machine resources are utilized to their fullest potential.

Financial Impact Assessment

- **Return on Investment (ROI):** Calculate the financial benefits gained from HMC.
- **Cost–Benefit Analysis:** Weigh the costs of technology implementation against productivity gains.
- **Budget Allocation:** Use analytics to inform spending on technology versus human capital.

Additional Applications

- **Integrated Performance Metrics:** Measure the combined efficiency, output, and quality improvements of human-machine teams.
- **Predictive Workforce Planning:** Use data analytics to forecast collaboration trends, model technology impacts, and plan for future talent needs.
- **Ethical and Compliance Monitoring:** Ensure data privacy compliance, detect AI biases, and maintain transparency in machine decision-making.

Implementing Enhanced Workforce Analytics

Consider these facets.

- **Data Integration:** Consolidate data from various sources, including HR systems, workplace/operational data, machine logs, and performance trackers.
- **Advanced Analytics Tools:** Utilize AI and machine learning algorithms to analyze complex datasets involving human and machine variables.
- **Cross-Functional Teams:** Involve stakeholders from IT, Finance, HR, and Operations to ensure a comprehensive approach.
- **Change Management:** Prepare the organization for new analytics practices through communication and training.

Conclusion   Incorporating HMC into WFA is essential for organizations aiming to stay competitive in an increasingly automated world.

By expanding the scope of analytics to include both human and machine factors, organizations can gain deeper insights into performance, optimize workflows, and enhance employee satisfaction. This integrated approach not only maximizes the benefits of technology investments but also ensures that human talent is effectively leveraged alongside machines.

1.3 Let HR (Get Better at) Help(ing) You

The best HR functions work hand in hand with the business. Only with that tight connection to the business will HR be able to iterate at the speed of business.

—Julia Stiglitz, CEO & Co-founder, UpLimit

Remember: the end game here is YOU improving YOUR business outcomes by taking advantage of the incredible power of WFA, a very worthy objective. It's about transforming what you can manage by changing what you measure.

And, that means letting HR help you. But how can you as a business leader help HR get better at that over time? First, understand what a partnership to achieve your key initiatives could look like, and then invite the partnership to happen. It's both not at all that simple and exactly that simple.

Understand the Through-Line

What does it actually look like to partner with HR and let them develop initiatives to support your business objectives? We suspect many of our esteemed readers have never seen it done (or done well).

Look to L&D as a Microcosm   Given our deep experience in Learning & Development (L&D), we know not all senior leaders understand how HR drives measurable results. Some haven't the foggiest idea that training can, in fact, yield business outcomes. Not surprisingly, we've also seen L&D professionals who are similarly unaware—mirroring many of the larger HR issues that prompted us to write this book.

How is that possible?

Let's say you're a smart, experienced L&D professional who has worked at profitable companies with solid leaders and positive company cultures. It's possible, or even likely, that you have *never* been asked by any stakeholder to actually *make a measurable impact*. Or been given the tools, skills, insights, processes and/or incentives to meaningfully move the needle on specific business issues.

Let's even say that you tried thinking outside the box and endeavored to link your learning initiative to concrete business outcomes.

- You may be shut down by a colleague or manager who is risk-averse, doesn't think such initiatives necessary, or has simply seen too many of them fail.
- Perhaps the stakeholders funding the program will not give you concrete targets, because they don't have any or fear being held accountable if objectives are not achieved. Maybe they won't share post-training outcomes.
- Also likely: you couldn't measure results due to a lack of tools, processes, institutional knowledge, or another barrier.

It is, candidly, shocking how often these scenarios happen, even at top-performing companies.

L&D professionals routinely come up against some or all of these challenges. What would *you* do? Based on our experience, you'd give up. Why bang your head against the wall when you can simply carry on doing what you always have?

This shines a (hopefully bright and helpful) light onto the persistence of L&D's (and HR's) status as a cost center that doesn't deliver value—and how the mediocrity merry-go-round can go on spinning itself indefinitely.

The following content is designed to help concretize how business leaders can grab that brass ring and get off the ride to nowhere.

Start by Knowing the End You Want   It may seem insane that we feel we have to make this explicit, but based on our research, our careers in L&D and HR, and our experience working with hundreds of clients around the world, we do. We have had far too many meetings with business unit leaders asking for "a three-hour training" without being able to provide a single KPI they want to improve, much less actual targets.

> *If you don't know where you want to go, no one in (or outside of) HR can help you get there.*

If you don't know where you want to go, no one in (or outside of) HR can help you get there. That said, a high-performing CHRO and HR function can and should help you define realistic objectives within a strategic priority, but truly, as a business leader, you bear much of the responsibility for setting HR up for success by defining your goals and setting expectations on outcomes.

Shift How You Connect the Dots   There are, in fact, many ways to get from Point A (business goal) to Point B (HR solutions to help achieve it). One straightforward approach to consider is below. This adaptation of the Human Capital Value Profiler (HCVP), developed by WFA expert Max Blumberg, is a flexible framework for aligning business objectives with HR processes.

As Blumberg explains in "A Strategically Aligned HR Operating Model," part of the CEO Working Paper series from the University of Southern California Marshall School of Business Center for Effective Organizations, "HR's key deliverable should be the workforce and strategic capabilities required to implement the business strategy. HR accomplishes those objectives through people processes which enable the capabilities."[21]

As depicted in Figure 1.6, the HCVP begins with the business outcomes. These translate into capabilities the organization must have in order to achieve the outcomes, and then the knowledge, skills, tools, and/or processes the workforce needs to power the organizational capabilities. This leads to HR determining how to get the workforce what it needs.

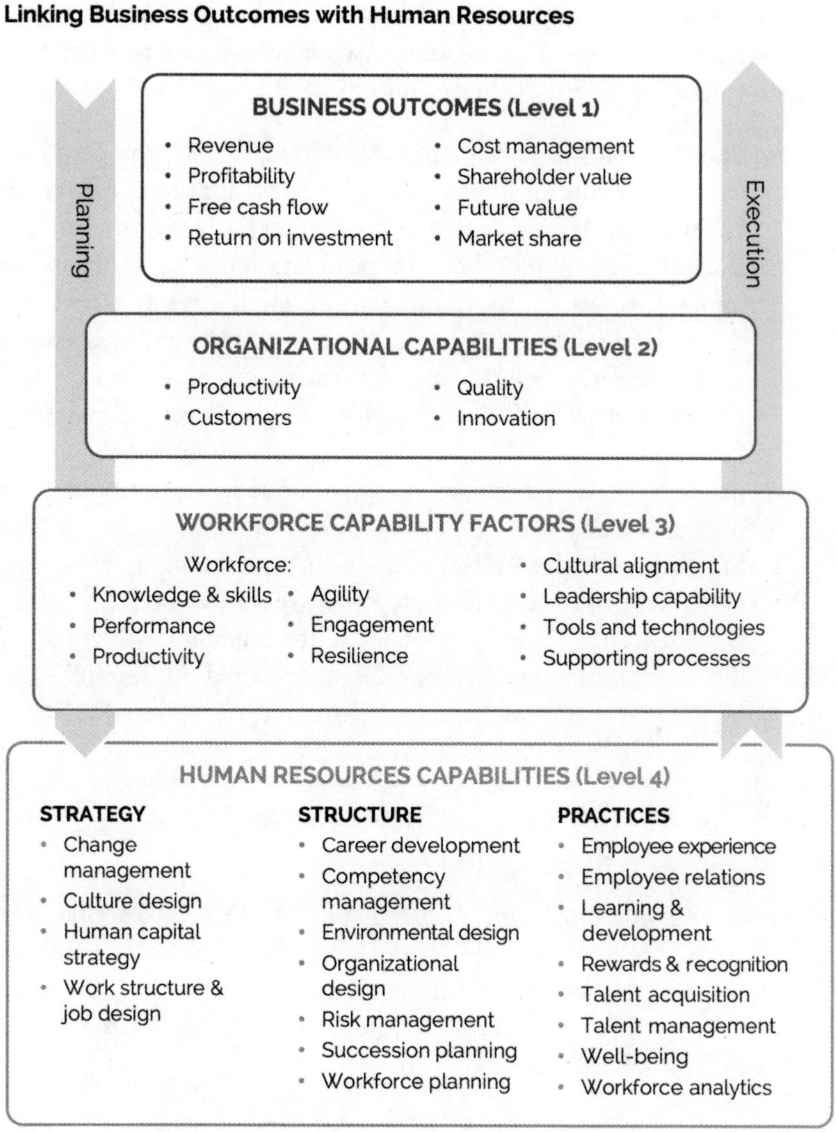

Linking Business Outcomes with Human Resources

Planning

Execution

BUSINESS OUTCOMES (Level 1)

- Revenue
- Profitability
- Free cash flow
- Return on investment
- Cost management
- Shareholder value
- Future value
- Market share

ORGANIZATIONAL CAPABILITIES (Level 2)

- Productivity
- Customers
- Quality
- Innovation

WORKFORCE CAPABILITY FACTORS (Level 3)

Workforce:
- Knowledge & skills
- Performance
- Productivity
- Agility
- Engagement
- Resilience
- Cultural alignment
- Leadership capability
- Tools and technologies
- Supporting processes

HUMAN RESOURCES CAPABILITIES (Level 4)

STRATEGY
- Change management
- Culture design
- Human capital strategy
- Work structure & job design

STRUCTURE
- Career development
- Competency management
- Environmental design
- Organizational design
- Risk management
- Succession planning
- Workforce planning

PRACTICES
- Employee experience
- Employee relations
- Learning & development
- Rewards & recognition
- Talent acquisition
- Talent management
- Well-being
- Workforce analytics

Figure 1.6 Human Capital Value Profiler (HCVP)

Adapted with permission from Max Blumberg, Alec Levenson, and Dave Millner, "A Strategically Aligned HR Operating Model" (USC Marshal Center for Effective Organizations, 2023), https://ceo.usc.edu/wp-content/uploads/2023/11/G23-02701.pdf, 4.

For example: A pest control company Blumberg worked with was struggling to increase sales. Here are two ways to look at what happened, through the lens of the HCVP:

1. **Starting with the "Business Outcome":** The company had trouble generating higher sales (**Business Outcome: Revenue Growth**), in large part due to challenges both maintaining and expanding its client base (**Organizational Capability: Customer Growth**). Overcoming those challenges required that their salespeople improve their prospecting, product knowledge, customer relationship management, and closing skills (**Workforce Capability Enabler: Sales Force Capability**). Based on findings from data analysis, HR improved these skills through a combination of enhanced recruitment and onboarding.

2. **Starting with the "HR Processes":** Improvements in recruitment and onboarding (**People Processes**) increased the skills of the sales reps (a **Workforce Capability Enabler**), which in turn drove customer growth (an **Organizational Capability**) and increased revenue (a **Business Outcome**).

Utilizing this model can help set the stage to enable HR to concretely support and deliver value to the business.

Extrapolate Dot-Connecting to HR Domains   You can apply/adapt the HCVP model to distinct HR domains, such as Talent Acquisition. Simply modify the Human Resources Processes to reflect that unit's strategies, structures, and processes, and similarly update the Workforce Capability Factors.

Involve HR Broadly in Strategic Decisions

Among the most important changes business leaders can make: including HR in all major strategic decisions, not just the ones that *seem* HR-related. As explained below and reflected in many of our case studies, HR provides expertise essential to addressing a range of business challenges.

Remember: Business Problems are People Problems All business problems are people problems at one level or another. Ah, but what about a broken machine? We're glad you asked. As it happens, the sector one might imagine is *least* impacted by people problems—U.S. manufacturing—is facing profoundly serious ones, namely a shortage of humans.

A 2024 study by Deloitte and The Manufacturing Institute (MI) projects that the sector may need to fill as many as 3.8 million jobs between 2024 and 2033, with around half (1.9 million) potentially remaining open due to two yawning gaps: skills (technical manufacturing, digital, and soft skills like critical thinking, problem-solving, and creativity) and job applicants. It's no wonder that 65% of respondents in the National Association of Manufacturers' 2024 Q1 outlook survey indicated that talent attraction and retention are their *primary* business challenges.[22]

If you are the CEO of a U.S. manufacturer, could you really afford to have anything but a high-performing HR team helping you address these issues head-on?

For additional evidence that business problems are people problems, look no further than the case studies and "cautionary tales" shared throughout this book. HR helped analyze, understand, and address a range of challenges that seemed unrelated to HR, something to keep in mind the next time you wonder whether you should ask HR for help (please do):

- Business transformation
- Customer loyalty
- Data security
- Digital transformation
- Location strategy
- Product launch
- Restructuring (*see* following)
- Revenue
- Safety
- Sales

And nearly every story depicts the benefits of enlisting HR's help as soon as possible and/or the pitfalls and price to pay when HR is overlooked, ignored, or dismissed.

Bring in HR from the Start   Engaging HR at the inception of business projects will help you take full advantage of WFA and ensure that people issues are incorporated into decision-making.

Below is one of several stories in which an HR professional got wind of a problem rather than being asked to help address it from the outset (you won't let that happen, right?).

Cautionary Tale | Penny Wise, Pound Foolish: Save Money by Asking HR

When a leading U.S. banking corporation decided to shut down a line of business (LoB) and launch a new one, the Finance team jumped straight to work. Their plan—made without HR's input—was swift: terminate hundreds of employees tied to the closing LoB.

By chance, the CHRO overheard the news. Acting quickly, the leader deployed the People Analytics team to determine alternative approaches. Analyzing the skill profiles of employees in the closing LoB, the results were clear. Instead of mass terminations, the company could redeploy talent into roles in the new LoB, and let attrition take its natural course over time. This approach would save millions in severance costs, retain valuable employees, and maintain the company's employer brand reputation—a win for both business and employees.

This near miss highlighted a critical flaw: the lack of a strategic partnership between the CHRO and CFO. Without the CEO insisting on Finance/HR alignment, the CFO overlooked HR's broader perspective on talent mobility and long-term costs, and simply viewed the restructuring as a financial exercise. Without HR at the table, the company was set to waste millions, lose key talent, and damage employee morale.

You may wish to review the stories about involving HR in Section 3, Take Your Preference, too. The following is an additional realm where HR can make an impact, if allowed.

Merge with HR for M&A Mergers &Acquisitions is notoriously difficult to do well. In fact, 70–90% of acquisitions fail.[23] And, very often, contributing factors are people related. "When it comes down to closing and signing the deal—it's always about people," says Lisa Blair Davis, Global Head of HR, Johnson & Johnson MedTech. In addition to planning fundamentals like global compensation, benefits, and employment contracts, her team is involved in processes including due diligence—assessing senior leaders and the board of directors as well as issues like pricing and product innovation—and partners closely with business development leads. Davis herself has met with target company CEOs to learn about culture and key talent. "It truly is an opportunity to deliver HR in a much more end-to-end way."[24]

A high-performing HR function can meaningfully contribute to M&A success in realms including:

- **Cultural Alignment:** Culture mismatches are fatal in M&A. HR can identify cultural gaps and similarities and design a plan to unify values and behaviors.
- **Protecting Talent:** Uncertainty during M&As risks losing top performers. HR can drive business continuity by implementing retention strategies and providing role clarity through transparent communication.
- **Managing Change Effectively:** Navigating organizational shifts without HR expertise is a recipe for chaos. HR can provide clear messaging to minimize resistance and keep engagement high, actively track satisfaction through surveys and feedback, and address concerns to maintain focus and motivation.
- **Streamlining Roles and Structures:** Misaligned roles or poorly managed restructuring can stymie operations. HR has the expertise to redefine job roles, ensure fairness in evaluations, and facilitate seamless onboarding for reconfigured teams.

- **Creating Unified Systems:** Redundant processes waste resources. HR integrates policies, systems, and workflows, streamlining operations and building a cohesive workforce.
- **Prioritizing Employee Morale:** Overlooking morale can derail productivity.

Even extremely basic details of a deal can be overlooked by leaving HR out of the planning. One colleague told us about a global professional services firm that acquired a company whose workforce included thousands of forklift drivers. The firm employed no forklift drivers and had no use for forklift drivers. Yet the deal team never consulted HR about the potential impact on acquisition success or how to negotiate the future of those employees. The deal got done, and HR was left picking up the pieces.

Give Workforce Data a Starring Role   As described elsewhere in this book, business leaders must proactively and thoughtfully champion new standards for data-driven decision-making. To maximize insights, they must also put workforce data at the center of the action. According to RedThread Research, C-level leaders should consider workforce data as they do finance data—"essential to nearly every business decision."[25]

The need to embrace workforce data will become increasingly clearer as you read on.

Clearly Communicate New Approaches   As with any change, communication is key. Business leaders can help key players understand HR's new role in driving strategy, new relationships, and new reputation. CEOs can share this information internally, and even externally, with shareholders, analysts, and the media.

1.4 Act on the Insights

This advice may seem obvious, but we have seen enough instances of data being ignored to know that it's a subject meriting attention. Just as data without insights has little value, insights will have limited impact if they "don't get seen by the right people, don't get exposed to the right people, or worst of all, don't get used to improve the quality of daily decision-making."[26]

In other words, insights without action will not move the needle on anything.

Commit to the Key Step

Yet the road from insight to adjustment can be challenging to navigate. HR professionals surveyed by HR.com on a range of WFA processes scored themselves lowest on making "constructive changes" in response to WFI, even those with more mature WFA functions.[27] This is another area where business leaders can help drive change by asking HR for the insights and partnering with them to determine how to move ahead.

Cole Napper, Principal Owner of Directionally Correct, observed that most HR data is "not actionable in the eyes of leaders," as it's either too simplistic or too complex. Data in what he calls the "Goldilocks zone" is sophisticated yet approachable enough that leaders actually used it, made decisions from it, and the business improved as a consequence. To Napper, "that is such a rare body of work, and it shouldn't be."

The important November 2024 study from renowned HR expert Josh Bersin, "The Definitive Guide to People Analytics: The Journey to Systemic Business Analytics," ties three of "15 Essential Practices for Systemic Business Analytics," to ensuring data "isn't just collected but used to fuel progress:"

- Make recommendations strategic, customizing solutions by business unit.
- Be systematic about how WFI are shared.
- Use WFI to drive truly consequential decisions for the company's sustained success.[28]

Reject the Enemy: Inertia

The payoff is significant: businesses that both generate sophisticated WFA and use them to act are 6.7 times more likely to effectively manage change and 7.7 times more likely to be innovative. The Bersin study counsels following the example of high-performing organizations, which "fall in love with the problem," rather than the solution, and focus analytics efforts on prioritizing, quantifying, evaluating, predicting, and nudging action.[29]

Below is the story of one executive especially committed to acting on insights. While we don't necessarily advise going to such extremes, it was effective, and we applaud the chief revenue officer's dedication to success (and, we admit, their stunning endorsement of the power of L&D).

Vignette | Acting on Insights: One Sales Executive's Insistence on Success

A global shipping and mailing company faced an existential threat. As digital communication surged, demand for traditional mail processing and postal metering equipment fell sharply, putting their market leadership at risk. To adapt, the company pivoted to sophisticated shipping technology systems aimed at helping businesses streamline operations and increase profitability. But selling these advanced solutions required retraining sales teams, long accustomed to selling simpler equipment.

The Learning & Development (L&D) team not only created a multifaceted program, but they also carefully tracked results to ensure that the knowledge and skills were indeed helping the reps succeed. Early data from the program revealed a critical insight: the 35% of reps who completed all program components, including learning assignments prior to the start of the course ("prework"), and strictly adhered to the sales methodology produced a 42% increase in sales. The remaining 65% did not complete all the coursework or apply the new methodology and saw no notable change in sales results.

Acting on this data, the Chief Revenue Officer (CRO) took extraordinary steps to ensure strict adherence to the training process. Reps who arrived at the next training without having completed their prework received a letter from the CRO instructing them to return home immediately. More than half the class was sent away, but the entire sales team got the message. Subsequent learners arrived fully prepared, and the sales organization was soon consistently exceeding their sales targets.

1.5 Key Takeaways

This section offers practical ways to start integrating **Workforce Insights (WFI)** and **Workforce Analytics (WFA)** into how you, and your HR function, think and work. WFI are the powerful revelations you can extract through WFA, which combines and studies data about your workforce (human + machine) and data about your business.

- **Commit to Insights, Not Metrics:** Shift your mindset from numbers (metrics) to the stories those numbers tell (insights). Consistently pursue HR reporting (all reporting, really) that conveys impact versus just activity. Know which HR metrics are truly meaningful so you can ask better questions and demand better answers. And, appreciate that if your HR team is not already providing the data we're suggesting, it is likely no one ever asked them. But you will.

- **Embrace Workforce Insights:** Understand the nuts, bolts, and benefits of WFI so you can understand and address impacts on workforce performance, improve critical talent and business outcomes, and achieve strategic priorities. Get to know "killer combos" of workforce and business data that can generate WFI.

- **Let HR (Get Better at) Help(ing) You:** Learn how well-designed HR initiatives can directly support your key business objectives, and how you can create the conditions for that success by being a better informed, more supportive, more consistent partner. After all, business problems are people problems at their core. So, bring in HR early and regularly, and use those "killer combos" to inform your strategies and tactics.

- **Act on the Insights:** Uncover important information and then do . . . nothing? You're too smart for that. Invest in your own success by making it a practice to consistently and concretely use WFI to improve your business and talent outcomes.

Bottom line: Prepare to extract insights from your data by shifting how you think about metrics (impact vs. activity), understanding how WFI are generated (killer combos), helping HR to help you achieve your goals, and committing to acting on what you learn.

SECTION

2

Enabling Workforce Analytics

CEOs AND OTHER business leaders can—and must—help their organization reap the rewards of Workforce Analytics (WFA) and Workforce Insights (WFI), partly through funding (that's you, CEOs) and partly from an awareness and appreciation of what's needed to advance top business priorities.

Start by deepening your own understanding of workforce data, then help ensure your company has the technology, guardrails, people, and collaborative spirit needed to make WFI a reality.

We'll also explore a topic that is relatively new as of this writing: analytics for human-machine collaboration.

2.1 Get with the (Workforce Data) Program

Raw HR data is not inherently meaningful. Its value comes from using it to understand, predict, and influence business relevant outcomes.

—Steve Hunt, PhD, Founder, i3 Talent, LLC

47

Enabling WFA requires that you (and all leaders, and HR) better understand workforce data and what makes it uniquely powerful—and complex. Appreciating these two seemingly contradictory characteristics will help to create the conditions under which combining workforce data and business data to yield actionable insights can begin to transform your business.

Appreciate Why "It's Complicated"

Enormous Volume   HR produces huge quantities of workforce data, encompassing details from throughout the employee lifecycle: hire date to post-exit "alumni" contact information and everything in between (*see* "Employee Data 101" later in this section). This is in addition to the enormous volume of business data overall, which increases by 63% every month, according to a recent Deloitte survey.[1]

Legally Protected   Much workforce data is sensitive and comes with special ethical, legal, privacy, security, and confidentiality considerations. HR departments must comply with local, federal, and regional data protection laws affecting employee information (*see* details as follows), including from "works councils," mandatory bodies akin to U.S. labor unions.

Compliance is critical for maintaining trust with employees and stakeholders as well as avoiding financial penalties and reputational damage.

Good Fences Can Annoy the Neighbors

Legally, HR must prevent unauthorized individuals from accessing employee data. This obligation can nevertheless cause or exacerbate garden variety data territorialism and may prompt other business units to prevent HR from accessing *their* data. Business leaders who wish to leverage Workforce Insights to help accomplish their goals must prevent this, starting with setting expectations within their team around data-sharing and collaboration.

No Standardization "In engineering, you have standards. In Finance, you have Generally Accepted Accounting Practices and standards set by Sarbanes-Oxley, but in HR, we have no measurement standards," Noah Rabinowitz, Chief Learning Officer, explained. "Every company, regardless of industry or sector, represents People Analytics differently." This can impede credibility, collaboration with other functions and alignment with business measures (among other things).

Bad Reputation Unlike data from Finance, Legal, Sales, Engineering, or Operations, workforce data is often seen as untrustworthy. This is due to unfortunate issues (past and present) with data quality, including:

- **Inconsistencies:** In addition to HR lacking overarching data standards, as explained above, inconsistent internal data like job titles or performance metrics further erode data reliability.
- **Fragmentation:** Most companies use multiple HR platforms with inconsistent data practices, which can lead to scattered data that's hard to consolidate and compare.
- **Limitations:** Privacy and security constraints impacting how HR collects and shares data can result in issues like incomplete datasets.
- **Isolation:** Data silos can seriously impede integrating HR data with other business functions, restricting analysis and limiting strategic insights.
- **Inaccuracies:** Systems that capture self-reported data and/or data entered manually can lead to human error, like when hiring managers, recruiters, or applicants themselves mis-enter candidate information.
- **Incompleteness:** Employees can be lax about updating their work experience and skills (if your company tracks such critical data; if not, add it to your list). They may also choose, legally, to withhold personal data such as demographics.
- **Unstructured data:** Text, images, and multimedia formats— all "unstructured"—require specialized processing to extract

meaningful insights. AI has transformed analyzing text-based HR data like engagement survey comments, emails, and talent reviews, using techniques such as advanced natural language processing and intelligent pattern recognition across complex data types, but has not eliminated all the challenges of accurately interpreting employee sentiment, behaviors, and performance.

Sometimes workforce data quality *is* poor, and when that happens, the impact is real. As Sergey Gorbatov, Managing Partner, Intalensight, shared with us, "If you show a beautiful dashboard but the data there is crap, then you undermine the effort very quickly . . . Without quality of data, your sandcastle just goes away with the next wave."

But sometimes HR data gets a bad rap because . . . it's from HR. And HR, as we've discussed, has baggage. Perhaps no story illustrates this better than The Case of the Disappearing Credibility.

The Case of the Disappearing Credibility

Lucy Adams, CEO of Disruptive HR, told us about a friend who was head of Logistics for a global media company. "And then, as often happens," she related, company leaders said, "Oh, you're an intelligent, capable person, we'll just give you HR."

As head of Logistics, he told her, when he presented to the board, no one questioned his work. "But now that I'm CHRO," she recalled him saying, "I present my findings and everyone just piles on going, 'No, no, that's not the right answer. We should do it this way.' And it's like, what happened? At what point did I suddenly become someone who wasn't of any credibility?"

Now Included: Machines   The era of modern human-machine collaboration introduces new complexities and opportunities to WFA. Machine-generated facts and figures, detailed in *Machine Data 101*, further below, present novel ways of measuring a host of productivity, efficiency, and impact metrics. And, like all data, it also brings compliance and data security challenges (*see* "Machine Data Privacy", later in this section).

Know Where It Lives

If that wasn't complicated enough, workforce data is also scattered throughout your company, a top technical challenge for the "killer combos" that power WFI. Appreciating this aspect of the complexity will serve you (and your data-driven aspirations) well. We provide advice on overcoming these challenges in "Support Data Integration" below.

Across HR   HR guru Josh Bersin estimates the average company has "30–40 HR-related and productivity systems."[2] These would include separate Software-as-a-Service (SaaS) solutions for HR realms (like Talent Acquisition), each with its own database, data model, and formatting. Figure 2.1 helps illustrate HR's many data support systems.

Figure 2.1   Human Resources Ecosystem

Credit: Actionable Analytics Group.

The most common HR systems:

- **Human Resources Information Systems (HRIS)** manage and automate core HR functions and processes including employee data management, payroll, benefits administration, and compliance reporting.
- **Learning Management Systems (LMS)** centralize and manage employee training programs and data, enabling the creation, delivery, and tracking of online or in-person training courses and helping employees track and meet learning requirements and goals.
- **Applicant Tracking Systems (ATS)** handle the entire hiring process, from posting job openings to tracking applicants, automating tasks like resume screening, interview scheduling, and candidate communication.
- **Employee Listening and Feedback Tools** enable organizations to gather and analyze employee feedback through surveys and sentiment analysis to understand employee satisfaction and engagement, helping inform responses to workplace concerns and improve employee experience.

Across the Company   Every company's unique tech stack houses different data types in multiple systems, including workforce data that resides outside of HR. Examples:

- **Finance:** Compensation, capacity utilization forecasts, cost per headcount, open positions
- **IT:** Personal activity, both online and physical, from time spent using one's keyboard to badge swipes; group activity including meeting schedules and email; number of helpdesk requests
- **Sales:** Time to quota, deal close rates, pipeline size, deal velocity
- **Customer Support:** One-call resolution ratio, escalations per employee, number of tickets opened and resolved, customer satisfaction ratings by team
- **Engineering:** Bugs resolved, points completed, points per employee, time to product delivery

"It's Complicated"—A Deeper Dive

"Fundamentally, the HR space is a classic multi-system problem. Even within Enterprise Resource Planning (ERP) that has a suite of solutions, each area of HR has massively different processes and concepts that require advanced data modeling.

For example, compare your core employee data from your HRIS, LMS, and ATS and then add an employee engagement survey. Each has different types of events, workflows, processes, and data structures that need to be understood and combined into a coherent logical model. Then you need to consider all of the events flowing across time, so you have a massively multidimensional data structure that may be held on many separate platforms.

On top of this we have the critical overlay of data privacy and confidentiality that is required when handling data about people. This is just the start—real impact comes when you combine people data with business data, and you have again extended the level of complexity.

There are also political challenges with sharing data across the enterprise and the lack of technology investment for People Analytics and IT teams thinking they can solve it with a general BI [business intelligence] approach rather than a deep understanding of the HR space and the unique nature of people data."

—Tony Ashton, Chief Product Officer,
One Model—People Analytics

Data, data everywhere—and turning that data into insights requires many steps, key among them integrating all those disparate data sources.

2.2 Support Data Integration

Of the many strikes workforce data already has against it, integration is a doozy. "Unlocking people data's value within organizations can be challenging," asserts a recent EY report. "Legacy systems, outdated and incompatible with modern tools, create hurdles for data analysis. Inconsistent practices across units result in data silos and conflicts over ownership."[3]

As this EY report implies, integration means both data and people, two factors that may be equally tricky to overcome.

Connecting the Right People

As explained above, data lives all over your company. So do the people who control that data. If you want to solve your business challenges through WFI, bringing together the right people is critical (hint: if your CEO isn't already on board, get her there ASAP).

Make collaboration table stakes. As a business leader, you already know well (perhaps too well) the extent to which human nature can give way to conflict, and how interpersonal tensions can stymie progress. Set expectations that your leaders and data experts will be among those playing productively in the sandbox.

We weren't surprised by this statistic: only 24% of 271 companies recently surveyed had established strong relationships between their WFA and Finance teams.[4] It reflects themes we encountered over and over again in our research.

Much needs to be done to reverse the trend.

Cultivating Collaboration   **The right people must be in the room where it happens.** The people with the motivation and skills to derive meaningful insights and drive meaningful change are typically **data owners, data users,** and **leaders** within and outside HR such as IT, Finance, Sales, Customer Support, Marketing, and Legal. The CEO must ensure these key players create a regular meeting cadence and set goals, and then meaningfully hold them accountable for achieving those goals.

Another player, if/when your company has one, is the **Chief Data Officer (CDO)** or **Chief Data & Analytics Officer (CDAO)**, an increasingly common role. In its inaugural year, 2012, an annual survey of data executives at Fortune 1000 and leading global organizations found just 12% had a CDO. By 2023, 82.6% of respondents had appointed a CDO or CDAO. Though they shared meaningful gains in CDO/CDAO impact, 43% still considered the role "nascent and evolving/struggling with turnover."[5]

Aligning incentives is essential. To ensure collective and individual accountability, players should set goals with quarterly targets that then transfer to their own performance targets, with rewards for achievement.

Recognizing progress builds momentum. Business leaders consistently praising data successes, large and small, will help motivate committed partnerships and inspire incremental progress while also aiming high for long-term gains.

Building Trust in People and Data

> People hold data grudges. If data was wrong once, the accuracy of that data source is forever doubtful in people's minds.
>
> **—Steve Hunt, PhD, Founder, i3 Talent, LLC**

Part of your role as a WFI believer is helping HR bolster—or in some cases, rehabilitate—its data reputation. Consistent, high-quality data, which a high-performing WFA team can deliver, will help. So will positive, collaborative relationships that you encourage among data experts and leaders making data-driven decisions. But your clear and unwavering support for HR, especially among other business leaders, is also essential.

Acknowledge the history. HR folks may have PTSD from past attempts to collaborate around workforce and business data, gain access to non-HR data, and/or have others trust their data.

Seal of Approval

The need to build trust can birth inventive solutions. WFA leader Suku Mariappan shared that his team developed a literal seal of approval—an icon they add to reports and dashboards to convey that the contents had been properly obtained, cleaned, analyzed, and approved. The seal reflects a discipline that gives people confidence.

Data is power—help channel it. Data can make people look incredibly good, or unbelievably bad. Some people would rather be blamed for being uncollaborative than look stupid by sharing data that could reflect poorly on their performance. Your goal as a leader is to keep data players focused on making the company successful—full stop (*see* incentives, discussed earlier).

Encourage iterative improvement. Business leaders understand that starting with imperfect data is sometimes necessary and can lead to improvements over time. Yet HR's struggles with data quality issues can paralyze efforts to use people insights effectively. Set expectations that imperfect initial data can be progressively refined.

Data Collaboration, Two Ways   The following two case studies illustrate divergent outcomes when teams must partner to create successful WFA. First, a cautionary tale conveys just how wrong things can go. The case study depicts how successful collaboration across functions—with senior leaders' support—can effectively solve expensive business problems.

Cautionary Tale | The High Price of Data Privacy Without Partnership

A CEO aiming to transition his organization from on-premise systems to Software-as-a-Service (SaaS) approved an ambitious HR technology road map proposed by the newly appointed Chief Human Resources Officer (CHRO). Designed to facilitate the company's internal move to the cloud, the road map also aimed to improve data privacy and security while enhancing operational efficiency.

As the CHRO prepared plans for the multi-platform rollout, she discovered significant data privacy risks. Both Finance and IT, which at the time owned and managed HR data governance, regularly ran reports containing sensitive and confidential employee information, and often distributed them via email, including to employees not trained to handle the sensitive data.

After consulting with and gaining approval from the company's Data Protection Officer, the CHRO removed Finance and IT access to confidential HR data, took over reporting and governance, and assumed responsibility for the HR tech road map implementation. While those actions removed privacy risks, they also caused major friction with Finance and especially IT. Both teams also lost access to some of their own dashboards, and IT was shut out of configuring and selecting a major new tech stack. Frustration and resentment grew and the opportunity for partnership was lost.

Finance and IT obstructed the tools' success, and HR worked to keep IT and Finance out of the loop, resulting in fractured workflows, delays, and morale issues. Well-intentioned efforts to protect employee data led to a painful lesson: HR data governance requires extensive cross-departmental collaboration and plenty of good will. By failing to establish productive partnerships, HR—and the company—paid a heavy price in strained relations, operational inefficiency, and lost opportunity.

Case Study | Integrating for Impact: How Data-Driven Insights Transformed Sales Success

In 2012, one of the largest enterprise software companies in the world bought a rapidly growing SaaS provider, "Acme." This acquisition brought exciting growth potential but revealed critical integration challenges, hindering revenue goals and leaving both sides dissatisfied. Faced with lagging sales numbers and high rep attrition, leadership engaged the Acme sales enablement team to help them understand and address the challenges.

The Problem

With the support of Acme's CEO and CHRO, the team launched a data-driven analysis to get the root causes at work. By combining sales data from the CRM (Customer Relationship Management) and ERP (Enterprise Resource Planning) and sales rep data from

(continued)

(*continued*)

HRIS (Human Resources Information System), among other systems, the team revealed serious challenges that were stymying financial success. New hires took an average of 42 months to meet quotas, more than triple the industry-standard of 11 months, and early-stage attrition was at 18%, well above the industry average of 14%. Worse yet, a small group of high performers generated most of the revenue. The CEO issued a stretch target to the team: cut time-to-ramp for new reps in half within one year.

The Solution

To address these issues, the company took an integrated approach, enabled by close collaboration between individual leaders and multiple business units and data integration from multiple systems. They began by interviewing the top sales reps to uncover their best practices, then designing a range of initiatives to teach these effective strategies to underperformers.

The enablement team **revamped the Sales Bootcamp** to target specific skill gaps. A **Sales Coaching Dashboard** provided managers with insights into critical metrics and tailored coaching recommendations, while a **new Mentorship Program** offering personalized guidance from Day 1, helping new hires quickly adapt to the sales environment and build confidence to accelerate new hire productivity. **Enhanced data analytics** allowed the team to monitor pipeline creation, deal size, and conversion rates, enabling real-time adjustments to optimize rep outcomes.

The Results

Boosted by collaborative partners and powerful data, the team easily met the CEO's challenge. Their accomplishments in just 12 months:

- **Time to Quota:** Reduced from 42 to 22 months.
- **Attrition Reduction:** Regrettable attrition among new hires dropped from 18–3%, saving more than $510,000 in rehiring costs and lost productivity.

- **Bootcamp Boost:** Within six months of completion, bootcamp graduates generated 36% more pipeline and closed 23% more deals than previous new hires.
- **Pipeline Conversion:** Improved by 79%.
- **Revenue Growth:** Average deal size increased by 65%.

Cutting to the Chase

With active involvement from the CEO and CHRO of this newly acquired SaaS provider, the sales enablement team was able to access multiple data sources, identify root causes, and design a holistic solution that completely turned sales around. Thanks to executive support, combining resources across Sales, HR, and IT accelerated ramp time, reduced attrition, and transformed sales outcomes.

Connecting the Right Data Sources

Aligning relevant parties creates a hospitable environment for connecting workforce data both within and outside HR, a major struggle for WFI. In HR.com's 2023–2024 State of People Analytics study, respondents named data integration as the most difficult of eight analytics processes, and only about a third of respondents agreed or strongly agreed that their *HR technology systems* are well integrated (41% disagreed or strongly disagreed).[6] Only 23% of organizations "often or always" integrate business data with HR data.[7]

The previously mentioned November 2024 research from The Josh Bersin Company paints an even starker picture: just 9% of companies integrate diverse types of data and standardize metrics across HR and business systems, and fewer than 10% are correlating or otherwise "directly linking HR and people data to business metrics."[8]

Investing to Get Returns Connecting data siloed in different systems, including across geographies with distinct privacy regulations, will require investment. No matter where your company is on your data integration journey, overcoming challenges to derive the benefits of insight-driven decision-making will need a budget from business leaders like you, and of course, your CEO.

Spending (Wisely) on HR Analytics Tools

Leaders need to champion the best-in-class consumer-driven talent analytics platforms that are now available.

—Shelly Holt, VP, Talent Development

HR organizations already spend about 8.4% of their total budget on HR technology, the highest investment area for three consecutive years, according to Gartner.[9] Your CHRO must determine how best to spend those funds on HR analytical tools, including **newer AI tools**, which Bersin sees as a powerful workaround to data integration challenges. "I've been doing data analysis and data management for 30+ years," he writes, "and these new tools are as groundbreaking as the spreadsheet was compared to an HP calculator."[10]

In addition to rapidly advancing AI tools, organizations must assess which HR analytics tools—more common and more sophisticated than ever—can help them integrate multiple data sources and provide actionable insights aligned with business objectives. Below are some insights into key choices to make.

Build: Companies with software development capabilities may choose to develop internal analytics platforms internally. Such systems would create new data pipelines and dashboards tailored to HR's data and needs, hooked up to general business intelligence software the company already has (if not, it's probably time).

- **Pros:** Control, customization.
- **Cons:** Resource intensive, with complex data governance constraints and maintenance.

Buy: Paying for a best-in-class point solution designed to handle WFA can help quickly launch a range of functionalities and metrics capture versus building dashboards one by one. Built-in security typically includes multiple access levels and compliance checks.

- **Pros:** Speedy time to value, robust security, customer support.
- **Cons:** Some customization limitations, high price tag (typically six figures).

Consolidate: Companies with an enterprise-level HR solution can potentially purchase a WFA add-on; however, its analytical capabilities may not extend to HR data living elsewhere, significantly reducing its usefulness.

- **Pros:** Reduces or eliminates need for integration; one-stop shop.
- **Cons:** May be limited to data in that system, fewer capabilities than point solution, some customization limitations.

Getting Dashboard Makeovers   Business leaders should demand dashboards that deliver value: well-designed, accurate, user-friendly data interfaces that comprehensively present employee and business metrics, compellingly visualize insights, and inform decision-making. Truly integrated dashboards are still aspirational for many companies, but a highly worthy goal.

Note: Like all tools, dashboards are a means to an end—generating Workforce Insights—not a final data destination. They are also living organisms that can and should change as business goals shift or programs are deprioritized.

Striving for Quality, Accepting Imperfection   Data quality is a worthy but highly technical topic, so we will keep this high-level. A few quick definitions:

- **"Clean" data: usable, accurate.** Clean data has been prepared to a level suitable for accurate analysis and insights, based on factors like data accuracy, consistency, completeness, and conformity to predefined rules or formats.
- **"Dirty" data: requires attention.** Dirty data, not fully processed or standardized, has issues like duplicates, missing fields, inconsistencies, or errors that can skew results or lead to misleading conclusions.

Dedicating budget to ensure "clean" workforce (and other) data is fundamental. That said, don't let perfect be the enemy of the good. Sometimes starting with imperfect data is necessary and can lead to improvements over time. "Most businesspeople understand that dirty data is the path to good data," HubSpot's Ben Putterman told us. "Since you have to start somewhere, you can start with dirty data as long as you're willing to iterate and learn from it."

Unblocking Access

Data owners being territorial will do absolutely nothing to advance your company's strategic priorities, whether those individuals are possessive because they think they can do more with the data than another team, aren't yet on board with a collaboration agenda, or simply distrust HR.

As a business leader, and here CEOs are critically important, clearly communicate that no one within your purview will block and tackle when it comes to your workforce or any other data. Be swift and emphatic in your response if it does happen. The exception, of course, is where access must be limited due to privacy and/or other considerations, as emphasized throughout this book.

Naysayers may request that HR data first go through what they perceive as a more trusted source, like Finance or IT. That's an inefficiency—as well as a trust killer—to avoid at all costs.

Business leaders: lobby your CEO to unblock access whenever/wherever needed.

2.3 Fall on the Sword of Data Governance

A Caveat

As a business leader, you surely know the importance of data governance. Because the topic is so broad and so crucial, and because we are neither data governance experts nor would we want to play ones on TV, we will highlight core issues and players relevant to workforce data.

Workforce Data 101

As we define workforce data as including both humans and the bots, automations, or other "machines" that support them, we cover both employee and machine workforce data governance.

Employee Data 101 The basics—a primer for beginners and a reminder for advanced WFA fans. "**Employee data**" encompasses a variety of information that organizations collect and maintain about their employees. **Personally identifiable information (PII)** is data that can uniquely identify an individual, such as a person's full name, a home address, or phone number, and online identifiers like IP addresses or cookie data. Other categories of employee data:

Financial	Bank account details, Social Security numbers, and similar sensitive data.
Medical	Health records, medical history, genetic data, psychological or behavioral health information, and any details about disabilities or medications.
Biometric	Unique identifiers like fingerprints, facial recognition data, iris scans, and DNA sequences.
Demographic	Age, gender, race, nationality, religious beliefs, sexual orientation, and other personal attributes.
Employment	Details about salary, benefits, performance evaluations, and disciplinary actions.
Criminal history	Records of arrests, convictions, sentencing, and related information.

Machine Data 101 The **employee data** counterpart would be **machine operational data** or **machine-generated data**: any information collected and maintained about the machine's identity, performance, and interactions within a system.

Identity Data	Would include unique identifiers (serial numbers, device IDs, IP addresses) and configuration data (model, firmware version, installed software).
Operational Data	Spans performance metrics (speed, efficiency, uptime/downtime), usage patterns (task types, frequency of operations), and diagnostics (malfunctions, failures).
Environmental Data	Covers contextual information (location, temperature, humidity) and input/output data from sensors (e.g., readings from IoT devices).

Behavioral Data	Pertains to interaction data with humans or other machines (task assignments, collaboration patterns) as well as learning and adaptation records (changes based on AI/ML algorithms).
Security Data	Is found in access logs (who or what accessed the machine) and cybersecurity events (unauthorized access, software vulnerabilities).
Lifecycle Data	Ranges from maintenance records (service dates, component replacements) to end-of-life or decommissioning data.

Key Governance Issues

Having defined employee and machine data, let's explore at a high level the key governance issues business leaders need to be aware of. Please consult legal and other experts for detailed guidance.

Employee Trust   Employee trust is in many ways the most important facet of data governance but the most easily overlooked since it is governed not by regulations but rather by integrity and empathy. Research shows that workers are actually willing to share data—with conditions.

- In one survey, 90% of respondents were willing to let their employers collect and use data about them and their work *if* it benefitted them.[11]
- In another, most employees surveyed were open to sharing personal data on "skills, interests and passions, preferences, and performance on informal work in projects or internal gigs" even if unrelated directly to their role, but for many, it depended on "whether their employer offered them benefits in return."[12]

These findings reflect what Insight222 calls a **Fair Exchange of Value**, a "key mantra" for WFA professionals: workers who know how their data will be used and believe it will benefit them are more likely to provide it, improving analysis quality and yielding mutual benefit.[13] Employees must also recognize their part in quality data, especially self-reported data, and its potential impact on company goals related to hiring, promotions, and recognition.

The key takeaway: Find ways to use employees' data for their benefit, and chances are, your company will benefit, too.

Bias   Bias in WFA refers to systematic errors in data collection, analysis, and interpretation that lead to unfair outcomes. It presents specific governance challenges that organizations must address to ensure equitable decision-making. And, as AI expert Bernard Marr points out, "Biased data means your insights will not be informed by objective reality." Marr is among many experts citing bias prevention as a key societal challenge if AI's potential is to be realized.[14]

Biased data inputs can result from historical workforce data that contains embedded biases reflecting past discriminatory practices, which can lead analytics tools to perpetuate inequities in hiring, promotions, and performance evaluations. **Algorithmic bias** happens when models unintentionally favor or disadvantage certain groups due to flawed design or training processes, potentially embedding systemic inequities.

Governance frameworks should:

- Monitor and correct bias with mechanisms including regular audits, predictive model validation, and incorporating diverse perspectives in model development.
- Commit to transparency and explainability to building trust and accountability regarding bias.
- Ensure compliance with anti-discrimination laws.

Ethics   Especially with the hyper-advancement of AI, ensuring ethical data use requires serious intention and resources. Insight222, a leading resource for insights and information about People Analytics, suggests building a "data ethics charter" to address ethical concerns. Their six recommendations:

1. **Define What's Important:** Clearly establish the purpose and weigh potential risks and benefits of collecting and analyzing employee data for both company and employees.

2. **Align Key Stakeholders:** Identify and collaborate with stakeholders to address their concerns and align ethical principles with broader organizational goals.

3. **Demonstrate and Communicate Specific Individual Benefits:** Transparently explain how analytics initiatives will benefit the company and employees. Insight222's advice if you cannot do so for employees: "be careful." If you cannot for either group, do not proceed.

4. **Create a Process:** Develop a structured approach for designing and implementing the ethics charter, ensuring it reflects stakeholder feedback and incorporates change management.

5. **Develop an Implementation Plan:** Establish actionable steps and checkpoints for each stage in an analytics project to guide the work while adhering to ethical principles.

6. **Translate the Charter into Action Questions:** Formulate practical questions to evaluate whether each stage of the analytics process aligns with agreed ethical standards.[15]

Diane Gherson, Board Director at Kraft Heinz, Centivo, and Tech-Wolf, BCG Senior Advisor, and CHRO Coach who drove the adoption of AI and automation as CHRO of IBM 2013–2020, said "one of the first things that we did when we started using it was to publish our own code of ethics around how we use AI in HR. The headline was, 'just because you can, doesn't mean you should.'"[16]

Collaboration is key for ethics. A recent study found that although in 89% of organizations the WFA function has a "working partnership" with legal and data privacy experts, only 36% have a governance body regularly meeting and overseeing the ethical use of its people data.[17]

In a similarly troubling finding, 99% of data leaders see a need for "safeguards and guardrails for governing Generative AI," yet only 63% have such measures in place.[18]

As a business leader, champion the powers that be to ensure that your company helps increase these numbers.

Sensitivity and Compliance   Business leaders must ensure their company's data practices comply with regulations on privacy, data protection, reporting, and more or face serious risk. If you are directly involved, *plan ahead*. If not, know and appreciate the significant resources devoted to complying with these regulations and support your colleagues wherever possible. For examples, *see* "Key Governance Players," further in this section.

Access and Security   Due to its sensitive nature, workforce data requires restrictive access controls and layered security protocols to prevent internal misuse or external breaches. Governance frameworks must regularly review access, design a highly regulated process to grant any exceptions, make certain only authorized personnel have access to specific datasets, and ensure employees know how to protect their own data. *See* the data security case study on Salesforce in Section 4, "Creating Your Insight-Driven Culture."

Integration Across Systems   Good governance practices can help integrate workforce and business data across systems, enabling more accurate, real-time WFI. Your company's CHRO and workforce data experts must be full partners in data governance bodies with authority to drive meaningful change.

Dynamic Nature of Workforce Data   Workforce data is constantly evolving thanks to hiring, promotions, terminations, re-orgs, and more. Governance must ensure systems manage ongoing changes and keep data accurate.

Machine Data Privacy   Yes, there are privacy concerns related to machine data, especially in the context of human-machine collaboration and increasingly interconnected workforce technologies. These concerns stem from the potential for misuse, unintended exposure, or exploitation of machine data, especially when machines are integrated into environments involving sensitive operations or human interactions (*see* Figure 2.2).

Mitigating machine data privacy concerns involves steps similar to other data types. Establish **clear governance policies** to define who

Data Linkage to Individuals	Machine data often overlaps with personal data when machines interact with humans, like IoT workplace devices that track employee behavior, location, or activities, raising concerns about surveillance and privacy intrusion.
Sensitive Information Leakage	Machines operating in secure or confidential environments like healthcare or finance may generate data revealing sensitive operations, workflows, or proprietary information.
Unintended Data Exposure	Machine logs and operational data can inadvertently include personal or sensitive information like keystrokes or customer data processed.
Security Breaches	Machine data is often targeted by cyberattacks, with risks of vulnerabilities discovered, operations disrupted, or confidential information extracted.
Behavioral Tracking and Profiling	Machines with AI or IoT sensors may track user preferences, habits, or performance data, potentially leading to unauthorized profiling of those individuals.
Ownership and Access Rights	Disputes may arise over who owns machine data, especially in collaborative environments involving multiple stakeholders (e.g., suppliers, vendors or contractors). Improper access controls could lead to privacy violations.
Ethical Use of AI and Analytics	Using machine data to train AI models may inadvertently perpetuate biases or make decisions that negatively impact human stakeholders without their knowledge or consent.
Cross-Border Data Transfers	Machines operating across international boundaries may generate data that is subject to varying privacy laws and regulations, creating compliance challenges.

Figure 2.2   Machine Data Privacy Concerns

Credit: Actionable Analytics Group.

owns, accesses, and uses machine data, especially when it intersects with human-related information. Embrace **data minimization**, collecting only what's necessary for operations to reduce exposure risks. **Encryption and security protocols** protect machine data at rest and in transit to prevent unauthorized access. Be **transparent** and inform stakeholders about what data is being collected, and why and how it will be used. Finally, ensure **regulatory compliance**, heeding privacy laws when machine data includes or interacts with personal data (*see* as follows).

While machines don't have privacy in the human sense, the data they generate can have significant implications for the privacy of the humans or organizations they interact with. Thoughtful management and ethical practices are critical.

Key Governance Players

> Regulatory changes are coming from different workforce regulatory agencies in the U.S. and worldwide—it's critical for business leaders to be aware and stay on top of these requirements.
>
> **—Keith Sonderling, Former Commissioner, United States Equal Employment Opportunity Commission**

In workforce data governance, various players contribute to setting standards, ensuring compliance, and protecting data privacy. We share this with you to raise your awareness of how serious and extensive workforce data governance truly is. As follows, some key players:

Regulatory Bodies Compliance regulations and authorities differ across the globe, with Europe in the lead in terms of privacy law maturity and strict enforcement mechanisms, followed by the United States.

Europe   The European Commission and related entities drive regulations covering data privacy, transparency, and reporting.

- The **General Data Protection Regulation (GDPR)**, considered by some the gold standard in data privacy (and by others a giant thorn in the side, given its extraterritorial reach and hefty penalties), requires secure employee data storage and entitles employees to access, correct, and delete their data.
- The **Corporate Sustainability Reporting Directive (CSRD)** obliges certain companies to disclose workforce data including employee development, wages, and labor conditions.
- Each EU country has a **Data Protection Authority (DPA)** to ensure GDPR compliance.

United States   Various agencies regulate how U.S. companies oversee workforce data.

- The **Department of Labor (DOL)** oversees workforce data including wage reporting, workplace safety data collection, and labor market statistics.
- The **California Consumer Privacy Act (CCPA)** requires state-level transparency about workforce data collection, data sharing opt-outs, and security measures.
- Regulated sectors require more standards for their employees, such as the **Health Insurance Portability and Accountability Act (HIPAA)** and **Financial Industry Regulatory Authority (FINRA)**.
- The **Federal Trade Commission (FTC)** regulates data privacy practices, including employers, especially around data misuse or security breaches.
- **Securities and Exchange Commission (SEC)** Regulation S-K requires since 2020 that public companies disclose "material" human capital information, without clearly defining "material." While designed for flexibility, wide variances in disclosure hinder comparisons, even among direct competitors.[19] In 2023, the SEC's Investor Advisory Committee recommended more

standardized metrics, such as demographics and turnover, to offer investors consistent insights.[20] As of this writing, the SEC has not mandated these.

- The **Equal Employment Opportunity Commission (EEOC)** has mandated EEO-1 reporting since 1966 to help ensure compliance with federal anti-discrimination laws and monitor for patterns that may indicate workplace discrimination. Keith Sonderling, EEOC commissioner from 2020 to 2024, anticipates increased scrutiny from agencies like the FTC and SEC, which are considering various mandatory disclosures (such as pay and demographic data) to modernize and enhance oversight and regulation of the employment space.

Oceania   Australia's Privacy Act and New Zealand's Privacy Act provide comprehensive frameworks for protecting workforce data.

Asia   **Japan:** The **Tokyo Stock Exchange (TSE)** requires that companies disclose specific data including workforce policies and efforts around human capital investments. The **Personal Information Protection Commission (PPC)** obliges companies to manage workforce data securely.

Other countries: Government authorities regulate issues like workforce data collection, storage, and privacy in countries including China, India, Malaysia, Singapore, and Thailand.

Other Regions   Workforce data regulation is still developing elsewhere. Countries with larger economies typically take the lead: Argentina, Brazil; Israel, Saudi Arabia, United Arab Emirates (UAE); South Africa, Nigeria.

Standards Organizations   **International Organization for Standardization (ISO):** The ISO 30414 global certification in human capital reporting may offer regulatory bodies a basis for future reporting standardization.

Corporate Governance and HR Leadership   **HR leaders** must ensure that data collection, storage, and usage align with legal requirements and company policies on privacy, compliance, and transparency. Many organizations establish internal **data governance committees** comprising IT, HR, Legal, and other leaders to monitor and develop governance frameworks that ensure compliance and risk management.

Each player contributes to ensuring workforce data is handled appropriately in compliance with local and international standards.

2.4 Understand Workforce Analytics Capabilities

As early as 2020, McKinsey reported that most large organizations had People Analytics teams, with 70% of company executives indicating People Analytics was a top priority.[21] Of course, executives checking a box on a survey is very different from those same men and women demanding, funding, nurturing, and otherwise ensuring the success of any given priority.

We've explored some of what needs to happen to make WFI a true business intelligence tool and performance enabler. Now, let's address what a WFA capability could look like for your organization.

See the Journey

We start by examining WFA maturity to provide context and perspective. As an overall philosophy, we found this advice from Deloitte apt. Considering WFA an *organizational imperative* (as we suggest) means "approaching it like its own business. Not a science project or an adjunct piece of the human capital puzzle, but a full-fledged internal service provider that directly affects business success."[22]

Considering Workforce Analytics an organizational imperative (as we suggest), means "approaching it like its own business. Not a science project or an adjunct piece of the human capital puzzle, but a full-fledged internal service provider that directly affects business success."

Components of Workforce Analytics Maturity Below are several approaches that, taken together, cover broad territory and should help identify key areas of focus for a company aspiring to develop their WFA capability. The common themes reflect key topics in this book:

- Data-driven culture
- Technology and tools
- Data governance and ethics
- People and skills
- Value and business impact
- Change management

Workforce Analytics Maturity "Dimensions": PwC offers these "dimensions" as part of a broader People Analytics Maturity Assessment Framework to help organizations assess current and aspirational future states. These progress along five levels of maturity, from Prefoundational (not yet begun) to Foundational (ad hoc), Aspiring (consistent), Mature (reflecting best practices), and Leading (cutting edge). *See other maturity progressions below.*

1. **Strategy:** A clear vision, mission, and initiatives aligned with the digital agenda and integrated into HR processes, widespread employee adoption of analytics-driven decision-making, robust operating model and sufficient budget.
2. **Technology:** Scalable IT systems and advanced tools that extract deep insights and improve decisions.
3. **People:** Cultural readiness for change, analytical skills, effective training, and clear team roles.
4. **Data:** Quality, governance, and security with sophisticated data analysis yielding actionable insights and consistent, well-developed reporting.[23]

Workforce Analytics Maturity "Characteristics": Insight222 offers "Eight Characteristics of Leading Companies."[24] It's no coincidence that value follows investment.

Investment

1. **Influence:** People Analytics leaders maintain a close reporting relationship with the CHRO, helping them effectively influence the C-suite.

2. **Business Priorities:** People Analytics targets advanced insights aligned with the organization's top priorities.
3. **Skills:** Investment is made in three critical skill areas: People Analytics consulting, data science, and behavioral science.
4. **Ethics:** Strong ethical standards guide People Analytics activities, with transparent communication of these standards to employees.

Value

5. **Measurement:** The function quantifies the financial value it delivers through its activities.
6. **Democratization:** Data is accessible to managers and executives to inform decision-making.
7. **Personalization:** The function creates personalized analytics tools and insights for employees.
8. **Data-driven Culture:** The CHRO ensures data and analytics are integral to HR strategy, and HR business partners enhance their data literacy.

Insight222 2023 research identified Ethics as the eighth characteristic, reflecting its growing importance; they'd listed the other seven in 2022.[25] Some companies create a dedicated data ethics role to "lead the case for all ethical standards and practice of people data across the enterprise."[26]

Progression of Workforce Analytics Maturity   Other approaches to understanding maturity plot progress along a scale, focusing more on the sophistication and impact of the analytics than the function's dimensions.

Levels of Impact   Visier offers a simple approach paralleling People Analytics maturity with "workforce intelligence" maturity, which aligns (more or less) with the four levels of analytics discussed in Section 1, Commit to Insights, Not Metrics. As shown in Figure 2.3, this model, fairly logically, links deeper analytics capabilities to an increase in business value delivered.[27]

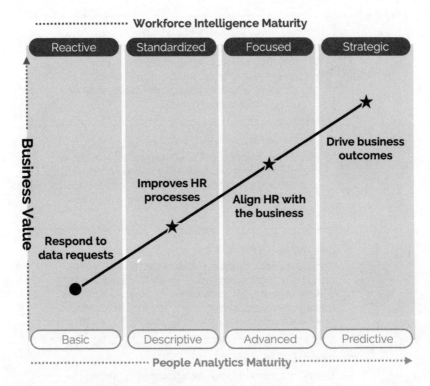

Figure 2.3   Workforce Intelligence Maturity Model

Source: Reprinted with permission from Visier, "7 Steps to Becoming a Highly Effective HR Organization: Using people analytics to drive better business outcomes" (Visier, 2023), https://www.visier.com/lp/people-analytics-data-driven-hr/, 13.

Levels of Performance   The Josh Bersin Company's November 2024 report, "The Definitive Guide to People Analytics," shares a model tracing four levels of performance (*see* Figure 2.4). Interestingly, the study differentiates between *systemic* **people** *analytics*—focused on improving HR processes and employee management—and *systemic* **business** *analytics*, using advanced data solutions to improve organizational performance overall (i.e., what we mean by "Workforce Analytics"). Note: Figure 2.4 mentions a "data dictionary," which is a single, authoritative source of truth for how data is understood and used across an organization; it catalogs detailed definitions, descriptions, and documentation of data elements, defining their structure, meaning, and business context.

Systemic Business Analytics

Focus on driving business transformations: data that solves business problems; team has AI and global talent intelligence data; highly business aligned; strategically focused; works with C-level stakeholders.

Systemic People Analytics

Focus on shaping people strategy: data that solves people problems; operational focus on integrated data dictionary; emphasis on governance and ethics; storytelling; centralized team and some business data integration.

Integrated HR Analytics

Focus on understanding HR: data that measures HR operations and investments; recruiting dashboards; service delivery; dashboards for employees and managers; solid data dictionary; advanced reporting tools; data privacy in place.

Sporadic HR Reporting

Focus on data monitoring and compliance reporting: manual data collection; optimizing for accuracy; ad hoc data encryption; HR team skills limited to reporting; sporadic data available; low-tech support; risk-averse culture; monitoring basic KPIs.

Figure 2.4   Systemic Business Analytics Maturity Model

Source: Josh Bersin, Stella Ioannidou and Kathi Enderes, "The Definitive Guide to People Analytics: The Journey to Systemic Business Analytics," 2024, 19, https://joshbersin.com/definitive-guide-to-people-analytics/. Reproduced with permission from Josh Bersin Company.

The report offers advice on how to advance from each level to the next, providing examples of companies that have successfully followed that path. For example, steps going from Level 1 to Level 2 include building the WFA team; standardizing data collection; creating dashboards; and establishing ethics and privacy measures.[28]

Stages of Development Deloitte's research and analysis identifies four stages of maturity: Fragmented and Unsupported; Consolidating and Building; Accessible and Utilized; and Institutionalized and Business Integrated. Describing characteristics of these stages across six pillars offers a robust reflection on WFA maturity. Our take on their model is Figure 2.5.[29]

STAGES OF MATURITY			
Foundational	Developing	Established	Excelling
Analytics Capability Basic reporting; focus on activity vs. impact	Standard reports and basic analysis	Regular insights using multiple data sources and AI	Advanced analytics enabling transformation
Technology Ecosystem Spreadsheets and manual processes	Basic reporting tools and dashboards	Connected systems with automation	Integrated platforms with predictive capabilities
Stakeholder Scope Core HR team only	HR function and initial business partners	Active business unit partnerships	Enterprise-wide strategic partner; external collaborations
Governance Minimal practices, basic data monitoring	Defined standards emerging	Established quality and ethics framework	Comprehensive governance model with controls
Data-driven Culture Limited data awareness	Growing data literacy, skills	Data-driven decisions common	Analytics embedded in organizational DNA

PILLARS OF MATURITY

Figure 2.5 Workforce Analytics Maturity Model

Source: Adapted from Deloitte.

Benchmarking Research on Workforce Analytics Maturity   The *level* of insights your WFA team can deliver depends on the progress of your company's data analytics journey. The benchmarking data below can help you locate where that is.

In their **2023 High-Impact People Analytics (HIPAN) research**, Deloitte surveyed more than 400 organizations in 18 countries to evaluate what characterizes effective People Analytics. They reported progress each year since they began their HIPAN research: in 2017, just 17% of companies were at levels 3 or 4, and by 2020 only 18% were at those levels. But in 2023, that number had risen to 40%.[30]

Notably, Deloitte also found that high-performing organizations "treat PA as its own internal consulting capability with a clearly articulated strategy, a fit-for-purpose operating model, and clear measures of success."

The **HR.com State of People Analytics 2024–2025** survey asked 256 HR professionals across industries worldwide to score their organization's effectiveness in five "specific and sequential steps" in a WFA process. Figure 2.6 depicts the results overall, for "PA Leaders," and for "PA Laggards," who rated their company's current ability to "get the most value out of their people analytics" as extremely or very effective, or somewhat effective or not effective at all, respectively.[31]

The most recent research, published in November 2024, offers the worst assessment of WFA maturity. In "The Definitive Guide to People Analytics," Josh Bersin analyzes quantitative survey responses from 469 organizations across 50 countries.[32] Most still focus on measuring HR vs. driving business improvements.

Do not conduct any analytics	3%
Use predictive analytics to prepare for changing conditions	2%
Recommend actionable steps	3%
Aggregate business and HR data	4%

Respondents were asked to rate their organization's current ability in each area. Below are percentages for "good" or "very good":

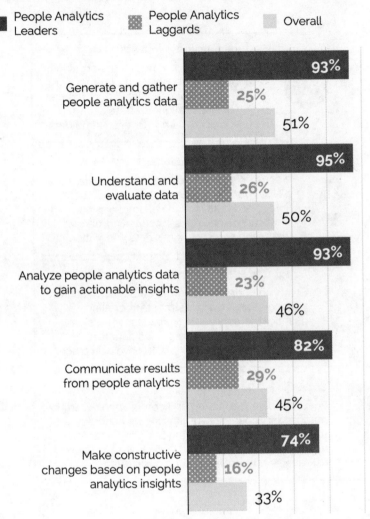

■ People Analytics Leaders   ▨ People Analytics Laggards   ▨ Overall

Generate and gather people analytics data — 93% / 25% / 51%

Understand and evaluate data — 95% / 26% / 50%

Analyze people analytics data to gain actionable insights — 93% / 23% / 46%

Communicate results from people analytics — 82% / 29% / 45%

Make constructive changes based on people analytics insights — 74% / 16% / 33%

Figure 2.6 Organizational Abilities Across People Analytics

Source: Adapted from HR.com, "HR.com's State of People Analytics 2024-25: Commit to Data-driven Growth in Your Workforce" (2024), https://www.hr.com/en/resources/free_research_white_papers/hrcoms-state-of-people-analytics-2024-25_m1g4f7he.html, 13.

Looking again at Bersin's Maturity Model (Figure 2.7), 75% of respondents reported being at Level 1 or 2, with just 10% at Level 4.

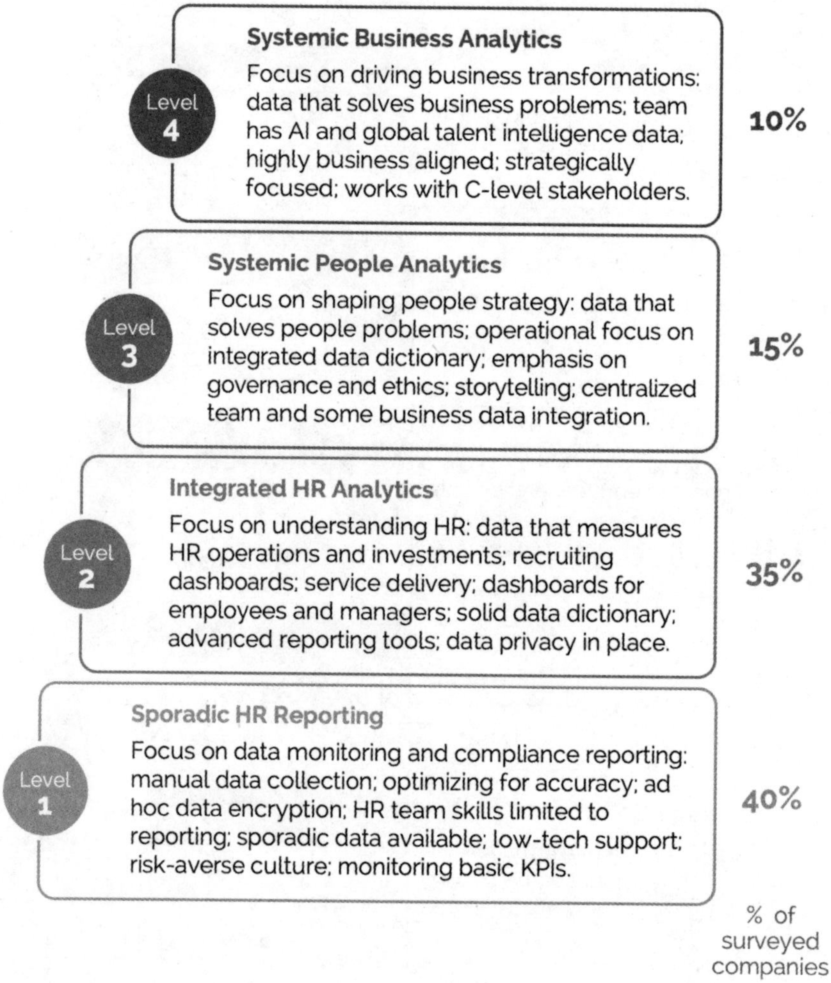

Figure 2.7   The Systemic Business Analytics Maturity Model with Benchmarks

Source: Bersin, Ioannidou and Enderes, "The Definitive Guide to People Analytics" 2024, 19. Reproduced with permission from Josh Bersin Company.

Though various benchmarking numbers differ, the message is the same: the enormous potential of WFA to transform business performance awaits most companies. Tapping it isn't easy, but few things worthwhile ever are.

Workforce Analytics Competencies   What skills would a WFA function need? Several sources offer frameworks for consideration, with key themes emerging. Importantly, technical abilities such as statistical modeling and database management are just one facet of a well-balanced WFA team skillset.

Six Skills for Success   This framework was developed by Nigel Guenole, Jonathan Ferrar, and Sheri Feinzig, authors of *The Power of People: Learn How Successful Organizations User Workforce Analytics to Improve Business Performance*, a resource we found enormously helpful.[33] Their findings, based on interviews with 60 practitioners, summarize the impressive range and depth of WFA capabilities.

1. **Business Acumen:** Quickly grasp and address business challenges. Key sub-skills include financial literacy, political awareness, organizational insight, and marketplace awareness.
2. **Consulting Skills:** Define problems, develop hypotheses, propose solutions, and manage change effectively. Stakeholder and project management are also indispensable.
3. **Human Resources Expertise:** Use deep HR experience and intuition, including domain specialization, to guide strategy and tactics.
4. **Work Psychology:** Bring scientific rigor in areas like individual performance (industrial psychologists) and team productivity (organizational psychologists) and domain expertise that can quickly help pinpoint causes of common issues.
5. **Data Science:** Extract and structure data for analysis via quantitative skills (building mathematical and statistical models of processes like attrition) and computer science skills (managing databases and programming).
6. **Communication Skills:** Share and inspire action on insights through deep skills in clear storytelling, visualization, presentation, and marketing.[34]

Four Core Skills   The Academy to Innovate HR (AIHR), an HR training provider, identified similar "core" skills for WFA: **business consulting** to identify critical issues; **analytical skills** to execute the technical side; **stakeholder management** to drive and enable collaboration; and **storytelling and visualization** to communicate effectively with the business and share results.[35] *See also* "Insist on Top Talent," below.

Examine the Options

Common Types of Set-Ups for WFA Teams   Workforce Analytics teams operate under a variety of models suited to their organizational goals, resources, and technological maturity. Figure 2.8 presents the most common operating models and associated pros and cons.

Smaller WFA functions may have a different set-up, potentially in combination with a model in Figure 2.8.

- **Embedded in HR/Dotted Line to Larger or Centralized Analytics Team (Most common):** Helps ensure alignment with HR priorities and goals while providing access to advanced analytics expertise and resources. Coordination between HR and larger function can require extra effort. Optimally, WFA leads report to CHRO or other senior HR leader.
- **Embedded in Larger or Centralized Analytics Team/Dotted Line to HR:** WFA professionals get access to data infrastructure, tools, and expertise—and cross-functional insights when on centralized team—but need clear, consistent communication and prioritization to remain aligned with HR-specific objectives.

Avoid isolating WFA professionals from HR by fully incorporating them into another team.

Help Evaluate Needs

It's a simple formula: Quality + Partnership (to the power of Communication). What matters most is whether your analytics team gives you the right insight into the right problems at the right time, delivered in the right way. To realize the vision, a realistic baselining of capabilities will provide the foundation for a talent strategy that combines consulting acumen with data science, analytical enquiry, and the capability to drive change.

—Mark T Lawrence, BA (Hons), MBA, FRSA, Head of Analytics & Reporting, Deloitte

	PROS	CONS
Centralized Model *(Most common)* One analytics team for entire organization	• High standardization, governance • Deep expertise in analytics	• Limited responsiveness to localized needs • Risk of isolation from frontline concerns
Decentralized Model Analytics capabilities embedded within individual business units or HR functions	• Tailored insights for specific units • Strong alignment with local priorities	• Inconsistent data practices • Difficult to scale solutions across organization
Hybrid Model aka Center of Excellence (Federated) *(More common for smaller teams)* Combines centralized oversight with decentralized execution	• Balances consistency and customization • Promotes innovation, best practice sharing	• Requires clear alignment between teams • Can be complex to manage
Front-Back Model (Consultancy) *(More common for larger teams)* Team divided into front office (strategy, business-specific needs) and back office (data consistency, operational efficiency)	• Front office can quickly adapt solutions to local or team requirements • Back office centralizes resources and streamlines processes, avoiding duplication of effort	• Miscommunication between offices can cause delays or inefficiencies • Over-reliance on back office can slow response times when overloaded • Strong governance needed to avoid inconsistencies

Figure 2.8   Common Models for Workforce Analytics Functions

Credit: Actionable Analytics Group.

Business leaders seeking WFI can help by advocating for appropriate investment and offering data, information, mentoring, moral support—whatever their HR partners may need. If your company is just getting started on its WFA journey, starting small and allowing for iterative improvements is fine.

To help your CHRO and team to identify what is most important in the short, medium, and long term, business leaders should communicate their priority challenges and work together to determine where to start.

Supporting WFA Capabilities   As HR prepares to ramp up operations (regardless of starting point), they'll have many considerations.

Skills: As outlined above, skills range from consulting to comms to collecting and calculating. They can be secured like any other:

- **Buy:** Your HR team may need to hire to ensure they have the data and analytics expertise needed to build out their capabilities.
- **Build:** No matter how good they already are, HR professionals will benefit from deeper skills in data and analytics and HR measurement overall. Your HR leaders and data experts will need to determine who should be trained first on the skills that are most needed to deliver value.
- **Borrow:** Temporarily bringing in expertise, whether from other groups like Finance or IT (potentially via a rotation) or hiring contract workers and/or consultants, may make sense.

Tech: Buying any technology solution (another worthy topic for a separate book) requires serious upfront investment—aligning stakeholders, identifying business objectives, defining success metrics, and more. HR should partner closely with IT and other analytics functions to help prioritize needs. Business leaders interested in seeing WFA succeed will find ways to be useful, even if it's as a sounding board or sympathetic ear.

Processes: Offer your insights to help prioritize goal setting, dashboard reviews, governance cadences, and other to-dos. A decision-making framework to help with prioritization may be useful.

Setting Goals   Here the CEO should step in to ensure that the CHRO is preparing the team for full accountability. They will need to capture objectives, leading and lagging indicators, dependencies, timelines, and more. Just like any other high-performing business function.

- **Rubber—meet the road.** Once priorities are identified, setting goals is an excellent time to road-test new relationships, collaborative frameworks, accountability parameters, and more.
- **Strike a balance.** Develop a road map that balances immediate business needs with long-term data and analytics goals.
- **Step by step.** Ensure that foundational data management practices are in place before pursuing advanced analytics projects.

Eye on the prize. The ultimate objective is to enable you, the savvy business leader, to make wise, data-driven decisions that help you achieve your priority goals. Benefits to HR are fantastic, and a source of excellent karma for you. But your focus? Workforce Insights for breakfast, lunch, and dinner.

Insist on Top Talent

Getting the best people will make advancing your company's WFI capabilities faster and easier. Below, needed skills are embodied in typical WFA team roles.

The Data Engineer	The Data Scientist
Builds and maintains data infrastructure.	*Extracts insights from data analytics.*
Data engineers design, construct, and manage the data pipelines and architectures that enable data collection and processing, ensuring data is accessible, reliable, and efficiently stored for analysis. They collaborate with data scientists by providing clean and well-organized datasets necessary for advanced analytics.	Data scientists analyze complex datasets to identify patterns, trends, and correlations that can inform strategic decisions, developing models and algorithms using statistical and machine learning techniques. They help translate data findings into actionable insights.

The Product Owner
Manages analytics tools and stakeholder needs.
Product owners configure, maintain, and oversee the systems and tools that generate insights. They work closely with stakeholders to understand their requirements and ensure the right analytics products are built to meet those needs, liaising between technical teams and end-users.

The Translator (aka The Storyteller)
Bridges technical and business communication, crafts compelling narratives from data.
As discussed in Section 1, Commit to Insights, Not Metrics, translators liaise between technical experts and business stakeholders, expressing complex technical jargon in business-friendly language and conveying business needs back to the technical team. They also weave data insights into engaging stories to inspire action to solve organizational challenges.

About the Workforce Analytics Job Market

A Role by Any Other Name   Despite the nice, neat descriptions in the previous table, naming conventions for WFA roles are far from settled. People Analytics platform provider One Model started tracking WFA job postings in January 2023. Within three months, their database contained more than 5,400 roles across 3,500 unique titles.[36] Forewarned is forearmed.

Beware of the Branding Issues   HR's persistent branding issues extend to hiring. Case in point: A Microsoft HR recruiter came to address a career course for first year MBA students at the UCLA Anderson School of Management. According to Class of 2026 MBA candidate Jack Tarlton, despite the recruiter presenting appealing work-life balance and compensation, "Most classmates said, 'No, thanks.' The general feedback was that HR wouldn't offer skills or experiences beneficial for long-term career growth."

2.5 Key Takeaways

Gain familiarity with key considerations and complexities of bringing WFI to life: organizational, governmental, human, and machine.

- **Get with the (Workforce Data) Program:** It's complicated—and there's a lot of it. HR data is sensitive, fragmented, and often plagued by quality issues. Some workforce data lives outside of HR; e.g., in IT and Finance, introducing additional technical, political, and other integration challenges.
- **Support Data Integration:** Integration challenges are a top WFI impediment. Business leaders seeking WFI must break down silos, build trust, actively cultivate collaboration and access, and encourage (and/or fund) investment in analytics and other integration tools. Also critical: drive toward progress, not perfection.
- **Fall on the Sword of Data Governance:** Know and help address fundamental governance issues and requirements specific to workforce data, from Employee and Machine Data 101 to ethics, access, and privacy to key governance players.
- **Understand Workforce Analytics Capabilities:** Understand WFA maturity, competencies, and options to help you benchmark your current capabilities and develop a road map to ensure you have the right people, skills, processes, and technology to be successful.

Bottom line: Your WFI success hinges on how well you and your company can address its many complexities, including data quality and data integration issues, human trust and other factors, legal and technical requirements, and needed WFA capabilities.

SECTION

3

Moving the Goalpost

HAVING EXPLORED CHANGING one's mindset about numbers in general and measurement in particular, and taken a deeper dive into the world of Workforce Analytics (WFA), we turn our attention to a closer study of the Human Resources function, where it's been, and what it could become.

Many business leaders, including CEOs, have low expectations of their HR team. But for WFA to become a true force for change, these same people will need to change their expectations, support, and accountability. If you want a team to run farther, moving the goalpost is the most obvious and concrete act.

Let's take time to appreciate first the other functions that have made the journey to a high-performing strategic partner. Following, we offer some perspectives on what good HR (outstanding, actually) can look like. Plus, some sojourning down that two-way street of accountability, with KPIs in tow.

3.1 Remember Yesterday's IT

Functions Evolve: HR Can, Too

In a fascinating chapter of corporate history, the C-suite was pioneered by none other than Alfred P. Sloan (1875–1966), who helped restructure General Motors over decades of leadership. Sloan had already formulated a "system of disciplined, professional management that provided for decentralized operations with coordinated centralized policy control," which he formalized into a new internal structure that—eventually—changed the face of GM and organizations worldwide.[1]

Since Sloan's structure took hold in the 1920s, the C-suite and the key functions it comprises have evolved significantly. The stroll down memory lane below will, we hope, be fascinating and easily called to mind whenever doubts about whether evolving your HR organization to achieve Workforce Insights (WFI) is worthwhile or even possible.

Leaders Evolve   As each function evolves, its leaders move from being "behind the curve" to being "on the curve," according to strategy consultancy firm BTS (*see* Figure 3.1). Those on the curve sit at the proverbial strategic table, helping accelerate enterprise business results and innovation proactively and with agility.

Those behind the curve are in reactive mode, service providers and order takers focused on operating cost effectively. They lag behind business needs.

Although the BTS chart in Figure 3.1 was developed for Chief Information Officers, with very few tweaks it could easily be adapted to the CHRO (replace "security issues" with "compliance issues," for example). But it could also be extrapolated to suit the evolution of Chief Finance Officers or Chief Marketing Officers.

IT and the CIO/CTO Evolved

From Fixing Projectors to Driving Digital Transformation   We begin with the namesake of this chapter because so many of us remember the IT of yore: the guy with the taped-together glasses and pocket protector who came to load software onto your desktop computer and connect it to the enormous printer down the hall. Most IT functions reported into Operations, and the most senior title was director. IT is also a close analogy to HR.

Today, a company's Chief Information Officer (or Chief Technology Officer) is—must be—among its most powerful and influential leaders (*see* Figure 3.2). CIOs and CTOs became prevalent in the 1980s, as computers replaced typewriters as (what we would now call) the knowledge worker's main productivity tool and something called electronic mail was starting to catch on. By the 1990s, the top IT leader had evolved from a data-processing expert to making executive decisions about hardware, software, and data management.

"Behind the Curve"	"On the Curve"
Struggling to align IT initiatives to business priorities	Working to shape business initiatives to take advantage of tech capabilities
Vigilant and chasing security issues	Vigilant and trying to anticipate security issues
Organizing and leading change efforts	Leading an agile organization in constant change
Striving for a seat at the table, struggling to show business relevance	Excited about their seat at the table but insecure or still striving to "fit"
Developing the right talent / skills	Keeping and investing in the right talent
Risk averse – show me where it has been successful before	Skeptical, confident, and self-sufficient
Hired as an Operator OR as a Change Leader	Hired as a Business Partner

Figure 3.1   Chief Information Officer

Source: Reproduced with permission from BTS.

The IT Operations Manager
1960s 1970s
Focused on overseeing mainframe computers and basic data processing for business operations.

The Technical Expert
1980s
Managed the growth of enterprise computing, software applications, and the shift to client-server models.

The Systems Integrator
1990s
Emphasized network development, infrastructure scaling, and integrating disparate systems.

The Digital Strategist
2000s
Oversaw the rise of the internet, e-commerce platforms, and early transformation efforts.

The Business Enabler
2010s
Aligned IT with business strategies, emphasized cybersecurity, cloud computing, and agile methodologies.

The Innovation and Transformation Leader
2020s and beyond
Focuses on driving digital transformation, adopting AI and emerging tech, and spearheading strategic innovation across the organization.

Figure 3.2   Evolution of the Chief Information Officer (CIO)/Chief Technology Officer (CTO)

Credit: Actionable Analytics Group.

Even so, throughout the 1990s (remember Y2K?) CIOs were "still largely IT operators rather than business executives," their teams treated as order takers, not innovators. The switch flipped in the early aughts, as social media, smartphones, search engines, and e-commerce made IT fundamental to business strategy and operations. This "consumerization of IT" was what finally transformed CIOs from running centralized computing to overseeing digital business strategy.[2]

The CIO role continued to evolve in the 2010s. Gartner's 2016 CIO Agenda Report of 2,944 respondents found that CIOs needed new styles of executive leadership, including collaboration, communication, and business alignment to exploit multiple platforms and build a network of digital leadership inside and outside the enterprise. "Digital leadership is a team sport," Gartner asserted, "with CEOs expecting their CIOs to be 'first among equals.' To succeed, CIOs must rethink and retool their approach to all the layers of their business's platform, not just the technical one."[3]

We could stop here, but the parallels to Finance and Marketing provide yet more support for the notion that evolving HR makes sense and is part of how savvy CEOs respond to changing realities.

Finance and the CFO Evolved

From Accounting to Strategic Stewardship   Ah, the bean counters. That's who Finance professionals were not so long ago. They served the business by handling accounting: bookkeeping, reporting, etc. Over time, however, factors including technological advances, globalization, and increased competition required that Finance, and its leaders, evolve to become strong partners involved in both shaping and executing on corporate strategy.

Today, CFOs are leaders in managing risk, guiding corporate investments, and ensuring compliance with increasingly complex, multi-geography regulations. The modern CFO is expected to optimize capital allocation and oversee growth initiatives such as mergers and acquisitions (M&A). *See* Figure 3.3.

CFOs also advocate for the company with shareholders and board members, and in some cases also manage investor relations. Underscoring the trust placed in these finance leaders, 23% of CFOs are board members of Fortune 500 companies. But these changes didn't come easily. CFOs grew up in an era where finance professionals focused on closing the books and managing balance sheets, not developing long-term growth strategies.[4]

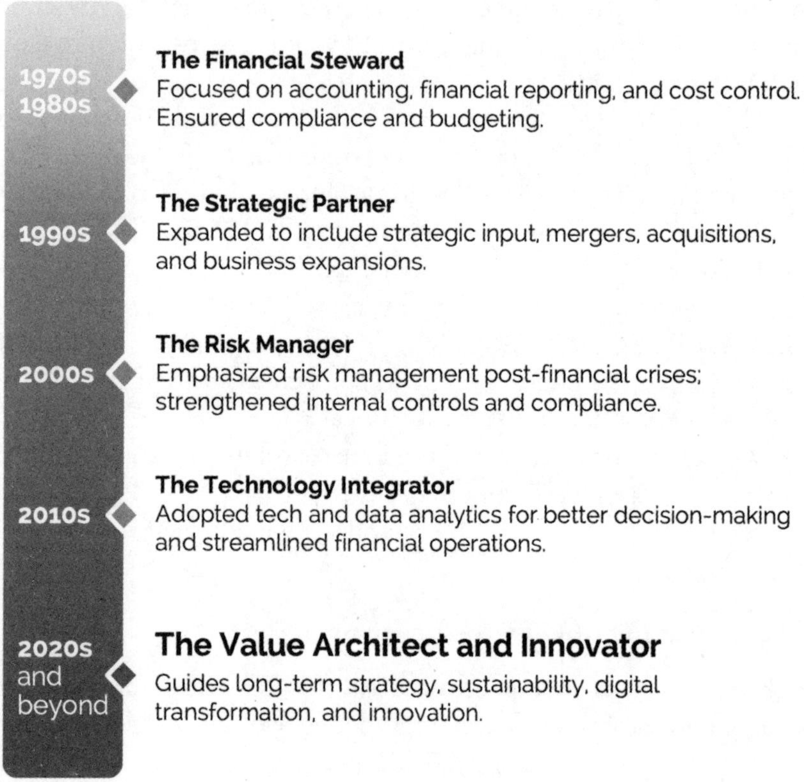

The Financial Steward
1970s
1980s   Focused on accounting, financial reporting, and cost control. Ensured compliance and budgeting.

The Strategic Partner
1990s   Expanded to include strategic input, mergers, acquisitions, and business expansions.

The Risk Manager
2000s   Emphasized risk management post-financial crises; strengthened internal controls and compliance.

The Technology Integrator
2010s   Adopted tech and data analytics for better decision-making and streamlined financial operations.

2020s   **The Value Architect and Innovator**
and   Guides long-term strategy, sustainability, digital
beyond   transformation, and innovation.

Figure 3.3   Evolution of the Chief Financial Officer (CFO)
Credit: Actionable Analytics Group.

They had to expand their mindset as well as their business acumen in order to meet the moment, elevated and empowered by CEOs and boards who granted them the influence needed to deliver on new expectations. And they had to engage with functions across the business—Operations, Marketing, IT, and, yes, HR—to understand and help develop holistic solutions to drive growth and performance.[5]

CFOs didn't get from there to here by themselves. CHROs won't, either.

Figure 3.4   Evolution of the Chief Marketing Officer (CMO)

Credit: Actionable Analytics Group.

Marketing and the CMO Evolved

From Public Relations and Parties to Brand and Customer Strategy Following a similar pattern to IT and Finance, Marketing once had a very narrow remit: advertising through storytelling, product promotions, and parties. Increased competition elevated the importance of more deeply understanding consumers and business customers, lead generation, building strong, memorable brands, and collaborating with Sales. *See* Figure 3.4.

Leads began joining the C-suite in the 1990s, as the rise of the Internet and early e-commerce transformed many Marketing fundamentals. As both commerce and everyday life increasingly moved online, the discipline evolved, too. Today's Chief Marketing Officer is also a major strategic partner to the CEO and board, helping drive long-term growth, which Gartner calls the "center of the bullseye" for most CMOs.[6]

Today, CMOs lead digital strategies, create customer experiences, and even shape corporate values.[7] Some Marketing functions also drive the "talent brand" and/or "employer brand," shaping perceptions of their company to attract top talent.

As with CIOs and CFOs, marketing executives also could not have made such a radical transition without empowerment from top executives, the CEO, and the Board of Directors.

Evolution in business is part of the natural order. This is true regardless of function. It was true of Finance, IT, and Marketing, and it is true of HR today.

HR Must Evolve Now

From Worker Protector to Workforce Enabler   A 2020 IBM study surveyed more than 1,500 HR executives regarding HR's reinvention. More than two-thirds of respondents said HR is "ripe for disruption." Executives from top-performing companies—leaders in profitability, revenue growth, and innovation—are "extremely confident" in the need to reinvent HR and eight times as many of those senior leaders are *already leading* their HR disruption, compared with other respondents.[8] *See* Figure 3.5.

Remember the Global Pandemic?

During the COVID-19 pandemic, HR was thrust into a much broader role, quickly needing to adapt its own operations while also helping their employers and employees adjust to the new reality.

HR teams coordinated with **IT** for remote work technology needs, **Finance** to address tax and payroll considerations, and **Real Estate** and **Operations** to ensure workplace safety. They took on new areas like health-related contact tracing and built external partnerships, collaborating with medical providers and navigating complex local, regional, and national health regulations. Some HR

1920s
1930s

The Welfare Officer
Focused on employee welfare, safety, and basic labor rights during the industrial era. Managed worker conditions and grievances.

1940s
1950s

The Labor Relations Specialist
Addressed labor unions and collective bargaining; managed strikes, labor contracts, and workplace policies.

1960s
1970s

The Personnel Manager
Expanded to include administrative HR tasks, payroll, hiring processes, and regulatory compliance.

1980s

The Human Capital Manager
Emphasized human capital as a valuable asset; focused on performance management and organizational development.

1990s

The Employee Relations Expert
Prioritized employee engagement, retention strategies, and conflict resolution; introduced structured feedback systems.

2000s

The Strategic HR Leader
Integrated HR strategy with business objectives; focused on talent management, leadership development, and succession planning.

2010s

The Culture and Change Champion
Emphasized fostering company culture, diversity and inclusion, and managing large-scale organizational change.

2020s
and
beyond

The People and Innovation Architect
Focuses on workforce innovation, data analytics in HR practices, employee well-being, and strategic workforce planning for the future.

Figure 3.5   Evolution of the Chief Human Resources Officer (CHRO)

Credit: Actionable Analytics Group.

leaders even established cross-company talent exchanges allowing organizations in struggling sectors, such as airlines and hospitality, to temporarily lend employees to high-demand industries, like healthcare and logistics.[9]

HR also co-navigated with **Legal** to address new regulatory and policy territory, determining company responses to a quickly changing landscape. Momentous decisions included employee requirements, guidelines, and enforcement: no coming to the office; coming into the office only with proof of vaccination; corporate social gathering allowed but only outside and in groups no larger than X; staying home for Y days if symptoms present; consequences for breaching policy; and more.

We will stop here to stave off any PTSD from those chaotic, scary times, but they help make the point that when HR needed to step up, they stepped up. HR helped keep people safe (and employed), shape new ways of working remotely, and sustain business operations.

And leaders seemed to recognize the difference: The percentage of executives "very confident" in HR's ability to navigate future changes doubled . . . from 12.5% in 2019 to 25% in 2020.[10] But no, we're not crazy about the notion that only a quarter of CEOs had that confidence AFTER witnessing how HR could turn on a dime. That's part of the reason we wrote this book.

We believe, and feel you will, too, that HR can and must evolve and that you as a business leader can help make it happen—and you'll get the strategic partner you need to achieve your most important business goals, through WFA.

3.2 Know and Demand Excellence

We now need HR to function like a professional services organization. The ultimate goal is not to "make HR better," but to help HR become ever-more effective at driving people strategies for the business. The best HR teams are bold, creative, and solution-oriented, and they don't just deliver "off the shelf solutions" but they listen, adapt, and add value in an integrated way.

—**Josh Bersin, Founder and CEO,**
The Josh Bersin Company

For many of you, the possibilities we are proposing may be new, unfamiliar, and possibly suspect. First things first. We titled this part of the book, *Know and Demand Excellence*. What does HR excellence look like?

The hallmarks of high-performing HR organizations, as you'll soon read, are clear and inspiring. But if you've never seen one in action, it may be hard to imagine what it can actually achieve. On the other hand, you may have no trouble thinking critically about any given HR function or HR overall.

Below, we delve into the function as a whole and three departments—Talent Acquisition, Learning & Development, and Compensation & Benefits—providing a broad range of perspectives. We look at the **cynical view** (beating our worst critics to the punch) and the **traditional view** (what HR has been known for), which we feel must urgently give way to the **strategic view** (where very good HR functions are today), and the **next-generation view**, reflecting advanced analytics and AI practices already happening at the highest-performing organizations and that will become pervasive in time.

Although these are general descriptions based on broad observations, you may see where your HR function is now, and where you'd like it to be. Bear in mind, of course, that not all HR functions are structured the same way, and that the maturity of domains will vary, even within the same company.

Human Resources Overall

HR plays a foundational role within any organization, but its impact varies widely depending on its approach. From a compliance-focused perspective to a fully integrated strategic partner, HR's evolution reflects diverse levels of influence on company culture, productivity, and long-term growth.

Cynical View

- The company's "rule enforcer" and compliance police, existing to protect the business from lawsuits, not to serve employees.
- A bureaucratic machine that generates endless paperwork, meetings, and policies, with negligible impact on business success.
- Attracts people who can't handle "real work," focused on "soft stuff" vs. contributing to the bottom line.
- Wastes resources on pointless initiatives like employee engagement surveys and wellness programs that no one asked for.
- Budget drainer, using empty buzzwords like "people-first" while employees feel disengaged and undervalued.
- Fundamentally out of touch, pandering to trends and perks instead of addressing genuine business needs or employee concerns.

Strategic View

- Positions HR as a vital partner in organizational success, aligning talent strategies with business objectives to drive performance and resilience.
- Develops a strong employer brand, comprehensive talent acquisition and development programs, and proactive engagement strategies.

Traditional View

- Focuses on essential administrative tasks such as payroll, hiring, and compliance, ensuring smooth day-to-day operations.
- Primarily manages employee relations, compensation, and benefits with a focus on consistency and policy adherence.
- Operates independently within its own scope, addressing issues as they arise and ensuring the organization meets legal and regulatory requirements.
- Viewed as a necessary support function, fulfilling operational needs and maintaining workforce stability, without broad involvement in strategic decision-making.

Next-Generation View

- Embraces AI, machine learning, and advanced analytics to automate routine tasks, predict workforce needs, and personalize employee experiences.
- Creates a dynamic talent ecosystem, utilizing digital tools to foster continuous learning, internal mobility, and a culture of agility and innovation.

- Uses data analytics to inform decisions, track workforce trends, and predict future needs, creating a more agile and responsive organization.
- Shifts from annual processes to continuous engagement, ensuring employee development and satisfaction are closely tied to business goals.

- Leverages predictive and prescriptive analytics to forecast trends, anticipate skill needs, and proactively address employee retention and engagement.
- Acts as a data-driven hub for talent strategy, aligning HR initiatives directly with real-time business performance metrics, enabling the company to stay competitive in rapidly changing markets.

Talent Acquisition

Talent Acquisition shapes the workforce by bringing in the right people to drive the organization forward. The approach taken by this function—from reactive hiring to predictive, data-driven strategies—affects not only the quality of hires but also the company's ability to adapt and grow.

Cynical View
- "Butts-in-seats" function, fills vacancies as quickly and cheaply as possible.
- Wasteful, hiring based on personal connections, or biases vs. meaningful assessments, leading to high turnover.
- Ineffective; most hires leave or underperform, regardless of recruitment efforts.
- Attracts same candidates as every other company, no unique employer brand or appeal.
- Runs endless interviews, with little regard for cultural fit or alignment with company values.

Traditional View
- Establishes processes for posting jobs, screening candidates, and scheduling interviews.
- Prioritizes filling open positions efficiently, with activity ebbing and flowing as hiring needs arise.
- Primarily evaluates applicants based on job requirements and qualifications, aiming to find suitable matches for specific roles.
- Focuses on addressing immediate staffing requirements, with limited integration into broader business planning.

Strategic View

- Positions Talent Acquisition as a partner in shaping the organization's future by aligning hiring with long-term goals.
- Builds a strong employer brand to attract high-quality, culturally aligned talent.
- Develops data-driven talent pipelines to meet anticipated needs, improving efficiency and readiness.
- Enhances candidate experience, boosting acceptance rates and strengthening employer reputation.
- Collaborates with business leaders to ensure hires contribute to innovation and growth.

Next-Generation View

- Utilizes AI-driven tools to streamline sourcing, screening, and candidate engagement, reducing time-to-hire and improving efficiency.
- Uses predictive analytics to identify talent gaps and forecast future needs, allowing for agile, preemptive hiring or talent mobility strategies.
- Leverages machine learning to analyze candidate data and match applicants with roles that align with both skillsets and predicted cultural fit.
- Integrates conversational AI for 24/7 candidate communication, creating an interactive and personalized recruitment experience.
- Implements virtual reality (VR) or augmented reality (AR) assessments for immersive evaluations, giving candidates realistic job previews and improving hiring accuracy.

Learning & Development (L&D)

L&D equips employees with knowledge and skills to succeed in their role and adapt within the organization. The function's approach, from compliance-driven training to a culture of continuous learning, should directly impact both individual growth and the company's competitive edge.

Cynical View

- Box-checking exercise to ensure regulatory compliance, with no real impact on business outcomes or employee skills.
- Money drain, providing training that employees forget or ignore, adding little value to actual performance.
- Low-priority function that only exists to satisfy HR requirements and avoid liability issues.
- Offers generic, irrelevant courses that waste time rather than developing any critical, job-relevant skills.
- Unnecessary "perk" for people who want to "learn" vs. get real work done.

Strategic View

- Aligns L&D initiatives with business objectives, building skills critical for the company's long-term success.
- Emphasizes upskilling and reskilling to help employees adapt to modern technologies and evolving roles.
- Uses data to identify skill gaps and create targeted, personalized learning paths.
- Helps attract, engage, and retain talent by making development central to company culture and employee offerings.
- Measures outcomes through performance data and demonstrates learning's impact on business results.

Traditional View

- Focuses on compliance training and onboarding to meet regulatory standards and basic job requirements.
- Delivers standardized courses on essential skills and company policies, addressing immediate training needs.
- Emphasizes completion rates and learner satisfaction scores, with limited measurement of training effectiveness or business impact.
- Functions in isolation from broader business planning, with minimal influence on long-term workforce development.

Next-Generation View

- Deploys AI-driven adaptive learning platforms that tailor content in real time to suit each employee's learning pace, skill level, and other preferences.
- Uses predictive analytics to anticipate future skill needs, proactively preparing the workforce for emerging demands.
- Employs VR and AR for immersive, hands-on training experiences, particularly for high-stake or technical skills, enhancing knowledge retention and engagement.
- Integrates with AI to provide bite-sized learning and real-time feedback that reinforce skills on the job, to build a culture of continuous improvement.
- Links L&D outcomes to performance metrics, providing real-time insights into ROI and productivity impact.

Compensation & Benefits (Total Rewards)

Compensation and Benefits (or Total Rewards) encompasses how an organization rewards and recognizes employees for their contributions. The approach taken in structuring rewards—from standard pay and benefits to customized, dynamic packages—affects employee satisfaction, loyalty, and overall alignment with company goals.

Cynical View

- Necessary evil, with minimal differentiation between roles or individuals—everyone is paid just enough to prevent them from leaving.
- Relies on rigid pay scales and generic benefits, with no attention to employee preferences or life stages.
- "One-size-fits-all" approach, with minimal investment in unique benefits or flexibility.
- Focused more on cost-cutting than enhancing employee motivation or loyalty.
- Superficial; benefits look good on paper but are rarely accessible or valuable in practice.

Strategic View

- Develops a comprehensive philosophy informed by company values and goals that drives the development of a Total Rewards strategy.
- Tailors rewards packages to appeal to diverse employee needs, offering options like wellness programs, remote work flexibility, and development stipends.

Traditional View

- Primarily focuses on meeting market benchmarks and ensuring fair pay within established salary bands.
- Offers standard benefits such as healthcare, retirement plans, and paid time off, designed to meet basic employee needs.
- Emphasizes consistency and equity across pay structures, with limited room for personalization or flexibility.
- Viewed as an operational requirement to attract and retain talent, with minimal alignment to company culture or broader employee engagement goals.

Next-Generation View

- Leverages AI and predictive analytics to design personalized compensation and benefits packages that adapt to individual employee needs and preferences.
- Uses real-time analytics to adjust rewards dynamically, ensuring they remain competitive and responsive to market changes.

- Links compensation to performance outcomes, rewarding high contributors and fostering a results-oriented culture.
- Uses data to monitor and adjust rewards programs, ensuring competitiveness and relevance across changing workforce demographics.
- Positions Total Rewards as a key driver of engagement and loyalty, reinforcing the organization's brand as an employer of choice.

- Employs digital platforms for flexible benefits selection, allowing employees to tailor rewards to their current life stage and goals.
- Integrates financial wellness tools and personalized financial coaching, supporting employees' financial health and overall well-being.
- Directly ties Total Rewards outcomes to business performance metrics, enabling a clear link between rewards, engagement, and productivity

We hope these contrasting descriptions have sparked your imagination and prompted you to question some of your own beliefs about what HR is for and can accomplish. Below, a final framework to consider.

A Model of Impact

This **Human Resource Competency Study (HRCS) model** is based on a study, co-sponsored by Ross Executive Education at the University of Michigan and The RBL Group, which has collected information on HR professional competencies every four to five years since 1987. The most recent model, from 2021,[i] affirms much of the positivity in the Strategic and Next-Generation views above. In this model, HR:

- **Accelerates Business:** Generating market insights, influencing performance outcomes, prioritizing effectively, and fostering agility, requiring a strategic understanding of both the business and its broader context.
- **Advances Human Capability:** Working to maximize talent, organizational culture, leadership, and the role of HR itself. HR extends beyond isolated tasks to building robust, people-centered strategies that propel the organization forward.

---

[i] Co-sponsors partnered with 19 global HR associations to gather data through 360 ratings on 3,594 HR professionals, assessing a total of 28,640 HR and business professionals.

- **Mobilizes Information:** Leveraging technology and data to align HR with broader social and strategic agendas.
- **Fosters Collaboration:** Influencing through relationship-building and self-management.
- **Simplifies Complexity:** Using critical thinking and adaptability in navigating competing priorities and providing clarity and focus amid uncertainty.

This is certainly a far cry from HR's reputation (among some) for simply keeping a company out of legal hot water and hiring enough employees to get the work done.

3.3 Take Your Preference

After sharing contrasting views of HR, here are some comparisons regarding HR as a source of WFA and WFI.

The Difference Really Is up to You

As business leaders, you'll determine how (or whether) a WFA capability develops at your company. As we've established, WFA relies on HR, and HR can't and won't change on its own—it needs leadership support as a forcing function. It's clearly in your best interest to drive the changes needed to harness WFI to advance your agenda and make a deep, lasting impact. We present for your considerations pairs of scenarios depicting potential implications for your choices.

Below are four stories from our primary research reflecting the hard fact that, at the end of the day, all business problems are people problems. That's why involving HR in major business decisions makes sense. These stories also underscore the power and importance of HR's role as a key driver of data-informed decisions, and how much you stand to benefit from WFA.

This series of two-pronged scenarios depict involving HR optimally versus sub-optimally: late in the game, minimally, or not at all, linking WFA and empowering HR as a strategic partner.

The Tale of Two Hotel Chains

In the first case, executives at a global hotel giant have come to rely on HR in general and their WFA function in particular to help solve a range of business challenges. In the second, the CEO of an industry competitor, of comparable size and stature, reluctantly engages HR, and hires a WFA consultant, to help figure out why his (not-so-) bright idea wasn't working.

Case Study | Unpacking the Guest Experience: How Software and Regulations Undermined Loyalty

A high-end multinational hotel chain faced a significant drop in Guest Satisfaction Scores (GSS) and declining revenue over three quarters in one region of the U.S. Worse yet, competitor data showed gains in customer loyalty while their guests reported disappointment. Despite extensive internal reviews of marketing and seasonal trends, leadership couldn't identify the cause.

The Problem

Suspecting workforce issues at the root, company leadership asked HR to put their well-established WFA team on the trail to understand why guest experiences had shifted so dramatically. Analyzing payroll data, the WFA team quickly saw that at hotels with sagging GSS numbers, property managers were increasingly filling open roles with contract workers for front desk positions instead of salaried employees. **These contract workers**, who bypassed the standard training provided to permanent staff, were **less experienced in customer service** and lacked commitment to the company. Visiting the properties to **investigate further with local teams**, WFA leaders learned that hiring contractors had become significantly easier than salaried employees for two reasons: new regional labor regulations, and changes to hotel software that required property managers to hand-enter hours for salaried—but not contract—employees.

(continued)

(continued)

The Solution

Within three months, the company updated its software to make it easier to hire and manage salaried employees. Leadership also limited the number of contractors each property could hire.

The Results

- **Improved Guest Satisfaction Scores (GSS):** GSS began to rise within one quarter after the company transitioned back to trained, salaried employees.
- **Increased Sales:** Hotels experienced higher sales within two quarters, indicating a positive correlation between improved guest satisfaction and revenue.
- **Enhanced Guest Reviews:** With improved service quality, guest reviews showed noticeable improvement, reflecting the impact of having a committed, well-trained workforce.
- **Reduced Dependency on Contract Workers:** By implementing administrative improvements and limiting contract hires, the company decreased reliance on contractors, prioritizing a more stable and skilled workforce.

Cutting to the Chase

By empowering HR with a robust Workforce Analytics function and trusting that team's advice, leadership of this global hotel chain rapidly uncovered the source of, and solution to, declining guest satisfaction and sales. The WFA team's expert investigation and insights enabled leadership to quickly reverse the trend toward hiring inexperienced contract labor, leading to an upswing in guest satisfaction and revenue within months.

Cautionary Tale | The Innovation Illusion: A CEO's Pricey Pitfall

The CEO of a prominent hotel chain, always seeking the next big idea, was dazzled after hearing a charismatic speaker introduce a new leadership model. Certain he'd discovered the key to outperforming competitors, he decided to overhaul how the company recruited and trained its General Managers (GMs) with this fresh approach.

Eager to implement his vision, he poured millions into reimagining hiring, training, and evaluation practices across the organization, all in the name of "GM effectiveness." It was a grand-scale commitment, complete with new metrics and revamped processes. Yet, months passed, and business results did not improve. Occupancy rates and revenue per available room (RevPAR) remained stubbornly flat. Nothing justified the investment.

Sensing something was off, the CHRO commissioned an external analysis to assess the impact of this model on the hotels' performance. The results were surprising: the new leadership traits actually correlated with *declines* in profitability. Confronted with data that challenged his vision, the CEO dismissed the consultants and held tightly to the model.

The costly experiment left employees disillusioned and profits stagnant—a sobering reminder of the dangers of unchecked executive overconfidence.

Analyze This: A Study in Contrasts

The following are two situations where HR—and advanced analytics—saved the day, although much later in the process than was necessary. In both cases, HR helped analyze, understand, and propose solutions to vastly different challenges: maritime safety issues for a shipping company and an office expansion decision for a tech start-up. And in both, that was only AFTER the company learned the hard way that ignoring the human side of their business was just as risky and ill-fated as underestimating the importance of data.

Cautionary Tale | Engineering Alone Can't Steer the Ship: The Human Solution to Maritime Risks

In the high-stakes world of maritime shipping—where 80% of global trade moves across sea routes—a leading cargo shipping company found itself grappling with rising safety incidents despite substantial investments in advanced ship engineering. Aware that human error was a factor, leadership were convinced that technology alone would resolve the issue. However, accidents and costs continued to mount.

The Problem

Leadership's reliance on engineering delayed the recognition that the real issue was human-centered. Once HR got involved and the People Analytics team began analyzing workforce data, they identified key factors driving the safety issues: **low training completion rates**, **inconsistent safety practices across regions**, and a **weak safety culture**, in which employees were reluctant to report safety concerns.

The Solution

Informed by the team's findings, the company took a **comprehensive approach** to addressing the human factors. They overhauled recruitment, which had historically been based on personal recommendations rather than formal qualifications. **Structured, skills-based interviews and certification requirements** ensured new hires were qualified for safety-critical roles. Safety discussions became a routine part of meetings, embedding **continuous learning** into daily operations. Clear career paths with **promotions and pay tied to safety performance** further incentivized accountability, fostering a proactive, people-centered safety culture.

The (Delayed) Outcomes

- Higher training completion and improved safety audit scores across regions.
- Accident frequency dropped by **40%**.
- Financial impact of accidents was reduced by **35%**.
- Client satisfaction improved by **40%**.
- Increased employee engagement, reduced downtime from human error, and a stronger reputation, resulting in increased contract renewals and lower insurance costs.

The Caution of This Tale

This shipping company spent tens of millions of dollars on unnecessary engineering upgrades before they finally conceded that technology couldn't solve their safety problems. Once leadership engaged HR, People Analytics experts quickly identified and created holistic solutions to the root causes of the issue: human error. Significant safety improvements, lower costs, higher contract renewals and enhanced client satisfaction soon followed.

Cautionary Tale | Data Versus Preference: A Location Strategy Gone Wrong

A high-growth B2B SaaS company faced a pivotal decision: where to grow its U.S. presence. With just one office in its founding U.S. city, where labor costs were rising, and a commitment to in-office work at least three days a week, company leadership would need to expand to another city to attract top talent. The only question was where.

(continued)

(*continued*)

The Problem

Senior leaders formed a working group, but only considered factors like which cities they felt were "hot" markets and their own preferences. Their personal biases risked compromising the expansion's effectiveness:

- Leadership failed to consider recruitment potential, infrastructure, or financial feasibility.
- The favored locations would not have supported the company's Diversity, Equity, and Inclusion (DEI) and talent acquisition goals.
- Forgoing data was out of step with the company's culture of transparency and logic-driven decision-making.

The Solution

When the CHRO learned of the company's expansion plan, it was clear this was more than just a numbers game—it was about making a choice that would support people, growth, and strategic goals all at once. Advocating for a rigorous analysis, the CHRO encouraged the Workforce Analytics team to dive in. Creating a two-part study, they evaluated which teams needed in-person collaboration and where they'd thrive together, while also exploring markets that could provide the best talent pool at competitive rates and align with the company's DEI goals.

After analyzing 30 U.S. cities against 25 factors, the team crafted a shortlist of five cities where the company's vision could truly come to life. It was a thorough analysis that would enable data-backed decisions and earn employee trust and respect, while ignoring the facts would damage morale.

The Results

Unfortunately, despite the thorough analysis, leadership dismissed the recommendations, opting for a location near several executives' residences. After announcing the new office in an all-hands meeting, the response was swift and overwhelmingly negative. Employees voiced serious concerns about transparency and leadership commitment to data-driven practices.

Company leaders eventually relented. After several months, they selected one of the data-recommended cities, aligning the expansion with both strategic and cultural values.

The Caution of this Tale

For this software start-up, selecting the location of their critical second office became a litmus test for letting HR and data—not personal preference—drive the way to strategic decisions. Ignoring the data eroded employee trust, and leadership had to backtrack to align the new location with well-researched insights that prioritized access to key talent, financial viability, and achievement of the company's DEI objectives.

3.4 Accountability as a Two-Way Street

A large company spent more than US$500 million annually on merit increases and bonuses. When the compensation director was asked about the return on investment, he replied, "To be honest, the only thing we know for sure is employees don't quit too often and don't complain too much." Imagine how a CFO would react if someone proposed spending $500 million dollars a year on a project where the success criteria was "people won't quit or complain." But when it comes to investing money in people, that is what companies do every year.

—Steve Hunt, PhD, Founder, i3 Talent, LLC

Self-evident, but worth making explicit: Accountability is a prerequisite for excellence. And accountability for workforce outcomes must be shared. So yes, we are asking you to move the goalpost for yourself, too.

Treat HR KPIs Like Financial KPIs

> We use (our data analytics platform) so that our top 600 leaders have all the people data from every system blended at their fingertips. Since it's all in that system, people leaders are required to have a high level of command and engagement in their BU people data.
>
> **—Jeremy Shapiro, VP, Workforce Analytics, Merck & Co**

No one questions that each business unit contributes to the company's financial performance, and therefore must include financial KPIs in their monthly, quarterly, and annual reporting, forecasts, and long-range planning. Yet while every business unit also contributes to the utilization and optimization of the *workforce*, directly managing employee productivity, development, engagement, and retention, somehow only HR is meant to drive people outcomes.

HR may create and facilitate the processes for workforce priorities like succession planning and promotions, but business leaders outside HR execute them and must take responsibility for them. Integrating HR data into your overall business accountability structure should not be radical. It simply is a more accurate reflection of how talent works: the metrics that matter most about employees—retention of top talent, talent mobility, engagement, and more—are most influenced by, and therefore the responsibility of, those who lead their business unit.

In fact, in terms of engagement, the link is even more intimate. Gallup performed meta-analytics on 100 million employee interviews and determined that 70% of the variance between the most engaged teams and "persistently disengaged teams" is *just the manager*.[11]

No one questions that each business unit contributes to the company's financial performance, and therefore must include financial KPIs in their monthly, quarterly, and annual reporting, forecasts, and long-range planning. Yet while every business unit also contributes to the utilization and optimization of the workforce, directly managing employee productivity, development, engagement, and retention, somehow only HR is meant to drive people outcomes

Making the success of a company's workforce everyone's responsibility rather than laying it at the feet of one group (to which the majority of that workforce does not report), can go an exceedingly long way in generating focus on critical KPIs that leaders have the power to influence and must do better at influencing. More equally distributing accountability for HR metrics could potentially even raise HR's esteem in the eyes of leaders who suddenly realize just how big a responsibility it is to move the needle on workforce metrics. And it would also help end HR's isolation and branding issues.

Accountability Can Be Transformative

Business leaders should consider a function where they feel they have had strategic success. Think about how they plan for it, how they invest in it . . . then hold that up against how they invest and think about their people.

—John Boudreau, PhD, Emeritus Professor and Senior Research Scientist, Center for Effective Organizations, University of Southern California

A 2023 study by i4cp, "Culture Fitness: Healthy Habits of High-Performance Organizations,"[ii] found that leaders being held accountable for employee outcomes is one of "Seven Habits of Very Healthy Cultures." In fact, organizations with "very healthy" cultures are 18 times more likely to measure leaders on their people outcomes like retention and training.[12]

Doing so, i4cp found, generates "a cascade of other benefits: higher market performance, increased wellbeing, better engagement, greater productivity, improved retention, attraction, and diversity, and positive change to the culture." By contrast, in organizations without leader accountability for employee outcomes, attrition is likely to be higher, with leaders more likely to "hoard talent and inhibit employees' overall career progress," which can create silos and stifle collaboration companywide.

[ii] The report reflects data from 449 large companies (employing >1,000 people) from 53 countries plus follow-up interviews with select practitioners and subject matter experts.

Perhaps unsurprisingly, i4cp categorizes this accountability as a "next practice"—even among organizations the study defines as high-performing, fewer than 16% reported following it "to a very high extent."[13] But if optimizing your workforce is on your bingo card for the foreseeable future, it's a change to seriously consider.

Put Workforce Metrics on Your Dashboard

> Hold leaders accountable for employee retention—this should be a company initiative, not an HR-only one.
>
> **—CHRO survey respondent,**
> **U.S.-based $500M+ public company**[iii]

So, what might this look like? Fundamentally, similar to financial reporting. Just as revenue numbers for various business units add up to the total revenue the CFO reports, the CHRO would present a roll-up of company-level people metrics (see below) while business unit and regional leaders share, via their versions of the same dashboards, the people metrics for which they are responsible.

One interviewee we spoke with told us that at the global technology giant where he works all people managers at his company are empowered to, and responsible for, the people metrics at their level. They all have access to the relevant HR reporting systems and can view their data at any time. They are also accountable for fixing people problems within their team. Below are some examples of people metrics that should be included in business-level reporting.

- **Attrition:** As discussed earlier, most senior leaders know attrition is bad, but few realize just how bad: as previously mentioned, 50% to 200% of an employee's annual salary according to Gallup and other sources: rehiring costs, lost productivity while the job is unfilled (and burnout among those carrying the extra weight), onboarding and ramp-up time for the new employee, in addition to hits to morale, loss of institutional knowledge, and more.[14] Shouldn't business units, teams, and managers who hemorrhage direct reports be flagged and held accountable?

[iii] For details on our CEO/CHRO survey, please *see* the Appendix.

- **Engagement:** The leading indicator for attrition is engagement, another rich, complex, and important topic. If a business leader doesn't know their unit's engagement scores, down to the individual manager level, something is very wrong. But if business leaders are only AWARE of their engagement numbers and are not held responsible for TRACKING, REPORTING, and IMPROVING them, then the CEO has an even more significant challenge to address.
- **Talent Mobility/Promotions:** Moving people into new roles, whether laterally or through promotions, helps improve engagement, retention, and productivity and costs far less than hiring externally. Tracking these metrics by business unit and team will help keep them top of mind. In addition, if a business unit has a manager whose direct reports routinely take lateral moves into other departments, the faster and more easily that information appears on a dashboard, the more quickly that bad actor can be set straight or let go.
- **Hiring Metrics:** Hiring managers most impact the candidate experience. If a hiring manager interviews candidate after candidate, taking months to decide, metrics like time to fill a role, number of interviews prior to offer, and candidate experience scores should absolutely appear on THEIR team's dashboard, not HR's. How else could persistent, problematic hiring scenarios be systematically identified?
- **Training and Development:** When it matters, leaders must be held accountable. At top performing companies, it is not unusual for completion numbers on mission-critical training to appear on senior leaders' performance dashboards. Extend this same philosophy at the business unit level to help ensure that employees are being equipped with the knowledge and skills needed to perform at a high level—which, logically, leaders should already care about (but alas, although we cannot fathom why, we know many don't).

Of course, because completion numbers are not proof of impact in any universe, contrary to unfortunate popular opinion, unit leaders must track the relationship between training completed and performance, in partnership with L&D professionals. Companies that are more advanced in the quest to become skills-based (also a robust and important topic for a separate book) should be tracking which skills they need, how many employees have those skills, and the gaps that must be filled, and again, L&D can and should be a partner in this process.

A company can offer world-class development all day long, but if a business unit cannot connect the dots between their KPIs and the capabilities of the people who must achieve them, L&D's job is impossible.

- **Incidents:** Many HR cynics say that the function's #1 job is keeping the company out of trouble. Let's assume, for argument's sake, it's true. How, then, is it preferable that only HR be responsible for tracking and responding to employee relations complaints? Dear CEO, if you hate risk as much as we think you do, get those metrics onto team dashboards and hold people managers accountable.

Take Advantage of the Opportunity   Distributing responsibility for people metrics among those best positioned to influence them presents other opportunities. As John Boudreau shared with us, transitioning to holding leaders accountable for HR metrics in their business units presents an opportunity to partner with HR to identify where investing in people can create a competitive advantage for each unit.

While certain metrics should be consistent across business units, new conversations about tracking workforce performance provide an opening for high-performing HR to do some of what it does best: advise the business on matters related to people (and, we would add, the machines they work with). This can lead to identifying unit-specific metrics that will be meaningful to its leaders and revealing for company executives.

For example, HR could work with Engineering to determine key productivity metrics that drive their ability to meet business unit and corporate goals (e.g., how many bug fixes per unit of time, lines of code checked in and out per employee, etc.), and assess current levels to identify where investment is needed to close gaps. HR and

Engineering leaders could also determine the profiles of the group's top and bottom performers, and how to train the latter to work more like the former. A high-performing HR Business Partner (HRBP) would be doing this anyway.

3.5 Key Takeaways

Get up to speed on the HR function, where it's been, and what it can become when—and only when—business leaders like you raise their expectations, support, and accountability.

- **Remember Yesterday's IT:** Functions like Finance and IT and their leaders evolved from administrative to strategic, and HR can and must do the same. All such transformations require staunch executive support.
- **Know and Demand Excellence:** Want to understand how your HR function measures up (and how great it could become with your support)? Compare and contrast four sets of perspectives about HR—"cynical," "traditional," "strategic," and "next-generation"—and you'll never view it quite the same way again.
- **Take Your Preference:** Business leaders play a critical role in shaping the future of HR by consistently integrating HR and WFA into problem-solving and decision-making. Four memorable case studies illustrate how to do that well, and not well at all.
- **Accountability as a Two-Way Street:** Achieving financial goals is a responsibility shared enterprise-wide, and that accountability helps drive results. Making all leaders similarly answerable for moving the needle on workforce metrics, too, can transform outcomes.

Bottom line: Based on our research and personal experience, you can get a lot more from your HR function (and, as a result, more WFI) with some perspective on what good looks like, how to get there, and the true costs of not aiming for excellence.

SECTION

4

Become Truly Insight-Driven

IT'S HARD TO be data-driven. It's even harder—but infinitely more impactful—to be insight-driven. For an entire organization, the journey is a long, winding road but one that must be undertaken to realize the potential of Workforce Insights. It's also, of course, key to a company's performance in all aspects of the business.

A key to becoming insight-driven is culture change. Even with sophisticated technology and the grandest, most advanced analytics function one can imagine, unless you're bringing the masses along, you won't get too far. Sure, analytics will happen, but in rarefied air with a select few, with little insight-driven decision-making elsewhere.

The journey likely also requires upleveling your HR function. We know about some very high-performing HR teams, and none are consistently insight-driven. Luckily, AI and automation will make that lift much, much easier (while still not *easy*).

Committed business leaders with vision and patience, like you, will make all the difference.

4.1 Why "Insight-Driven" Matters

A note on language: As explained near the beginning of the book, we believe "insight-driven" emphasizes, advances, and makes explicit the aspiration behind "data-driven." The research and concepts we cite on data-driven initiatives, cultures, companies, etc., align with our intent.

Business leaders surely know intellectually that being insight-driven, with a healthy obsession with data and all it enables, *should* be a given today. After all, as Michael Dell, CEO of Dell Technologies, has said, "Almost anything interesting and exciting that you want to do in the world revolves around data."[1]

But actually *becoming* insight-driven—with being data-driven as a prerequisite or parallel effort—is complex and requires serious, sustained effort. Clear, persuasive evidence that an insight-centric culture will make such efforts worthwhile is essential motivation for CEOs and others who will need to dedicate significant resources (including their reputation) to making it happen. Let us provide some of this evidence.

Now Is the Time

The rise of Generative AI is hastening the true embrace of being *insight-driven*, after years of business leaders saying data mattered but not actually managing to become *data*-driven.

The 2024 Data and AI Leadership Executive Survey shows a dramatic increase for the first time since it started tracking the progress of data and analytics. Survey respondents reporting that they had "created a data-driven organization" improved sharply, from 23.9% to 48.1%, and those saying they'd "established a data and analytics culture" jumped from 20.6% to 42.6%.[2]

A 2023 study from Harvard Business Review Analytic Services shared similar findings: 75% of pulse survey respondents reported "having a data-driven culture" as very or extremely important to their company's success.[3] And, "leader" organizations, which successfully transform data into business value, were more likely than other respondents to report performance improvements in the past year:

Performance Areas	Likelihood of Improvement: Leader Organizations	Likelihood of Improvement: Other Respondents
New product/service introduction	83%	59%
Operational efficiency	81%	58%
Customer satisfaction	79%	51%
Revenue	77%	61%
Customer loyalty/ retention	77%	45%
Profitability	72%	50%
Market share	70%	49%
Employee satisfaction	68%	39%
IT cost predictability	59%	44%

For Your Business

Many benefits await—and have been waiting. McKinsey reported already in 2014 that data-driven companies were 23 times more likely to outperform the competition in customer acquisition, around 19 times more likely to remain profitable, and almost 7 times more likely to keep their customers versus other companies.[4] Ten years later, McKinsey called data "the fuel for everyday innovation," asserting that any kind of innovation has a better chance of success if "grounded in data and facts" and that companies embracing data-driven decision-making are about two-thirds more likely than others to "adapt to a changing business environment."[5]

KPMG, too, cites the benefits of "embracing a data-driven mindset"—indicating that it makes clear "the connection between their data assets and firm performance," enabling companies to improve how they use their data, collaborate, accurately predict changes in the market, and gain returns on their investments.[6]

We found this line from *Forbes* an apt summary: "Smart bets can be made on a hunch, of course, but data-driven businesses make the

We found this line an apt summary: "Smart bets can be made on a hunch, of course, but data-driven businesses make the most informed guesses possible before putting their money where their mouth is."

most informed guesses possible before putting their money where their mouth is." The article also points out that data helps companies lead in their industry by better predicting competitor movements and customer wants and needs, and responding accordingly with products and services that can bring in additional buyers.[7]

For Workforce Insights

Think of using Workforce Insights as channeling the heat and light from a fire. Some of the biggest logs in that fire will come from HR building its Workforce Analytics capabilities. But making data the core of your culture—creating an environment that will be optimally hospitable to evidence-based, outcome-generating work across your organization—adds both slow-burning wood and kindling while also fanning the flames. Remove wood and the fire will go out. And keeping the fire roaring requires continual tending, prodding, and adding more fuel. There's no getting around it.

Research from Deloitte confirms it: "A data-centric culture remains the single most influential factor" in driving Workforce Analytics maturity.[8] Research also shows that deeply embedding Workforce Analytics into your culture decreases HR professionals' resistance to using it.[9]

Also, the more everyone uses data and AI, the more comfortable and proficient they get, leading to even greater utilization and innovation.

4.2 Making Culture Your #1 Strategic Asset

Culture plays a critical role in achieving business goals, yet business leaders often overlook the power of culture as a strategic asset. Understanding and leveraging culture can drive significant business performance improvements.

"Our ambitions are bold and so must be our desire to change and evolve our culture," Satya Nadella wrote in a memo to employees titled "Starting FY15 – Bold Ambition & Our Core" on July 10, 2014, shortly after becoming CEO.[10] According to Aon, companies whose culture is "aligned to their purpose and business goals" tend to show better-than-average performance. In Aon's Engagement 2.0 Study, companies with high cultural alignment had: 440% higher revenue; 400% higher EBITA; and 4% lower attrition. They were also "13% more likely to have employees recommend their company."[11]

Know That Culture Is Power

Mike Sievert, president and CEO of T-Mobile, brings the point home in a *Fortune* interview with Diane Brady, "How T-Mobile's corporate culture powered it to become the world's most valuable telecom company":

> [T]he thing that allows us quarter after quarter after quarter to outperform everyone and outgrow them is our culture. ... [A]s the leader, that's my job to build that, to perpetuate it, to foster it, to jealously defend it and guard it when it gets challenged.[12]

"Culture is the reflection of the behaviors, decisions, and values a company lives by, shaped by what it rewards and tolerates," says Brigette McInnis-Day, a CHRO and COO who has worked at UiPath, Google, and SAP. "Leaders must recognize that culture cannot be outsourced to HR or used as a scapegoat for company issues. The culture employees experience is a direct manifestation of leadership behavior, making it crucial for leaders to embody and model the company's values."

Because culture is constantly evolving, having a data-driven culture must be pervasive throughout the entire organization and reinforced. Like tending the fire.

Avoid the Risks

Not investing in a positive workplace culture can have grave consequences. According to a study by HR platform Dayforce, 48% of employees have left a job due to a toxic or negative culture. Among the 9,489 participants, 70% said they have rejected, or would reject, a job offer because they disliked the company's culture. Among respondents younger than 34, it was 75%. But when employees are content, they "produce better work, are more likely to speak highly of the organization to others, and will stay longer."[13]

In 2024, tax and advisory firm KPMG surveyed 400 interns about their top professional priorities. They ranked a strong company culture at the top (64%), followed by positive team dynamics fostering a sense of belonging (37%), volunteer opportunities (34%), and manager mentoring (32%).[14]

An Accenture study emphasizes what's specifically at stake regarding a company's data culture. They measured the impact on employee trust of 31 workforce data practices, then developing an economic model to estimate impact on revenue. Their findings: companies that lose their people's trust risk losing 6% of revenue growth, but higher trust would be valued at greater than a 6% gain in revenue growth.[15]

Culture Can Doom Data-Driven Efforts   We weren't surprised that Wavestone's annual "State of Data and AI in Leading Companies" has consistently found since at least 2018 that the top challenge to becoming data-driven was "human factors," listed as "culture, people, process change, and organizational alignment." Nearly 78% of respondents in 2024 cited human factors as #1, versus just 23.4% choosing technology limitations.[16]

In the case study below, business transformation efforts to digitize a Fortune 500 financial services company failed until leaders examined, and responded to, serious issues in their culture.

Case Study | Overcoming a Resistant Culture to Achieve Business Transformation

A Fortune 500 financial services company, known for its stability and consistency, struggled to adapt to a rapidly changing digital landscape. Despite multiple organizational restructurings and leadership changes, transformation was elusive—and sales were stagnant.

The Problem

Evaluating the company's Organizational Health Index[i] revealed that the executive team ranked in the bottom quartile in three out of the four practices necessary for organizational success. The OHI data indicated that companies with even one underperforming power practice had nearly zero chance of achieving top quartile performance. This served as the burning platform for the CEO to act, particularly concerning critical areas like employee trust, essential for driving change.

The Solution

With the CEO's commitment to boosting trust by 10% within a year, the company set out on a bold transformation, putting cultural change at the heart of its mission. They turned to OHI data, finding clear paths forward by identifying and tracking critical competencies—**data wasn't just numbers; it became a guide** to rebuild trust and transparency. More than 900 leaders stepped into a **six-month program**, developing skills not just for themselves but for the future they wanted to create for everyone around them. Accountability and incentives solidified their commitment to this digital and cultural evolution.

At the executive level, a **unified C-suite** joined forces, proving that real change takes cohesion and unwavering support from the top. Through **revamped messaging and clear rewards**, employees everywhere began to feel part of the transformation, with an understanding of their role in this vision.

(continued)

---

[i] **Organizational Health Index (OHI):** Comprehensive diagnostic tool that evaluates a company's internal effectiveness, typically measured through rigorous surveys, interviews, and objective performance metrics that assess dimensions including cultural dynamics, strategic alignment, leadership quality, employee engagement, and operational agility.

(*continued*)

The Results

Trust was no longer an abstract goal; it was the heartbeat of a shared, revitalized future. Within a year of implementing these initiatives, the company achieved impressive results:

- **Improved Organizational Health:** The OHI score improved by 12%.
- **Enhanced Engagement:** The company observed higher levels of employee involvement.
- **Financial Growth and Recognition:** The company reported its best financial performance in years, moved up in the Fortune 500 ranking, and was recognized as one of the "World's Most Admired" companies in 2023.

Cutting to the Chase

For this large financial services company challenged by digital transformation and stagnant growth, restructuring alone could not drive change. Data from evaluating the company's organizational health revealed a path to a winning culture: preparing and incenting leaders to drive change, and re-engaging employees and their trust in leadership, all coordinated with united C-suite efforts. Within a year, the company increased employee trust, improved financial performance and rose in their market standing. This case underscores that when leadership aligns culture with strategy, real transformation follows.

"Culture eats strategy for breakfast"

As the adage goes, culture eats strategy for breakfast. You can have the best mission, vision, values, sales, and product, but if you haven't won hearts and minds, you will not be successful.

—CHRO survey respondent, U.S.-based $10–50M+ company

This maxim, widely mis-attributed to management guru Peter Drucker may provide further persuasion. (Drucker actually said, "Culture—no matter how defined—is singularly persistent."[17])

4.3 Upleveling HR

As organizations increasingly rely on diverse productivity resources beyond full-time employees, including outsourcing, gig workers, artificial intelligence, and robotics, HR faces both challenges and opportunities. For HR to be a true strategic partner, it must evolve its understanding and management of these varied resources, shifting from traditional people processes to more comprehensive productivity processes.

—**Max Blumberg, PhD, Founder,
Blumberg Partnership**

You are not surprised to find yourself here, right? We've made it plain by now. Part of your journey to exploiting Workforce Analytics (in the best possible ways) is using your clout and positions of power as business leaders to help HR get where you need them to be: as automated as possible through tools like chatbots and AI so they are free to become top performers in all aspects of their work.

The HR professionals who will make Workforce Insights a reality for you have an instinct for people and HR domain expertise, of course, but also strong business acumen, a deep understanding of your company and the nature and levers of its performance, and the curiosity and facility with data and analytics tools to meaningfully measure the impact of strategic initiatives that drive business value.

Think of it as being part of history. Your efforts are certainly timely.

Run, Don't Walk, to Automate HR

As with virtually all functions, AI (Generative and otherwise) and automation are transforming HR. Given the pace of change, we assume that by the time this book is published, most of this section will be outdated. We will, then, focus briefly on key trends and use cases. Wherever automation is headed, HR leaders and individual contributors alike must gain the skills and mindset to seek out and implement solutions to outsource routine HR tasks to non-human resources.

Realize What's at Stake   A wealth of data from reliable sources indicates that HR benefits significantly from using AI for automation. Yet the potential is mostly still unrealized. An August 2024 survey of HR and People Analytics leaders found that while 45% of respondents reported already tracking "great impact," most organizations are still "testing the waters" and determining ways to get the most from their AI investments.[18]

Analytics expert Max Blumberg highlights a range of benefits from AI in "Slashing HR Costs: The Ultimate Blueprint for Implementing GenAI in HR." These estimated benefits should motivate even the biggest automation cynics:

- **McKinsey** estimates **cost reductions of up to 40%** within three years for companies implementing AI in HR functions.
- **Deloitte** found an **average ROI of 200–300%** for organizations utilizing AI in HR in the first three years.
- According to **Gartner**, AI can cut time-to-hire by up to half and improve quality-of-hire by one-fifth.
- **PwC** estimates AI could reduce **HR administrative tasks by up to 30%**, freeing up resources for more strategic initiatives.[19]

Blumberg also captures key examples of traditional versus GenAI approaches to HR domains (*see* Figure 4.1). Examining benefits by industry, the report presents a representative sample (*see* Figure 4.2).

Prioritize High-Touch, Let Machines Do Low-Touch   The key to efficiently automating HR is clearly defining which activities require human intervention (high touch—involving judgment, empathy, and strategic insight) and which can be outsourced to bots, automations, and other "machines" (low-touch—routine operational tasks). Easier said than done? Possibly not by the time this book comes out.

AI utilization varies across HR functions. Automation is a godsend for the admin-intensive, high-volume, speed-needy processes of Talent Acquisition (TA), making them early tech adopters. Consider them the gaming industry of HR. Seventy percent of respondents to a 2024 survey said they are testing and/or using AI to automate TA. L&D and Workforce Analytics were the next most common users, at 65%, then Compensation and Payroll (30%) and Diversity & Inclusion (20%).[20]

Overall, the end goal is efficiency. Wavestone's "2024 Data and AI Leadership Executive Survey"[21] reported that nearly half (49.1%) its study participants said exponential productivity gains was their top GenAI business opportunity, followed by liberating knowledge workers from "mundane tasks" (23.6%). Both align exactly with where HR needs to go.

Different industries may experience varying levels of cost reduction potential based on their specific HR challenges and existing processes.

	People Process	Potential Cost Reduction
Healthcare	Workforce Scheduling	**25–35%** *(Deloitte, 2023)*
Retail	Recruitment and Onboarding	**30–40%** *(McKinsey & Co., 2023)*
Financial Services	Employee Development	**35–45%** *(PwC, 2023)*
Manufacturing	Performance Management	**20–30%** *(Combined Analysis)*
Technology	Talent Acquisition	**40–50%** *(LinkedIn, 2023)*

These projections highlight the significant cost-saving opportunities across various industries, with technology and financial services potentially seeing the highest reductions due to their data-rich environments and complex HR processes.

Figure 4.1   GenAI in HR: Potential Cost Reductions by Industry

Source: Reproduced with permission from Max Blumberg, "Slashing HR Costs: The Ultimate Blueprint for Implementing GenAI in HR" (Blumberg Partnership, 2024), https://blumbergpartnership.com/.

	Traditional Approach	GenAI Solution	Potential Cost Reduction
Recruitment	Manual screening	AI-powered candidate matching	**30–50% reduction in hiring costs** *(LinkedIn, 2023)*
Training	General e-learning	Personalized AI-generated content	**40–60% reduction in training expenses** *(Deloitte, 2023)*
Performance Management	Annual reviews	Continuous AI-assisted feedback	**20–35% reduction in review-related costs** *(Combined Analysis)*
Employee Relations	Static policies	AI chatbots for instant support	**30–40% reduction in query handling costs** *(IBM, 2023)*

Figure 4.2   GenAI in HR: Potential Cost Reductions by HR Domain

Source: Reproduced with permission from Max Blumberg, "Slashing HR Costs" (2024).

Find Inspiration in Use Cases   Below, we present both general descriptions and examples of leading companies embracing, and handsomely benefiting from, HR automation.

Overall: HR Automation in Action at Microsoft   HR at Microsoft is leveraging AI to optimize both its operations and employee experience. Key initiatives include developing AI-powered tools like the HR Virtual Agent, which saved 160,000 hours of productivity, and Copilot in Dynamics 365 Customer Service, which improved HR service response rates by 26% and cut case resolution time by 7%.

Microsoft also trained HR staff to become "citizen developers," enabling them to build AI solutions without coding. The initiatives have resulted in higher job satisfaction, with a 16% increase in HR employees enjoying their work.[22]

Talent Acquisition   Companies of any size can use AI to create job postings, screen resumes, and send emails. Hiring is certainly an area where companies should not eliminate human participation in the process, but large corporations, especially those hiring manual labor, are taking full advantage, and have gone beyond standard automation.

- **Chipotle:** Chipotle Mexican Grill is streamlining its hiring process through a conversational AI platform. This system helps general managers by handling administrative tasks like gathering candidate information and scheduling interviews, allowing them to focus more on daily operations and guest hospitality. The technology is expected to cut hiring time for restaurant positions by up to 75%.

  In addition, the platform's virtual assistant, named "Ava Cado," interacts directly with candidates, answering questions, gathering details, arranging interviews, and sending offers to selected applicants in English, Spanish, French, and German.[23]

- **McDonald's:** AI-driven hiring has already proven itself at the Golden Arches. In 2019, McDonald's rolled out McHire, an AI-enabled hiring platform. Prior to its launch, the majority of hires needed to complete an application in a restaurant and return later for an interview; now, application and scheduling have been slashed from three days to three minutes. McDonald's also doubled job applications, earning a near-perfect candidate satisfaction rate. In just more than a year, time-to-hire was reduced by 60%, freeing up four to five hours a week of restaurant manager time.[24]

Learning & Development   AI uses include helping to automate scheduling and calendars, generate custom content (inside your company's firewall) to expedite production and maximize ongoing relevance, provide personalized recommendations based on skills and career paths, and even bot-driven coaching and role plays. And AI has made it possible within minutes to interpret and find trends within qualitative learner feedback.

Talent Management　HR can automate tasks that support the performance management process, including issuing reminders to managers and their direct reports and helping answer questions related to key performance activities.

HR Business Partners　To free up your HRBPs to do the kind of strategic work described above, AI can assist in tracking employee performance and provide insights based on data analytics. By analyzing performance metrics, HRBPs can identify patterns and trends, helping them advise managers on personalized development plans, promotions, or performance improvement initiatives.

Champion AI for Workforce Analytics

The dual advancement of HR tech and AI is something akin to putting a Workforce Analytics rocket pack on HR professionals' backs. Even with minimal training, HR staff can use AI-driven tools to analyze data, uncover insights, predict trends, and prescribe actions. One simple example: utilizing bots to regularly monitor and analyze exit interview transcripts for causes of attrition among high performers and suggest effective responses. Such solutions are, without exaggeration, transformative. HR can be efficient AND effectively respond to business leaders' priority challenges.

Imagine the Possibilities　Like automation, uses of AI for data analytics are many and varied. Priority areas reported by HR.com are flagging talent at risk of attrition (53%), identifying best-fit job candidates (47%), predicting high-performing recruits (47%), handling employee support inquiries with chatbots (47%), and driving data-informed decisions (47%).[25] The following story demonstrates what's possible when HR uses AI, in this case for salary recommendations, with the ultimate goal of retaining top talent.

Vignette | IBM: Achieve More with AI-Driven Talent Strategies

IBM faced a serious workforce challenge: how to retain top talent in a fiercely competitive landscape. The solution: using AI to reshape their approach to compensation.

A cross-functional team at IBM developed an AI tool to support managers in making fair, skills-based salary decisions. It analyzed numerous factors—skills, market demand, performance, and growth potential—providing managers with tailored salary recommendations. The result? Managers could now have transparent, data-driven pay conversations with their teams.

With insights laid out like a "nutrition label," IBM ensured employees understood how pay decisions were made and could access their own salary relative to the market. Managers received salary increase recommendations tailored to each of their employees with a detailed rationale, including links between pay decisions and the employee's skills. Fairness was ensured through bias-detection tools, and robustness through rigorous data privacy protections.

The system not only enabled better compensation decisions but also helped managers proactively retain employees with critical, hard-to-replace skills. The AI-powered approach reduced attrition by a third, a powerful example of using AI to enhance data analytics and address serious and costly workforce issues.[26]

IBM has long made news for its use of AI in Workforce Analytics. Back in 2017 CEO Ginni Rometty described its predictive attrition software as 95% accurate in forecasting when employees are likely to quit, allowing IBM to act before they leave. Proactively working to improve retention saved IBM an estimated $300 million. IBM further uses AI-driven tools to assess employee performance and predict future success, with reported accuracy rates as high as 96%. These tools became part of IBM's external offerings.[27]

What a Great CHRO Can Accomplish

When a CEO boasts externally about HR, as Ginny Rometty did, that's a "tell" that an exceptional CHRO is at the helm. The CHRO of IBM during that period (2013–2020), Diane Gherson, redesigned IBM's overall approach to people and processes to support a business transformation. Gherson, who holds a U.S. patent in the field of predictive analytics, led the charge to bring AI and automation to an HR function responsible for a global workforce of 350,000+.

As a result, she said, the HR team was no longer "buried in transactions" but rather "spending time on helping them be greater leaders, helping their teams develop the skills that they need and adding real value to the business." The outcome: HR moved "from executing on the basics to truly helping talent become the competitive advantage in the market."[28]

In 2022, Coca-Cola Europacific Partners (CCEP) launched a talent intelligence platform to address concerns about limited growth opportunities, skill gaps, and manual succession planning. The "Career Hub" focused on 100 key business skills, using AI to provide targeted learning and development. Succession planning was digitized, consolidating employees' experience, aspirations, and development plans into "talent cards." This increased talent profiles from 2% to 80%, enabling real-time talent management. With more than 70% adoption, the Career Hub boosted engagement, addressed skill gaps, and improved organizational performance, highlighting how AI-driven workforce analytics enhance talent management and business outcomes.[29]

Spotting Issues on Autopilot   Perhaps the most significant benefit of leveraging AI in WFA is monitoring for patterns and insights. This makes possible AI-automated anomaly detection and alert, enabling the right people to receive notification whenever something is out of sorts, with a broad range of applications.

Scenarios can include mission-critical teams not holding a regular status meeting for three consecutive weeks, a high percentage of new hires not completing certain onboarding activities, or high-performing talent exhibiting signs that they are considering leaving, such as less time spent on company laptop, reduced productivity, rescheduled 1:1 meetings with their manager, or a recent promotion request turned down.

Remember, though, that even if issues can be identified without human intervention, one or more humans will need to analyze, understand, and act on the discoveries.

Evolve HR's Non-HR Acumen

Why we wouldn't, as an HR function, want to measure the impact of what we do is kind of beyond me. But historically, we've not done that very well. So, let's be like any other business function and measure our impact. We'll get the ear of the CEO and the rest of the leadership team if they see that we're making an impact on the business. They'll invest more time and effort in how People Analytics or HR generally can actually move the dial for them as a business.

—David Green, Managing Partner, Insight222

Understand HR's Range   High-performing HR professionals have a particularly broad set of sharp tools at their disposal. The upskilling we advise you to undertake requires an appreciation of this skill range. We found the framework in Figure 4.3 immensely helpful.

Business   Top-performing CHROs tend to have a background in business and/or a business degree. A few CHROs have even gone on to lead major corporations: Mary Barra, CEO of General Motors, Leena Nair, CEO of Chanel, Tricia Griffith, CEO of Progressive, and Anne Mulcahy, former CEO of Xerox.

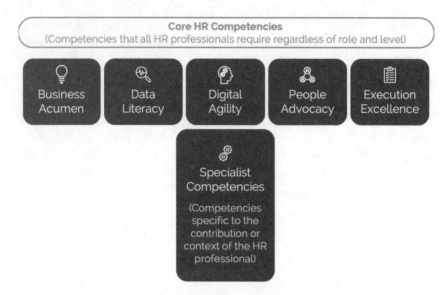

Figure 4.3   T-Shaped HR Competency Model

Source: Dieter Veldsman, Marna Van Der Merwe, and Annelise Pretorius, "HR Competencies for 2030: A Future Standard" (Academy to Innovate HR [AIHR], 2024), https://www.aihr.com/blog/hr-competencies/. Adapted with permission from AIHR.

Learning other disciplines can not only help HR professionals better understand their colleagues and their role in the organization but can also improve skills that can be applied within HR as well. For example, HR professionals can deepen their business understanding and gain new competencies by learning from their peers in Marketing and Communications, Finance, Operations, IT, and Sales.

Industry   Your HR colleagues should also have at least a working understanding of your industry's trends, key players, and regulatory issues as well as a deep familiarity with the talent market and related challenges and opportunities.

Company Picture, too, how much more strategic your HR function's focus and output would be, and the benefits to workforce performance, if the entire team understood your company's:

- **Strategic priorities:** Long-term planning and goals from the CEO
- **Competitive landscape:** Highly relevant to recruiting, so TA likely already has insights here via talent intelligence
- **Financials:** How your company makes money, interpreting quarterly earnings statements (and attending earnings calls)
- **Customers:** Key customers, customer types, customer trends, etc.
- **Products:** Know the product lines, and use them as feasible
- **Business units:** What each does, how it makes money, current challenges, etc.

Driving Strategy Home at SAP

During our tenure at SAP, Chief Strategy Officer Deepak Krishnamurthy exemplified how internal expertise can help drive transformation. All business leaders can learn from his response to low scores on the employee engagement survey for the question, "I understand the corporate strategy and how my work aligns to achieving our highest priorities," which reflected serious risks to SAP's evolution from on-premise to cloud.

To align employees with the strategy, Krishnamurthy's team provided a five-slide summary of key insights after each quarterly earnings call, complete with speaker notes and discussion prompts, to all of SAP's people managers. People managers then used the summary and notes to guide team conversations and help employees understand the shift and their role in its success. Within five quarters, survey scores for the strategy question had risen by 23 points.

Upskill HR in Workforce Insights

People Analytics should transform HR to become more evidence based. We should play a role in solving bigger business problems by helping business leaders understand the people angle to it.

—Craig Starbuck, Co-founder & CEO, OrgAcuity

Upskilling your company's HR team in Workforce Analytics, commensurate with each professional's baseline knowledge, role, and career aspirations, will not only advance their ability to help you solve your business challenges and achieve your most important goals. It will also position HR to help drive your company's overall movement toward AI and the Future of Work. That's a win-win you don't encounter often.

In the words of Insight222's David Green, "HR can't lead the charge on AI, skills and new ways of working, if it doesn't upskill itself."[30] Plus, all the cool kids are doing it.

While the CEO must dedicate the resources (both budget and work hours) and set expectations that training will happen, all self-interested business leaders should champion this development.

There's plenty to do. According to Bersin's November 2024 report, most HR professionals have "very low" People Analytics capabilities. Fifty percent identify as "mere beginners." Yet high-performing organizations develop "full-stack analytics capabilities," enabling those in HR to "analyze data, produce KPIs, tell data stories, and consult with the business."[31]

Establish Data Literacy as Table Stakes

HR has struggled to understand how to change themselves. They hear things like, "you need to be more tied to business strategy," but they often don't know how to execute that directive, be analytical, or look at the right data.

**—Kelley Steven-Waiss, Chief Transformation Officer,
ServiceNow**

Working knowledge of data fundamentals is essential to HR's success across its domains: which data is important; how to gather, interpret, and present it; formulating good questions; structured problem-solving; and more.

Experts report that **data literacy will be THE key skill of the future**. Both leaders and employees were found to believe that by 2030, data literacy, defined as "the ability to read, work with, analyze, and communicate with data" would be the skill most in demand.

In addition, 85% of executives believe it will become "as vital in the future as the ability to use a computer is today."[32] Ensure the basics.

Flair for HR Metrics HR people should firmly grasp key metrics across HR domains, not just their own. They should understand HR reports and their implications and connect dots in new ways to uncover collaborations that can enhance the impact of multiple teams. They may also need primers in "rear-view mirror" (aka activity) versus impact metrics, as explored in Section 1.

Setting Objectives Back in the day, Marketing might have run campaigns without setting goals enabling them to measure impact. That wouldn't happen now. Goal setting must also be part of HR's evolution. After all, if you don't set goals, assessing success quickly becomes elusive. If your company culture is risk-averse and experimentation is not encouraged, your HR professionals (and the stakeholders they serve) may squirm at the notion of being held accountable for delivering on goals. We have seen that happen over and over (and OVER) again.

But would you ever accept a no-accountability attitude from your sales team? Or allow them to not set goals? You wouldn't. Ever. Stop allowing excuses for HR.

> *Would you ever accept a no-accountability attitude from your sales team? Or allow them to not set goals? You wouldn't. Ever.*

Presenting Metrics Meaningfully Storytelling with data is such an important skill that it bears repeating. Indeed, "Being a storyteller with data, is becoming an important part of every business-facing HR toolkit."[33] Your entire HR team must learn how to present data in a way that resonates with business leaders, providing context, uncovering trends, and speaking in language their colleagues can understand.

Tying HR Metrics to Business Measures As we've discussed extensively, it's past time that HR transitions from merely reporting data to showing direct correlations between HR initiatives and business outcomes.

If you could make only ONE change as a business leader, it may be persuading your employees that problems are most easily and effectively solved by first truly knowing how they became problems in the first place.

Asking Good Questions to Get to the Root Cause If you could make only ONE change as a business leader, it may be persuading your employees that problems are most easily and effectively solved by first truly knowing how they became problems in the first place. "If I were given one hour to save the planet," Albert Einstein is widely quoted as saying, "I would spend 59 minutes defining the problem and one minute resolving it."

HR people must always ask the right questions—and TOUGH questions—to get to the root cause, and business leaders must be prepared to both answer those questions and accept that their HR counterpart may just know more about HR than they do.

The next vignette illustrates these points. Company leaders thought training was their salvation, and without examining the data would have wasted significant resources on it.

Vignette | Striking Oil: How Digging into Data Uncovered the Real Safety Issue

An oil company was facing mounting production delays due to repeated safety incidents. Although no one was hurt, every stoppage cost time and money. Leaders assumed it was a training problem and that they needed to reinforce safety protocols. But when the Workforce Analytics team dug into employee data, they found something unexpected: the problem wasn't training; it was exhaustion.

As they peeled away at the problem, the WFA team discovered that operators were consistently working long hours because of a severe staffing shortage, made worse by high production demands. So why hadn't they hired more people? As they dug deeper, data analysis revealed two truths: there weren't enough local qualified candidates, and the company's wages weren't competitive enough to draw talent from outside the area.

With this insight, the company faced a choice: continue paying the price in lost production or increase wages to attract skilled workers. Comparing costs, the decision became clear. Raising pay, targeting regional talent, and offering relocation benefits was the real solution, not more training. Workforce Analytics didn't just reveal the problem; it reshaped the company's entire approach to staffing.

NOTE: The case study, "Engineering Alone Can't Steer the Ship: The Human Solution to Maritime Risks," presents the opposite scenario: company leaders invested millions in sophisticated technology, thinking it could substitute for training. Both cases underscore the fundamental importance of HR asking good questions, and stakeholders both helping to discover the answers AND listening to the resulting advice. *See* Section 3, "Take Your Preference."

Leverage Success Factors　Insight222 research identified important steps organizations should take when upskilling HR in data and analytics.[34]

- **HR leaders who set examples get results.** Companies reported stark differences in daily use of workforce data and analytics by HR teams: 79% of companies where the CHRO and direct reports model that behavior, and only 22% of companies where they don't.
- **People Analytics leaders get the job done.** When the People Analytics leader takes responsibility for upskilling HR, those professionals "actively develop their data literacy skills to become more data-driven" at a far higher level versus if that training is led by anyone else (60% vs. 31% of companies surveyed).
- **Effective upskilling requires a multi-year investment.** The study estimates that an effective data literacy program—including change management, project management training,

and coaching—will cost on average $600 to $800 per full time HR employee over two to three years. Per-person costs naturally increase commensurate with the individual's seniority and role, with the highest investment in the CHRO and HR leadership team.[35]

Insight222 research also identified five skills as the "core of data literacy for HR." Our sense is that this set of skills is closer to Workforce Analytics essentials for HR, but we get that for some professionals "data literacy" necessarily includes analytics. They are similar to the skills shared in Section 2, "Understand Workforce Analytics Capabilities," but importantly, the study found these five skills more useful for the average HR practitioner than technical skills like statistics or data extraction:

1. Turning insights into "actionable recommendations"
2. Stakeholder management
3. Partnering with the business to ask the right questions and develop hypotheses
4. Extracting insights from data
5. Storytelling with data[36]

A New Kind of HR Business Partner (HRBP)

Imagine how dramatically your company could uplevel its workforce decision-making if the professionals who work most closely with functional leaders, day in and day out, had advanced analytics tools and training and a deep understanding of business operations. HRBPs savvy in the ways of Workforce Insights can better identify root causes of your business challenges and guide strategic, data-driven decisions.

In Brief: HRBPs align people strategies—talent development, workforce planning, and more—with business goals to drive organizational performance, collaborating closely with senior leadership. Top-performing HRBPs serve as trusted advisors and foster a high-performance culture.

Enable All HR to Support WFA   Although heavy lifting will be done by dedicated professionals with deep expertise, everyone in HR needs to have baseline skills in order to make the shift to being data-driven pervasive and lasting.

According to Insight 222, "Only through a partnership with data-driven HR colleagues can the people analytics team ensure it is working on the most important business challenges and scale solutions across the enterprise."[37]

Activating AI for WFA

> Non-data experts can use AI to synthesize data faster and create compelling visuals for storytelling. The utilization of AI across the enterprise enables HR professionals to identify patterns within the workforce.
>
> **—Lydia Wu, VP of Products, MeBeBot**

As mentioned above, the HR tech+AI combo is transforming how HR professionals, even those without an analytics background, embrace Workforce Analytics as a way of doing business. Josh Bersin calls AI "the most integrating, systemic, and easy to use data management technology we've ever seen."[38]

This is a no-brainer, golden opportunity to upskill your HR team without extensive training and get them WFA-enabled: analyzing data, uncovering insights, predicting trends, and prescribing actions to help business leaders accomplish their most important goals.

Yet so far, according to Bersin's 2024 November research report, only 4% of respondents said they have put into place a strategy to make Generative AI part of their Workforce Analytics practices, a "missed opportunity for gaining nuanced insights." Just 2% are using more advanced analytics simulating long-term HR outcomes and achieving adaptive talent management through machine learning.[39]

Remember Spreadsheets   Yeah, it may seem contradictory to even mention spreadsheets in nearly the same breath as AI but consider it analogous to being able to add when no calculator is available. Sometimes a spreadsheet can work well (or well enough) in lieu of a more advanced tool, as a temporary solution, need-it-right-now solution, and/or temporary workaround while planning a more sophisticated and costly solution.

If your HR team is not already making effective use of this still-useful analytics tool, upskill them now.

Remember, too: "It's Complicated"   In terms of using GenAI for data and analytics, recall that due to privacy regulations and concerns, some workforce data must remain siloed and not accessible even to internal Large Language Models.

4.4 Creating Your Insight-Driven Culture

Organizations that have a positive organizational culture . . . want to listen to their employees, want to see trends, want to use that data to make people decisions and business decisions.

—**Gargi Bhattacharya, PhD,**
Behavioral Scientist

There's no way around it: becoming insight-driven is not easy. At all. But investments in Workforce Insights are unlikely to pay off if the rest of the company has no appetite for data. "Employees need to be analytically willing and data savvy," as a report from Deloitte India puts it.[40]

Building a data-centric culture certainly has plenty of fans. In fact, 89% of C-suite leaders expect their people to be able to show the role of data in their decision-making, according to one study. Yet that study also found that only 11% of employees "feel fully confident" in their data literacy.[41] There's clearly much to do.

Many paths lead to an insight-driven culture, but they must be paved with more than good intentions: business leaders must commit themselves to changing (no one's favorite activity) their own way of thinking and working AND bring the rest of the company along. We aim to hit the major notes of the journey, including ones you may hear less about. Better get cracking.

To whet your appetite, here's a case study about *protecting* data that illustrates what cultural change requires and can achieve.

Case Study | Salesforce: Embedding a Culture of Security and Trust

In response to significant security breaches in 2010 and 2013, Salesforce recognized a critical gap in its security culture. Although "Customer Trust" was a core value, security was often viewed as a compliance task rather than a shared responsibility. This perception left vulnerabilities that technology alone couldn't address.

The Problem

In exploring why security was not an organization-wide priority, Salesforce identified three key challenges:

- **Cultural Misalignment:** Security measures were seen as barriers to innovation, conflicting with Salesforce's mission of customer trust.
- **Low Employee Engagement:** Security was perceived as the IT and Trust team's domain, leaving other employees detached from security goals.
- **Limited Awareness:** Without regular engagement, employees were more vulnerable to threats like phishing.

The Solution

Salesforce's "Detection Everywhere" initiative transformed security from a checklist item into a companywide culture of vigilance and collaboration. **Phishing simulations** kept employees on their toes, and **real-time data** revealed vulnerabilities that guided specific training. **Leaders stepped up as advocates**, integrating security into Salesforce's DNA, while employees found camaraderie on their **internal communication channels**, sharing stories, tips, and celebrating successes. **Rewards** like "Jedi Status" and "trust points" turned security practices into a source of pride

(continued)

(continued)

and engagement, creating a community empowered and aligned around the shared responsibility of keeping Salesforce safe.

The Results

- **82% Increase in Phishing Reporting:** Employees measurably increased their vigilance.
- **52% Reduction in Risky Clicks:** Trained employees showed greater caution.
- **11,000 Additional Security Course Enrollments:** Employees voluntarily enrolled in extra security courses over 18 months, showing commitment.
- **Continuous Readiness:** Bi-monthly simulations kept employees prepared, with real-time data driving relevant training updates.

Cutting to the Chase

With "Detection Everywhere," Salesforce took a multifaceted approach to changing its culture, transforming security from compliance to a shared responsibility. The measurably more secure organization that resulted demonstrates how leadership, engagement, and adaptability can drive lasting cultural change, empowering the organization to protect customer trust.[42]

Have the Guts to Go with the Data

To create a data-driven culture . . . requires clear, consistent decision-making structures that define how decisions are made and what data is needed. A truly data-driven approach means sticking to data for all decisions, not mixing gut instincts with data or using data to justify pre-formed opinions.

—**Kady Srinivasan, Chief Marketing Officer, Lightspeed**

Trust starts at the top—literally. But too many senior business leaders still prefer to make decisions based on instinct, and/or may leverage data to confirm their biases versus reveal new truths. For them, trusting facts is a significant mental shift that should not be underestimated.

A recent study of C-suite executives paints a fairly grim picture. Although 52% reported being "fully confident" in their data literacy, 45% said they "frequently make decisions based on gut feeling rather than data-led insights."[43]

That's why it's essential that every business leader, especially the CEO, commit to and model insight-driven decision-making; otherwise, there's little chance that others will.

When you consistently demand data to support decisions and remain open to insights that may challenge existing assumptions or preferences, you model data-driven decision-making and set a standard for data-driven culture within your organization.

The following vignette offers a powerful snapshot of how leaders can model being insight-driven.

Vignette | Beyond the Dashboard at Protective Life: A CEO's Data-Driven Moment

The journey to a data-driven culture for Protective Life benefited significantly from strong CEO support. Even relatively early on, the People Analytics team had created a powerful dashboard displaying real-time data on company trends that every senior leader could access. The People Analytics lead worked closely with the C-suite, guiding them to not just view the data but to truly understand it.

Then came a litmus test for the top executive: at a companywide town hall, an anonymous question surfaced: *"With the great resignation looming, what are we doing to keep our people?"*

Without hesitation, the CEO cited the company's resignation rate down to the decimal, explaining current trends and adding perspective on what might be driving the shifts, using precise data terminology. He showed employees that he understood and valued the data deeply. It wasn't rehearsed or planned—it was real.

In that moment, the CEO did more than answer a question; he set a tone, and a new expectation.[44]

Set Expectations

> In any meeting with the CEO, her first question was, "Show me the data, let's have a look." And if you didn't have the data, you wouldn't be invited back . . . [But] it's not just about one person having a strong, forceful personality. How do you win those hearts and minds? How do you help people feel, "This is the way I want to work?"
>
> **—Mark Lawrence, Founder and Executive Consultant, Data Driven HR**

With any change, business leaders must model for their teams. Promote a culture where insight-driven decision-making is valued and practiced across all levels of the organization. Take a deep look into how your organization is using data to inform decision-making and raising expectations for leaders to come to the table with data insights as part of strategic planning, reporting, and prioritization.

This is especially important within HR.

Engage the Entire Organization

From planning to implementation, actively engage employees in transforming your company to become insight-driven. In the words of Rolls-Royce Chief Transformation Officer Nikki Grady-Smith, "People drive a transformation. It's a human activity."[45] From top leadership to individual contributors, involvement fosters a sense of ownership and accountability, without which any wholesale culture change is, to put it plainly, doomed.

Democratize Data   It's a curious phrase you may never have heard, but it's critical to living in a world where data and insights rule the day. Data democratization means "giving everyone in an organization the ability to access data (appropriately) along with the tools and training necessary to understand it," according to data intelligence platform Databricks.[46] Enabling your entire workforce to easily find and use data to derive actionable insights may seem aspirational, but like so many aspects of becoming insight-driven, it can be done one step at a time.

One example of democratizing data would be to provide both managers and employees with self-service analytics tools that can be used independently, without support calls to the data team or IT, supported by in-depth training for employees at all levels.

Open Access, Welcome in Value   Creating "a more digitally connected and empowered workforce" yields measurable differences in performance. In a 2020 Harvard Business Review Analytic Services survey, 72% of leaders said productivity had increased "at least moderately" by empowering frontline workers, while 69% reported increases in customer AND employee engagement/satisfaction and 67% improved product and service quality. Another 16% said they had increased revenue by more than 30%, with a third reporting 10% to 30% revenue growth.[47]

Centralizing data for broader access can help break down silos while also removing bottlenecks and over-eager gatekeepers' sticks from the wheels of progress. Self-service data analytics frees analytics teams from their administrative work (of fulfilling requests) to do higher value work. Sound familiar? They could, for example, invest those hours in developing even more advanced, user-friendly analytics tools, creating a virtual cycle of innovation and efficiency.

And leaders who give "those closest to the work the autonomy to make their own decisions" are 85% more likely to increase organizational decision-making quality versus peers, according to McKinsey. They cite Indonesia-based Bank Mandiri, which rolled out a self-service system through which employees can access data to "make better, faster decisions" in days instead of weeks.[48]

The most robust data we have seen on what business leaders can gain from broadening access to data is, not surprisingly, from the 2024 "Definitive Guide to People Analytics" from The Josh Bersin Company. Practicing what he preaches, Bersin presents compelling analytics on the impact of data democratization strategies on nine "outcome areas" like financial performance, innovation, and customer delight. He cited data democratization as the largest differentiator in four of the nine.

For example:

- Companies granting access to "people data" (specifically) for **senior executives** are more likely to excel in engagement/retention and productivity: 2.2 times and 2.5 times, respectively.
- Those enabling **line managers** to access people data are 2.4 times more likely to excel in change adaptability,
- Granting access to **employees** made companies 1.8 times more likely to excel in financial performance.[49]

Transparency Matters   Democratizing data may require more transparency than you currently provide to your employees, but the return for that investment of trust is that employees can be productively engaged in seeking out and applying data insights.

Involve Leaders   It's essential that data democratization involve managers at all levels. "Get the right data into the hands of the right people in the organization who are most accountable to team performance and in the best position to take meaningful action to improve outcomes—leaders," advises Ian O'Keefe, Founder & CEO, Ikona Analytics.

Provide Incentives

It's really about offering more carrots than sticks. You've got to give people something to get excited about. It's not enough to tell them they have to change; you have to make them want to.

**—Meg Langan, Founder, ML Consulting & Advisory,
Previously, Chief People Officer, Turbonomic**

Creating an insight-driven culture requires efforts to win hearts and minds. Communicate clearly the WIIFM, the question every employee asks when faced with change: *What's In It For Me?* Do so in ways that will resonate for your workforce, speaking differently as needed to appeal to distinct groups (managers, individual contributors, consultants, assistants).

They will need to understand the reasons for coming changes, what they entail, new expectations for their job performance, and again, the WIIFM. Communicate again. And again.

And again.

Offer More Carrots Than Sticks   Recognize contributors and enthusiasts. Amplify leaders instead of chasing laggards. The laggards will follow.

Reward Problem-Solving   You'll need your workforce to help spot issues that hinder progress and productivity. That may involve simplifying processes to enhance efficiency and employee satisfaction. Becoming insight-driven offers broad opportunities for growth. "To me, organizational change and change management is actually about friction fixing," Huggy Rao, PhD, Atholl McBean Professor of Organizational Behavior at the Graduate School of Business at Stanford University told us. "Implement friction-fixing strategies that streamline workflows and remove unnecessary barriers, thereby giving employees the time and space to be more creative and productive."

Spotlight Insight-Driven Wins   Recognize leaders, individuals, and teams who successfully harness insights. Fund, support, or otherwise embrace their initiatives and innovation.

Equip EVERYONE *for Success*   One key to getting everyone on board is giving people the right knowledge, skills, and tools. Train your entire workforce on how to interpret and use data effectively—not just HR and business leaders. There's plenty to do. According to 2024 research from The Josh Bersin Company, only 12% of organizations offer training in how to interpret data. Given that just 6% of managers can analyze and explain data, business leaders must advocate loudly for corrective action.[50]

This includes both formal training as well as drop-in clinics, plenty of user-friendly digital resources, mentors, data buddies, coffee corners with Workforce Analytics leaders, crowdsourced tips, and more shared via whatever channel(s) are most effective at your organization.

Including data and analytics as part of onboarding is another way to not only provide knowledge and skills right away, but also cement your insight-driven culture. Critical, too, is making data literacy and analytics skills development as ongoing enablement. Lasting change won't happen with one-time training.

To those who may wonder whether employees might be tempted to take their valuable new skills elsewhere, we share the words of Sir Richard Branson: "Train people well enough so they can leave, treat them well enough so they don't want to."[51]

Get Creative   In our 100+ interviews for this book, we collected some genuinely innovative efforts to drive the adoption of data and analytics.

- **Discreet support:** Facing resistance to adopting a data mindset because employees feared looking foolish, HR formed a People Analytics Consulting Team offering discreet, nonjudgmental support, allowing employees to seek help with their projects without feeling exposed or inadequate. Providing that safe environment made a significant difference.
- **Credentials:** We learned about an internal "People Analytics certification" offered to anyone who signed up, in or outside of HR. Although the program was rigorous and included requirements like teaching peers the essentials of what you'd learned, many more employees than expected took the opportunity to uplevel their skillset. The investment paid major dividends.
- **HR all in.** One company made Workforce Analytics training mandatory for all HR employees, regardless of role. The training then became part of new hire onboarding.
- **Crowdsourcing innovation.** Going beyond data, a professional services firm incented AI upskilling through initiatives including a bot repository where any employee could contribute their own automation for access firm wide. Leaderboards tracked top downloads, ratings, and more across categories related to both

client work and internal efficiencies. This was an ingenious way to encourage an embrace of AI while also generating—and spreading—innovation. And which team got trained on AI first? Yep, Learning & Development, so they could then teach others and lead by example.

Empower Evangelists

In any organizational change, there are always people in different roles who really get the mission and love helping others buy into it. Find these individuals, give them the right training, and empower them as data "champions" to promote data-driven decisions and help you lead a cultural transformation.

—Preeti Lokam, AI Skills Lead, Microsoft

Ambassador programs are common at large companies. If yours hasn't yet tried turning employees into influencers roaming your (digital or actual) hallways ready to convert true believers, we encourage you to try it. Remember, your workforce is a powerful cultural force—harness it.

Ask for—and Respond to—Feedback Employees are also your best sources of insights about how well your data change initiative is or isn't working.

Assess progress. Some success against goals can be tracked with hard metrics, including how employees are embracing new data-centric processes and policies (*see* Pinpoint Needed Behavior Change, below). But progress is also emotional, and it's essential to track how much (and whether) employees believe in the change and its potential benefits. Use a range of "employee listening" tools—including engagement surveys, focus groups, feedback tools, and sentiment analysis on both internal conversations and external social media (as legally allowed) to gauge how, and whether, becoming insight-driven is impacting engagement and satisfaction, productivity, and performance.

Respond to inputs. Having a positive culture, about insights or anything else, requires actually doing something about employee feedback. Ensure you have processes in place to (a) analyze, understand, and act on feedback, (b) hold managers accountable for addressing team issues, and (c) regularly communicate that you are doing so.

Show employees how their input is being used to prioritize business decisions. Include the topic in regular all-hands meetings, functional leader meetings, on your intranets and internal social media, wherever you can.

Listening to Employees Is Serious Business   A UKG global survey of 4,000 employees, managers, and business leaders across 11 countries found that 86% of employees don't feel people are "heard fairly or equally" at their company and 63% said their manager or employer ignored their voice in some way. More than a third of employees said they'd prefer to quit or switch teams rather than honestly share concerns with higher-ups.[52]

Responding to your employees is not just the right thing to do. The UKG study also found that companies are far more likely to see positive financial performance (88%) when "their employees feel heard, engaged, and a sense of belonging."[53] McKinsey found companies that "actively listen and act on" frontline employee recommendations are 80% more likely to "consistently implement new and better ways of doing things."[54]

Remember: perception is reality. If employees report that policies are unfair or processes are poorly run, address and correct those perceptions, whether or not they mirror facts on the ground.

Earn and Generate Trust

Trust is a meta condition. In a high-trust environment, people are more willing to share data, which enriches the insights that can be derived.

—Ian O'Keefe, Founder & CEO, Ikona Analytics

Trust in data and analytics is essential and takes two equally important forms: trust in data accuracy, and trust in how data is being used. High-trust environments facilitate better data sharing and richer insights; conversely, low-trust environments hinder the effectiveness of People Analytics.

Trust is also at the heart of culture change. Employees are more likely to embrace change if they trust that their leaders have workers' best interests at heart, not just organizational good. Employees feeling safe to express concerns, ask questions, and offer suggestions without fear of retribution is critical to driving change.

Regular, transparent communication helps alleviate all these potential fears and uncertainties. In terms of new ways of working required by a newly data-driven culture, employees also need to understand the reasons for the change, what it entails, and how it affects them, including new expectations for their job performance.

A Prime Example of Trust Generating Employee Benefits

The Cleveland Clinic, with 77,000 employees, spent a decade risk-stratifying tens of thousands of workers based on factors like BMI and chronic conditions (e.g., asthma, diabetes, hypertension). This enabled targeted chronic disease and weight-reduction programs, enrolling 55% of eligible employees—far surpassing the 20% national average. Financial incentives tied to weight loss goals yielded average losses of 14 pounds per participant and flattened annual weight gain companywide. Overall, hospital admissions dropped 25% and annual cost savings reached $120 million.[55]

On Leaders, Trust, and Data Leaders must also understand and accept that workforce data will never be perfect. And since perfection is the enemy of the good, that's fine, but in the words of Preeti Lokam, AI Skills Lead at Microsoft, "Ninety percent of the battle with analytics is getting . . . the buy-in to trust the data that [leaders are] seeing."

Reward Calculated Risk-Taking

To drive change, leaders, data professionals, and others must be encouraged to experiment, take bold risks, and be willing to make mistakes in pursuit of innovation. By rewarding calculated risk-taking and embracing learning from failure, HR leaders, too, can adopt an agile mindset and make more informed, iterative decisions based on Workforce Insights.

—Kathryn Clubb, CEO, BTS North America

Creating the conditions for change requires actively encouraging bold experimentation. Leaders and employees at all levels must be willing to be wrong and make mistakes in order to drive change. Starting with the CEO, senior leaders must encourage and praise learning from failure to boost motivation and drive innovation.

Welcome Bad News A correlation to encouraging failure is insisting on being informed of unwelcome news that results from deeper, richer data analysis. As Cindi Howson, Chief Data Strategy Officer at analytics platform provider ThoughtSpot, advises, "confront brutal facts."[56]

This is especially important for the top executive. "CEOs often don't realize they're creating the very culture they claim to oppose," Annette Templeton, Partner at Trium Group, told us. "When they react angrily to bad news, it reinforces a fear-driven environment where employees delay sharing problems, perpetuating the cycle." Imagine some of the catastrophes that could have been avoided if leaders had the courage to share bad news (we're looking at YOU, Enron).

Celebrate Success

Business leaders already know, but may appreciate a reminder, that transformational change usually happens gradually. As longtime L&D analytics expert Peggy Parskey, Owner of Parskey Consulting and Co-author of *Measurement Demystified: Field Guide* and *Learning*

Analytics, told us, "In terms of a best practice, I see organizations who don't let perfect be the enemy of the good. They recognize that they are going to grow over time."

To sustain energy and enthusiasm over the long haul: communicate, communicate, communicate—especially good news. "It is important to recognize success along the journey, because that creates the momentum, the motivation; that also enables people to *see* 'the art of the possible' that they might not have seen previously," Rolls-Royce's Transformation Chief Nikki Grady-Smith told McKinsey.[57]

See How It's Done   For a peek behind the curtain of a company taking seriously its journey to becoming insight-driven, look no further than Lloyds Banking Group.

> ### Case Study | Lloyds Banking Group: Modeling Data Culture Change
>
> Lloyds Banking Group, plc, a 325-year-old British financial institution with 2023 net income of £17.9B and 66,000 employees, is on a journey to become the world's most data literate bank AND rank as a top 10 data and analytics employer of choice. After interviewing Josh Cunningham, Group Head of Data Culture, and John Fiore, Senior Manager in the Chief Data & Analytics Office, and reading online about their activities, we were blown away by their smart, comprehensive strategy.
>
> Lloyds is betting the bank, as it were, on a transformation that's placing data and analytics at the core of their strategy, operations, talent development, workforce planning, and decision-making processes. As Ranil Boteju, Group Head of Data Strategy and Innovation, observed in a company blog, "There's no shortage of interesting problems to solve or ways to make an impact on our 26 million customers" with data.[58] Our money's on them.
>
> *(continued)*

(continued)

Highlights from their extensive initiatives mirror the themes of this book:

- **Strategically Aligning Data Initiatives:** Business and analytics teams collaborate on KPIs aligned with strategic goals and data insights help iteratively refine critical strategies.
- **Embedding Analytics Practitioners Within Business Units:** These pros help weave data into the fabric of the organization and ensure data insights inform strategic and operational decisions.
- **Harnessing Advanced Analytics, AI, and Machine Learning:** Lloyds is committed to integrating advanced technologies to modernize operations and improve customer interactions.
- **Democratizing Data Access:** Lloyds invests in centralized systems and user-friendly self-service platforms, enabling real-time data access for both technical and nontechnical staff while reducing dependence on specialized teams.
- **Prioritizing Data Literacy, Modeled by Leaders:** To help scale data-driven decision-making, literacy "learning journeys" are companywide, tailored to different business units and roles, including senior leadership.
- **Communicating, communicating, communicating:** Supported by nearly 300 strategy and culture champions, a range of channels amplify, recognize, and advocate for data culture initiatives.[59]

Developing Analytics Talent

Maybe we're just HR nerds, but we were especially impressed with Lloyds' forward-thinking strategy to secure top analytics professionals. A strategic multiyear workforce plan outlines skill paths and standardizes hiring channels. A skills capture tool enables practitioners to benchmark their capabilities and personalize an upskilling plan; their Data Academy provides 3,000 hours of curated learning content. A data graduate program for young professionals helps build their data leadership

pipeline. And they're connecting more than 4,000 data practitioners to create cohesion and encourage knowledge sharing
and collaboration.

For business leaders looking to transform their organizations,
Lloyds offers an inspiring road map.

Help Bring HR Along

*In HR, change resistance may stem from the function starting at a
disadvantage—often facing skepticism from the organization before
they've even begun.*

—Shelly Holt, VP Talent Development

As you've read throughout this book, Human Resources is a function
with baggage. That baggage tags along on any change journey. Business
leaders who crave the efficiency, productivity, and problem-solving that
Workforce Insights can deliver can help lighten that load.

Admin order-taker to analytics superstar is a big, big leap. Many
in HR have far to go—a challenge all on its own. As Pamay Bassey,
Chief Learning and Diversity Officer at The Kraft Heinz Company,
told us, "If I am born and raised in HR, then chances are I'm doing
all the things that are administrative, I'm just chopping wood and
carrying water. The shift to strategic thinking in HR is a major shift
in mindset."

But HR folks have a few additional barriers to change. Self-
proclaimed "recovering HR director" Lucy Adams thoughtfully covers
this topic in *HR Disrupted: It's time for something different.*[60] Like us, she
endeavors to call a spade a spade for both business leaders and HR (*see*
Figure 4.4).

In our conversation with her, Adams challenges the mindset of
some in HR who may be perfectly content exactly where they are. "It's
so much easier to produce a new process than it is to change how people work. It's so much simpler to implement a new organizational
structure than it is to improve people's performance. And it's so much
quicker to tick boxes than it is to delve into the messy reality of people's minds and emotions."

Originating from Business Leaders	Originating in HR
Leaders find it hard to accept changes in HR for these main reasons:	HR finds it hard to envisage things differently for these main reasons:
1. Their ingrained assumptions about what constitutes good HR practices	1. The pressure to justify HR financially
2. Their lack of interest in, or understanding of, the "people agenda"	2. The ease of staying as we are vs. difficulties associated with change
3. Pressure from external regulators	3. The challenge of proving ahead of time that the change will be beneficial
4. Their preference for dealing with numbers and process rather than people	4. The difficulty of unraveling processes that are inter-dependent on each other

Figure 4.4   Barriers to Change for HR

Source: Adapted with permission from Lucy Adams, *HR Disrupted: It's Time for Something Different* (2nd Ed.; Northwich, UK: Practical Inspiration Publishing, 2021), 193.

Business leaders, fight what may be a natural urge to put up barriers—hopefully easier with the insights and information in this book:

1. Tuck into bed your assumptions about "good" HR and instead work to realize the vision you want for your workforce. For inspiration, re-read the divergent views on HR in Section 3, "Know and Demand Excellence."
2. Get to know and appreciate your workforce in all its (sometimes maddening) complexity. They're the best source of competitive advantage you'll ever have.
3. Accept that external regulator pressures have no impact on the human nature of your employees, but YOU can motivate them to come to work every day excited to help you accomplish your most important goals.
4. Numbers tell the story of the people behind the business. Fall in love with the process of revealing what that's all about—that's Workforce Analytics in a nutshell.

Thank you.

HR today is not HR of the past. I see HR making an enormous difference in many (not all) companies by creating stakeholder value through human capability. Our data, with over 120,000 respondents over 35 years, shows enormous progress of HR professional competencies. I am very positive about the emerging HR agenda.

—Dave Ulrich, Co-founder & Principal,
The RBL Group

4.5 Key Takeaways

The right technology, WFA capabilities, governance, etc. are essential but insufficient to become insight-driven. The linchpin: your company culture. Also pivotal: upleveling HR, including embracing AI for automation and data analysis.

- **Why "Insight-Driven" Matters:** Integrating evidence-based decision-making into any company's daily operations is well worth the effort. Especially with Generative AI's rapid advancement, data-driven organizations are outperforming their competitors, and now is the time to act.
- **Making Culture Your #1 Strategic Asset:** Companies with strong cultures enjoy advantages like superior financial performance and better employee retention. Likewise, business leaders who ignore culture's impact do so at great peril.
- **Upleveling HR:** Business leaders must not only raise expectations for HR but also provide the necessary support for transformation. By using GenAI to automate administrative tasks and advance data analytics, fostering skill development, and enabling evidence-based problem-solving, HR can become the strategic business partner you need.
- **Creating Your Insight-Driven Culture:** This multi-phase, multi-faceted transition requires that senior leaders act swiftly and consistently, including: establishing clear expectations,

engaging the entire workforce, democratizing data, generating trust through transparency, providing incentives, and celebrating progress.

Bottom line: Using WFI is like channeling the heat and light from a fire. Among the biggest logs? HR's WFA capabilities. But creating a data-centric culture adds slow-burning wood AND kindling AND fans the flames. Forget to tend that fire? It will go out, every time.

SECTION

5

Higher Math—Workforce Analytics at the C-level

LET'S FACE IT: no major change will happen at any company without the CEO's support and direction. And no HR department will change without the right Chief Human Resources Officer (CHRO) in place.

Further, the rest of the C-suite and Board of Directors must be in on the action. That's why we are dedicating an entire section to topics directly related to, and requiring input and advocacy from, the C-level.

5.1 All About the CHRO

The CHRO enhances the company's ability to deliver on key business metrics by developing a strategic people agenda that drives performance, fosters engagement, and builds organizational capability. Their efforts align the workforce with business goals, optimize human capital, and create a competitive advantage through people.

> —CEO survey respondent, Europe-based $1–10M private company[i]

---

[i] For details on our CEO/CHRO survey, please *see* the Appendix.

Jack Welch, one of the most influential—and controversial—business leaders of the last century, championed the head of HR, the individual most responsible for HR supporting business leaders and the company as a whole to achieve their key strategic objectives. "Without a doubt, the head of HR should be the second most important person in any organization," he counseled. "From the point of view of the CEO, the director of HR should be at least equal to the CFO."[1] For more about how Welch's thinking on HR evolved, *see* "Import Skills, Export Skills" later in this section.

If your CHRO has not already arrived at that position of power at your company, maximizing how Workforce Analytics can help you achieve your most important goals may be at risk. Certainly, the leader with the most power and influence here is the CEO. But any business leader can advocate for a head of HR with the right skills, acumen, and savvy to help raise HR to be a key strategic partner, thereby helping elevate Workforce Analytics to a fine art.

What's in a Title?

Just as HR goes by many names, so does the leader of the function. We are using CHRO because it's the most common title for that role, and because that leader must have a "C" in their title and report directly to the CEO.

Understand What's Possible

The Savvy CEOs and savvy CHROs realize that the role of the CHRO is multifold . . . to be a consigliere to the CEO, help the CEO run the C-suite, have a role with the Board, be a cheerleader for the employees, and not just a program administrator.

—**Huggy Rao, PhD, Atholl McBean Professor of Organizational Behavior, Graduate School of Business, Stanford University**

What IS possible in a CHRO? We explore the potential below.

According to an article on *Forbes* entitled, "The Most Important Hire a CEO Will Make: The CHRO," a great CHRO "possesses the strategic vision, trusted advisory skills, culture-building, prowess, and data-driven mindset to drive an organization's success. By prioritizing these qualities, avoiding common pitfalls, and actively supporting their CHRO's success," the article asserts, "CEOs can unleash the power of their people and create a competitive advantage in the ever-evolving business landscape."[2]

Accenture research calls outstanding CHROs "growth executives," accelerators of positive change who operate at the core of their organizations. These leaders bring data into focus, understand technological and business challenges, and zoom in on the skills and culture of their teams. They are, in other words, key C-suite players who foster positive change. However, according to their findings only about a quarter of CHROs fit this description.[3]

Why would only 25% of CHROs be operating at that level? Especially when in the same study, Accenture reports that 89% of CEOs say HR "should have a central role in the business"? Apparently, CEOs are not walking the talk, as only 45% of those same CEOs say they are "creating the conditions" for HR to lead business growth successfully.[4]

These contradictions are part of what spurred us to author this book. We know phenomenal, strategic, growth-driving CHROs do exist—and we are convinced that any company can have an incredible CHRO and HR function, if business leaders are willing to advocate for it, and if CEOs invest in realizing their potential as change agents and value creators.

Upgrading the CEO's Vision

The CEO's low expectations of HR are holding back the function. Unfortunately, they get what they expect.

—Robert O. Brinkerhoff, Professor Emeritus, Western Michigan University, Director of Research & Evaluation, Promote International

So, What Should Leaders Expect from Their CHRO?   Consider the perspectives of CEO participants in the 2024 CEO Academy, created and run by the Society for Human Resources Management (SHRM) and the Wharton School of the University of Pennsylvania. Attendees of this invitation-only, two-day immersive leadership experience said the CHRO qualities they look for are, in essence: "what most humans want—someone smart they can trust who will genuinely help them." They cited "three Cs: competency, confidant, and courage":

- **Competency:** CEOs expect CHROs to be "HR experts" who can guide them on critical issues such as talent acquisition, AI integration, and wage inflation strategies. They must have deep knowledge and foresight into HR trends.
- **Confidant:** A CHRO should be a trusted advisor, providing CEOs with confidential counsel. "The CHRO is someone who offers psychological safety and a sounding board for difficult decisions."
- **Courage:** CEOs look for CHROs with the courage to speak truth to power, ensuring ethical standards and guiding tough decisions even when challenging.[5]

In addition, here are key themes revealed by the CEOs we surveyed[ii] about how CHROs contribute to their success:

1. **Attracting and Developing Top Talent:** CHROs play a crucial role in recruiting top talent and building future skills within the workforce to drive company success.
2. **Building a High-Performance Culture:** By fostering accountability and aligning culture with business goals, CHROs create an environment where teams are focused on delivering results.
3. **Driving Revenue and Growth through People Strategies:** CHROs enhance revenue growth by building high-impact teams and partnering with revenue leaders to create performance and incentive systems.
4. **Using Workforce Analytics for Strategic Decisions:** CHROs leverage data to identify trends and proactively address talent gaps, optimizing workforce planning and performance.

[ii] For details on our CEO/CHRO survey, please *see* the Appendix.

5. **Leading Change and Promoting Agility:** In dynamic environments, CHROs guide change initiatives and build adaptable teams to support business agility.
6. **Serving as a Trusted Advisor:** As strategic partners, CHROs advise CEOs on people and culture issues, ensuring alignment across the executive team and organization.

CHRO *as a Key to Delivering on Priorities*   Several respondents to our CEO survey also spoke about the ways CHROs can help align HR with key business priorities. Below are a few wise responses.

Addressing the question, "How does a CHRO increase a company's ability to deliver on the most important business metrics?"

> The CHRO boosts a company's capacity to hit its most critical business metrics by acting as a bridge between the organization's strategic goals and its workforce capabilities. They focus on creating a high-performance culture that aligns with business priorities. This includes designing and implementing HR strategies around talent management, leadership development, and organizational structure that support business growth and innovation.
>
> **—CEO survey respondent, Europe-based private company (less than $1M annual revenue)**

When asked how a CHRO might diminish a company's achievement of key metrics:

> If the CHRO is focused on an agenda that is not directly aligned with the company's clear objectives, they are likely to be attracting the wrong employees for the wrong reasons and lead to organizations which are not unified or capable of success.
>
> **—CEO survey respondent, U.S.-based private company ($50–500M annual revenue)**

If you need more convincing that the CHRO can and should be a high-performing leader driving these kinds of impact, this may not be the book for you.

Times Have Changed

The CHRO role has evolved from providing a service to leading enterprise and organizational change—culture shaping, being a talent architect, workforce planning for the future including AI, and dealing with activism both inside and outside the company. CHROs are now handling real estate decisions, crisis management, internal communications, IT, Environmental Social Governance (ESG), and more. The role's complexity has skyrocketed, and many CHROs are being asked to take on tasks well beyond traditional HR responsibilities.

—**Brad Warga, Global Managing Partner,**
Heidrick & Struggles

As explained in Section 3, "Remember Yesterday's IT," the CHRO role continues to evolve, just like the CIO/CTO, CFO, and CMO previously. Most CHROs today spent their entire careers in HR, but expectations are changing.

In interviews with about half a dozen CHRO headhunters from top executive search firms, we consistently heard that CEOs seek HR leaders with different standards. Brad Warga, Global Managing Partner at Heidrick & Struggles, summed up the two most in-demand candidate profiles:

Profile 1: Business-First, HR-Second	Profile 2: HR-First, Business-Second
Business-savvy, data-driven, and creative problem-solvers who proved themselves outside of HR.	True HR experts who proved themselves through exceptional HR achievements.
• **Non-HR experience:** Considerable time in consulting: skilled at stakeholder management, rigorous analytics, storytelling.	• **Non-HR experience:** None.
• **Education:** Excelled as undergraduate, ideally science or math major; MBA from top business school.	• **Education:** Any undergraduate degree.
• **Path to CHRO:** Lateral move after proven success advancing another function; bringing strong "street cred" to the role.	• **Path to CHRO:** "Grew up" in HR, with deep experience building, scaling, and/or evolving their function to meet a company's changing needs, including major expansions.
	• **Has likely:** Architected an entire function from the ground up.

Unfortunately, according to Warga, the talent pool for both profiles is thin, with a shortage of HR talent who meet these new criteria, despite a down market. This underscores the importance of CEOs and other business leaders helping HR address their branding issues. Raising expectations and conveying the new standards can help make the top HR job more attractive.

The Influence Paradox

We've heard about it many, many times: CHROs who spent their entire careers in HR (Profile 2: HR-First, Business-Second) struggle to influence their C-level peers and other senior leaders, but Profile 1 leaders (Business-First, HR-Second) moving into the top HR job from "the business" enjoy instant credibility in the role despite having little or no HR experience. This near-automatic influence is, in fact, a key reason they succeed where the Profile 2 CHRO may have failed: they speak the same business language as their peers and have a track record doing "real" work.

This can be infuriating to watch for the HR team. After all, CEOs wouldn't hire a CFO who had never worked in Finance, or a CIO with no technology experience. It's also demoralizing and stressful for senior HR professionals hoping to one day lead their function (if you know any, please recommend this book).

And yet, this is the trend. Possible silver linings? An HR profession with more CHROs who have deep experience BOTH in and outside HR may just:

- Encourage HR professionals to gain business acumen and experience in other functions
- Generate more CEOs with CHRO experience, like Ford's Mary Barra and others
- Attract more high-performing talent to the field

Get the CHRO You Need

When searching for my CHRO, I make sure to only interview candidates who have reported to a CEO and have worked closely with the Board. If they reported to the COO, it meant their remit was transactional and focused on operational efficiency. Or if they reported to a CFO, it meant that talent as a cost, vs. a strategic differentiator.

—CEO survey respondent, Europe-based
public company, $500M in revenue

Getting the "right" CHRO for your company, its stage of growth, strategies, and aspirations—an individual with best-fit skills, experience, temperament, vision, cultural outlook, and other factors—is essential. But who is "right" for *your* business?

As discussed in "Get on the Same Page," previously, it's important to honestly assess whether you actually do want a top-performing, business-minded CHRO. If you're not interested in taking advantage of Workforce Analytics, we suggest you hire (or retain) a content leader to focus on administrative excellence (the "traditional view" in Section 3, "Know and Demand Excellence").

But if you do want to grab the brass ring, please consider the model in Figure 5.1. This model synthesizes CHRO best practices and models from leading consulting firms and CHRO headhunters and is informed by other primary and secondary research for the book and our own vision of high-performing HR leaders in the role. Use it as a tool for discussion to align on expectations, focusing on the areas most important to your business.

Help Your CHRO Keep Growing   Regardless of the path your CHRO took to the top HR role, continued support for that leader is crucial. All executives, including the CEO, must continue to learn and grow. And the CHRO has unique, additional challenges as discussed throughout this book. In addition to rotations into other departments and deep involvement with other C-suite leaders, cross-functional teams, and your Board of Directors, you can further support your CHRO in other key ways.

The Human-Centric Strategist

FIRST-PRINCIPALS INFLUENCER

First Consiglieri: Board partner, confidant, and coach, aligning human capital strategy with business objectives and outcomes.

Culture Keeper: Aligns values, purpose, and strategy to build engagement, centered around a core of robust learning as DNA.

Fact Seeker: Digital strategist using AI, tech, and advanced analytics to solve problems with actionable Workforce Insights.

Brand Ambassador: Thought leader and deft communicator whose vision and innovations boost both corporate and employer reputations.

SYSTEMS THINKER

Strategy Developer: Aligns organization, workforce, and incentives to navigate global trends, execute on priorities, and achieve core objectives.

Business Leader: Optimizes systems and deploys key talent to improve profitability, customer outcomes, and stakeholder returns.

Organizational Architect: Reimagines structures and leverages technology and analytics to adapt work design to evolving business needs.

Change Champion: Pulls structural and cultural levers to effectively execute pivots in strategy, mindset, and workforce processes.

FUTURE CATALYST

Stakeholder Manager: Balances conflicting demands from diverse stakeholder groups (leaders, employers, board, shareholders).

Technological Enabler: Forward-thinking digital strategist using AI, technology, and analytics to advance workforce planning and HR operations.

Resilience Inspiration: Develops systems that enable workforce responsiveness to disruption, building capacity to thrive amid uncertainty.

Human-Machine Collaborator: Maximizes productivity and human potential while optimizing impact of AI-driven technology and automation.

FUNCTIONAL EXPERT

Succession Guide: Partners with CEO and Board to build robust pipelines and plans to ensure future-ready leaders.

Job Architect: Reengineers labor around tasks and skills to quickly deploy talent and machines as needed, with employees doing high-value work.

Talent Magnet: Crafts compelling human-centric/tech-enabled employee value proposition centered on purposeful, engaging work.

Belonging Innovator: Builds trust and safety for all to nurture creativity, performance, and competitiveness across the workforce.

Figure 5.1   The Future-Ready CHRO

Credit: Actionable Analytics Group.

These may include: CHRO certifications; executive coaching; mentoring with Finance, Operations, and/other functional leaders; networking with other HR leaders; and potential partnerships with external consultants who specialize in HR.

If you bring in an HR leader from outside HR, include in their remit upleveling the team (*see* "Support New Skills," further below in this section) and grooming an internal successor.

5.2 CEO: Be a True Partner, Get a True Partner

Looking at my experience as a Chief People Officer, I can probably count on one hand the number of times my CEO wanted to have a strategic conversation that genuinely looked at how we were getting the people to do their best work. But what else is HR there to do? It's to create an environment where people can be more agile, more productive, more collaborative, more innovative, to enable the business to thrive.

—Lucy Adams, CEO, Disruptive HR

No leader is more integral to HR success than the CEO, and we aim to make plain that it's in the CEO's best interest to drive that success. "CEOs who miss the mission criticality of HR do so at their peril," reports Korn Ferry. "HR drives the people-related systems of the company just as the chief information officer (CIO) drives technology; this is equally mission critical. CEOs must empower HR."[6]

In Figure 5.2, we illustrate the progression to great HR, starting with administrative work done in isolation, advancing to working throughout the organization, and finally becoming a strategic partner to the business by working and aligning with the Chief Executive. Great HR happens when the CEO and CHRO are aligned and working together to understand, plan, and drive organizational success.

Following, we endeavor to map out what that close partnership can look like, and how to achieve it.

Siloed Administrator

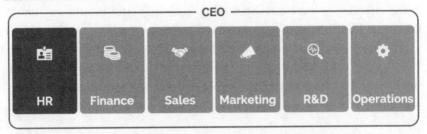

Integrated Operator

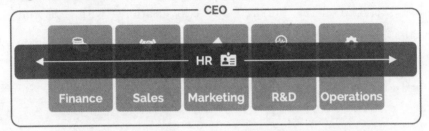

Strategic Partner

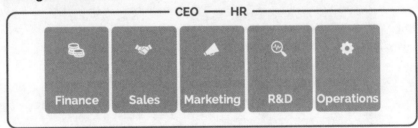

Figure 5.2 Good to Great HR

Credit: Actionable Analytics Group.

Get on the Same Page

Align on expectations that the CHRO job is to grow a healthy company.

—CHRO survey respondent, U.S.-based $500M+
public company

Our research—expert interviews, CEO and CHRO surveys, and a trove of books and articles—revealed repeatedly the importance of the CEO and CHRO being like-minded in terms of goals and expectations. A mismatch between a CEO who wants an order taker and a CHRO who wants to be strategic is just as doomed as a CEO seeking a big thinking HR partner and an HR executive focused on tactical excellence.

Welcome to the Matrix   To illustrate our point, Figure 5.3 is a framework Jenny developed to depict this alignment, or lack thereof. She has sketched it in hundreds of conversations with academics,

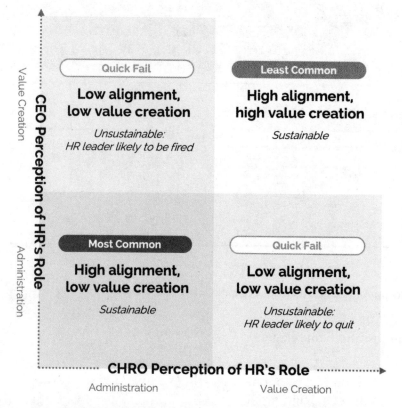

Figure 5.3   CEO/CHRO Alignment: Welcome to the Matrix
Credit: Actionable Analytics Group.

researchers, other CHROs, business executives and anyone who will listen to her evangelize about correcting historical wrongs and injustices through better HR.

The consensus was not just that it is on point, but also that the percentage of companies where the CEO and CHRO are in the upper right quadrant—both see HR as a value creator—is 10% or less. That's even lower than that 25% of "growth" CHROs we cited earlier.

Typically, CEO/CHRO pairs in the "Quick Fail" quadrants end up there due to one of two scenarios: a new CEO comes on board with HR philosophies and priorities that diverge from their predecessor's; or a new CHRO is hired without clear expectations set. To understand some key differences between the leaders in these paradigms, *see* Figure 5.4.

One HR leader we interviewed for the book (let's call her A.) recently found herself in a Quick Fail scenario. This high-performing CHRO, who exhibits the characteristics in the lower right corner of Figure 5.3, had been seen as a promising talent by a previous employer, and was sent to do a two-year stint in Operations to gain new perspective and skills, returning after to HR.

A. was then hired by the CEO of a cloud software provider with whom she partnered closely and who involved her in a number of highly strategic projects. She also made significant strides upleveling their HR function to be data-driven and strategic. When the board replaced that CEO, however, her new boss, whose view of HR was somewhere between "Cynical" and "Traditional," as outlined in Section 3, Know and Demand Excellence, asked her to essentially unwind the transformation and focus on operations and administration. A. soon left, unwilling to go back, or be held back, from what she knew HR could and should be.

Despite the somewhat pessimistic picture that the CEO/CHRO matrix in Figure 5.3, and A.'s story, presents, we do believe that some mismatches can be ameliorated when both parties are willing and able to change, compromise, and/or concede as needed. We are hoping that our CEO readers will be persuaded and inspired to lead the way, with vision and commitment, to that upper right quadrant, and that this book will help guide you.

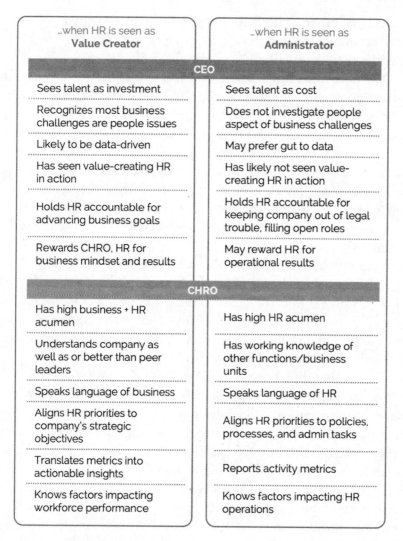

Figure 5.4   CEO/CHRO Alignment: Common Characteristics
Credit: Actionable Analytics Group.

We invite CEOs to consider which characteristics might describe them, and determine where they are on the matrix, where they might like to be, and how to bring their CHRO along or, if that is not feasible—with apologies to our HR colleagues who may feel this is unfair—hire a new one.

> Identify a business minded, agile and courageous CHRO and partner with them to drive the business AND talent strategies.
>
> **—CHRO survey respondent,**
> **private U.S.-based company**

To Align, Get Strategic AND Specific   When a CEO is ready to lay out the parameters of their working relationship with the CHRO, we advise they look both broadly and at details, aiming to align on:

- CHRO responsibilities to both develop and execute workforce strategies aligned to business goals
- CHRO interaction with and support of C-level peers and Board of Directors (more on this below)
- Which workforce challenges and outcomes the CEO and CHRO will manage together versus solo
- Expectations for the CHRO to challenge the CEO's thinking where needed
- Success metrics for which the CHRO will be held accountable
- Regular touchpoints

Dear CEO: Be Honest   We'd like to address CEOs directly for a moment. As you assess your vision and goals for HR and your CHRO, be honest with yourself about what you want and what kinds of change you can manage. Here's why.

Near the end of our writing process, Jenny shared her matrix at a CHRO roundtable sponsored by BTS. "I am living that right now!" exclaimed an attendee (let's call her B.). A senior HR leader at a Fortune 500 company, she had just witnessed the arrival, brief tenure, and departure of a CHRO who, like the one who found herself in the Quick Fail situation mentioned previously, was exceptionally high performing, with both deep HR expertise and broad business leadership experience.

The CEO, whom B. admired, had said he wanted a strategic CHRO who could transform HR, and she had helped him recruit just such an individual. Yet at every turn, the CEO missed opportunities to aid his new CHRO's success or undermined him outright. Finally, the CHRO left in frustration. Much to B.'s surprise, when the CEO asked for her help recruiting the new CHRO, he again declared his desire for a highly strategic HR leader. B. was astonished, and perplexed. Why would he sabotage himself—and another C-level executive—again? She chalked it up to an unfortunate blind spot: despite his many talents as a top executive, he couldn't see these limitations.

A. has been interviewing for CHRO roles. To her dismay, several CEOs rejected her explicitly because, they said, her extensive business experience made her over-qualified to lead their HR function.

Of course, not all CEO/CHRO matchups end badly. We have seen all the combinations. Below is a study in contrasts: two tech companies in transition, each led by a CEO engaging a new CHRO to help realize their vision.

Cautionary Tale | Vision Versus Reality: Lessons from a Stalled Transformation

It was two months before COVID-19 reshaped the world. The CEO of a mid-size tech provider that was transitioning from on-premise to the cloud hired the company's first CHRO. The sweeping mission: mirror the company's product shift to the cloud by bringing HR online and evolve it from a back-office role to a strategic powerhouse. The new CHRO created an ambitious two-year plan to modernize HR and prepare the workforce for the CEO's cloud-focused vision.

Trouble began when the pandemic struck, and the newly appointed CHRO had to pivot to crisis management while also advancing the road map, including hiring a new HR leadership team. Then, the CEO's vision of HR as a strategic force collided with entrenched internal dynamics. HR had historically reported to Finance, under a Head of Finance who had been the CEO's primary advisor for more than 20 years. This legacy created complex internal resistance, especially as the pandemic amplified demands on the CHRO's immediate attention.

Although modernizing HR was his vision, he had hired the CHRO to execute on the vision, and was fully aware of the demands the pandemic placed on all of HR, the CEO did not set up his new leader to succeed. He hadn't communicated his HR vision or set expectations with the rest of the C-suite, especially the Head of Finance. And he chose not to mediate mounting tensions among C-level peers. The CHRO found herself shut out of key strategic conversations, and struggling to overcome roadblocks to advancing the CEO's HR agenda.

The lack of CEO support made success impossible. The CHRO and her leadership team departed after two years of frustration, costing the company significant investment and momentum in addition to the time and expense of replacing HR leadership, lost productivity, and disruption of the broader business transformation.

Case Study | The Powerful CEO/CHRO Partnership that Helped Transform Microsoft

Microsoft has long been a leader in technology innovation. By 2024, the global powerhouse employed more than 220,000 people across 200 countries with a market capitalization exceeding $2.5 trillion. Yet beneath this impressive exterior, it hasn't always been an easy journey. In the early 2010s, Microsoft's market leadership and innovation legacy was in jeopardy.

The Problem

By 2013, Microsoft was struggling to stay competitive in crucial sectors like mobile and cloud computing. The company's once-admired culture had devolved into a rigid hierarchy, stifling

(continued)

(continued)

creativity and collaboration. Employees felt trapped in a work environment that prioritized individual success over teamwork. Internal feedback painted a stark picture: a culture characterized by fear of failure and a diminished reputation for innovation, as competitors surged ahead in adapting to changing market demands.

The Solution

In 2014, Satya Nadella took over as CEO, and immediately formed a powerful partnership with CHRO Kathleen Hogan, whose impressive background uniquely positioned her to drive cultural change at Microsoft. With an undergraduate degree in Applied Mathematics and Economics, 9 years of top consulting experience, an MBA, and 12 years in go-to-market business operations before pivoting to HR, Hogan brought a robust business acumen that complemented Nadella's vision.

Together, they recognized the urgent need for change and embarked on a cultural transformation aimed at revitalizing Microsoft's operational approach. They **co-created a shared vision that aligned cultural transformation with business objectives**, ensuring a unified direction across the organization. They introduced a revised mission statement—"to empower every person and every organization on the planet to achieve more"—that emphasized customer-centric solutions. Key to this transformation were new cultural attributes like "Customer Obsessed," "One Microsoft," and "Diverse and Inclusive," fostering collaboration and inclusivity across teams.

Nadella and Hogan implemented **leadership principles centered on transparency and motivation**, promoting a results-oriented culture. They relied on **data-driven decision-making** to assess employee engagement and track the effectiveness of cultural initiatives, demonstrating accountability. The **overhaul of the performance management system** shifted from competitive rankings to one emphasizing continuous feedback and teamwork, breaking down silos and encouraging collaboration.

Additionally, they established **mechanisms for continuous feedback** from employees at all levels, ensuring that voices were heard in decision-making processes. This emphasis on open communication fostered a culture of transparency and responsiveness. Leadership development programs were designed to emphasize emotional intelligence and adaptive leadership, equipping managers to model new cultural values and effectively guide their teams through the transformation. Furthermore, initiatives such as the One Microsoft hackathon spurred cross-team innovation, allowing employees to collaborate creatively on projects.

The Results

- **Revenue Surge:** Microsoft's revenue skyrocketed from $86.8 billion in 2014 to $143 billion in 2020.
- **Profit Growth:** The company's net profits increased from $22.1 billion in 2014 to $44.3 billion in 2020.
- **Employee Engagement:** Nadella's approval rating soared from a low of 74% in October 2014 to 98% on Glassdoor in 2020, reflecting renewed employee satisfaction.

Cutting to the Chase

Microsoft's transformation journey was significantly influenced by the powerful partnership between CEO Satya Nadella and CHRO Kathleen Hogan. By leveraging Hogan's extensive business background and recognizing the necessity of cultural transformation, they implemented a clear mission and cultural attributes that prioritized collaboration, innovation, and inclusivity. Their strategic overhaul of performance management and leadership development fostered an environment of trust and empowerment among employees. As a result, Microsoft not only achieved remarkable financial growth but also reignited its reputation for innovation and engagement.

Have the CHRO Report to You

The reporting structure of HR significantly impacts its effectiveness. If the CEO wants HR to play a strategic role and contribute meaningfully to achieving business goals, the CHRO must have direct access to strategic discussions and decisions.

Join the Club   Not surprisingly, 473 of the Fortune 500 have a Chief Human Resource Officer.[7] As Phil Cognetta, SVP IT Enterprise Technologies at PTC, Inc., observed in our conversation with him, "When a CHRO reports directly into the CEO, HR is seen as a much more strategic role, a function that can actually drive and influence adjacent functions."

In the past, HR often reported to Finance because HR was seen as a back-office function, and its involvement with salaries was considered a natural connection to Finance. If a CHRO reports to Finance today, however, "it's an immediate red flag," said Judy Kopa, CEO of Arroo, Inc., emphasizing that "it signals that HR is still viewed as an administrative cost center rather than as a strategic thought partner."

Build Trust Like Your Success Depends on It

> Listen to the advice we're giving—we understand the importance of the bottom line and we're not going to let you, or the organization, fail.
>
> **—CHRO survey respondent, U.S.-based $500M+ private company**

Like all key relationships, the CEO/CHRO connection depends on an elevated level of trust and understanding. Below are some simple reminders to CEOs about how to build that trust to develop the strong partnership foundational to HR becoming a value creator.

Meet Regularly   It might seem dumb to actually write this in a book for business leaders, since you know this as well as we do, but if your boss blows off your regular one-on-ones, you are not their critical thought partner. Your CHRO will never prove himself if you don't give him a fair shot. Stay aligned, proactively address challenges, and build a real partnership.

Encourage Transparency   Transparent communication is essential to building trust. Encourage open dialogue with your CHRO and create a more responsive and adaptable HR function that can deliver on your priorities.

Ensure the CHRO Meets the CEO (at Least) Halfway   While trust relies on rapport, it also requires mutual commitment to building a strong relationship. CHROs must demonstrate a commitment to both a partnership with the CEO and to focusing on the larger strategic goals of the company, with a willingness to move away from simply fulfilling the immediate needs of HR and an eagerness to innovate, especially through Workforce Analytics.

On CEOs, CHROs and Trust   Bill McDermott, SAP's CEO during our tenure there, often said, "Trust is earned in drops and lost in buckets." Another CEO Jenny worked for proved it: he regularly berated and belittled employees, then apologized, creating a cycle of fear and frustration and stifling innovation. No CHRO can counteract the impact of a CEO whose behavior is misaligned with the desired future state.

Don't Outsource People or Culture

> Your people and the culture in which your people thrive or fail will determine your business results and business growth. Be an active participant and serve as a key point of inspiration.
>
> **—CHRO survey respondent, Europe-based**
> **$500M+ public company**

CEOs can empower their CHRO, while also driving a high-performance culture, by actively engaging in issues impacting their workforce, and bringing other C-level leaders along. CEOs must personally be involved in people, leadership, culture, and other concerns considered by some to be HR's exclusive purview, rather than outsourcing these responsibilities to HR.

As Kathleen Hogan, CHRO of Microsoft, said of CEO Satya Nadella, "The most important thing Satya did as a CEO is he made all of the people priorities—that you might think are typical for HR to work on—he made those first-class problems for the [Senior Leadership Team] to work on. If anything, sometimes on the culture change, he's pushing and I'm trying to catch up with him."[8]

Unfortunately, as explained to us by CEO coach Doug Randall, partner at The Trium Group, many top executives don't get it right. "It's a big challenge when CEOs try to outsource people and leadership to HR. It does not work when the head of HR becomes the proxy for the CEO as the person who cares about the humans, the leadership team, and the culture."

Acknowledge and Champion HR

HR needs help from the CEO and other business leaders to step up and deliver. Praise goes a long way for any employee, or group of employees, and Human Resources professionals are no exception. Back them up, talk them up, and generally be their cheerleader. You may be surprised at what a difference your endorsement can make, both for the HR team and those who partner with them.

Don't Just Say It, Do It

The best CEOs appreciate the expertise of their CHRO and rely on them to help guide important decisions or implement a big change. The human impact is more than an afterthought, it is part of how the work gets designed from the start.

—CHRO survey respondent, U.S.-based $500M+
private company

Giving lip service is not enough. "CEOs must position CHROs as central to the priorities, processes, and decisions that impact P&L, and shape long-term profitable growth," asserts Accenture's research, referring to the 45% of CEOs who do create the conditions for their CHRO's success.[9]

5.3 Evolve the Power Structure

> You can change HR all you want . . . If the C-suite doesn't change its expectations of what it wants HR to do . . . then nothing will really change.
>
> **—Stan Slap, CEO, SLAP**

Raising expectations for HR is essential and nonnegotiable. But to enable HR to rise to those expectations, its leader must have visibility and real influence. That may require CEO influence to redistribute power within top leadership, to make room for the CHRO to become a true partner to other senior leaders. That's a huge shift. Yet it's indispensable to enabling a high-performing HR function that can generate the Workforce Insights needed to transform performance.

That includes giving the CHRO a seat at the biggest strategy table of all.

Bring the CHRO into the Boardroom

> In the boardroom, CHROs offer invaluable expertise in areas like talent acquisition, culture, succession planning, and compensation. As the nature of work evolves due to automation, AI, and shifting employee expectations, CHROs play a pivotal role in guiding boards to align strategies with future workforce needs. They are transforming what were once considered "soft" HR issues into critical strategic imperatives to drive sustainable business success.
>
> **—Coco Brown, Founder & CEO, The Athena Alliance,**
> **Corporate Board Director**

CHROs have yet to earn the place of honor that their C-suite counterparts already occupy in many companies: consistent and valued attendees at Board of Directors meetings. Often, the Chief Financial Officer, Chief Operating Officer, and Chief Revenue Officer attend the entire meeting, but the CHRO simply slips in to discuss the HR metrics members received in their quarterly Board book and slips out again. To change mindsets about HR and transform the impact HR is empowered to make, CEOs should bring CHROs into the room where it happens and keep them there.

"CHROs have valuable experience in developing talent strategy and cultivating corporate culture," says Annalisa Barrett, Senior Advisor with KPMG's Board Leadership Center, "making them well suited to ask the right questions in the boardroom to identify concerns and encourage strong human capital management practices."[10]

According to EY, CHROs are now "arguably as crucial to CEOs as the Chief Financial Officer (CFO)—and their strategic value needs to be unlocked." EY's report identifies three areas where CHROs and boards "can support and challenge each other": "rethinking and facilitating" the CHRO's role; talent governance; and developing a human-centric strategy, culture, and employee value proposition. The report also suggests five questions for Boards to consider as they determine how to help their CHRO advance key corporate priorities:

1. Do they strategically support the CHRO through formal and informal talent governance?
2. Does CHRO collaboration help proactively address talent issues and enhance responsiveness to evolving employee sentiment?
3. Do management and the workforce measurably uphold the organization's values and culture?
4. Is the organization securing any critical talent to fulfill its business strategy, especially within its leadership pipeline?
5. How can individual Board members advance the talent agenda, especially vis-à-vis reskilling, employee experience, retention, and hybrid work?[11]

Consider the Impact of a CHRO on Your Board

To truly be a people-first organization, CEOs and Boards must prioritize data-driven decision-making that considers the impact on people. Without robust people data, decisions lack the insight needed to sustain HR's strategic value and ensure people remain the greatest asset.

—**Brigette McInnis-Day, CHRO & COO,**
Former UiPath, Google, SAP

In addition to the CHRO becoming a consequential boardroom presence, adding a Board member with CHRO experience may help further accelerate your company's HR transformation through advocacy and expertise. Traditionally, points out Coco Brown, corporate Boards have included a CIO and CFO, to bring in experienced strategists in those domains, and a CEO to guide the company's top executive. Today's challenges, she argues, justify adding a CHRO as "another must-have" to advise on issues including talent acquisition, culture, succession planning, compensation, and the structure of the Board itself.[12]

There's plenty of room for growth. According to executive intelligence solutions provider Equilar, the percentage of Russell 3000 Board Directors with CHRO experience steadily increased from 2012 to 2021 . . . from 1.1% to 3%. Equilar's tracking methodology shifted in 2021, but recent increases have been similarly snail-like.[13]

Keep Top Performers Top of Mind

Companies have finally come to the conclusion that talent is at the center to achieving financial results. Getting talent to the right place is one of the most important roles of the CHRO.

**—Ram Charan, PhD, Professor Emeritus,
Harvard Business School**

A range of experts we spoke with while researching this book emphasized the importance of HR's role in attracting, developing, advancing, and retaining top talent, a topic we imagine is already a priority for any Board (or leader). The CHRO can help examine data around top performers in new ways. For example:

- **Retention trends:** As emphasized in Section 1, Commit to Insights, Not Metrics, the CHRO can explore trendlines over time, emphasizing regrettable departures of top employees. Poor employees getting fired isn't anything to celebrate but high-potentials quitting is a grave issue—Board-level serious if numbers are high and persistent.
- **Key roles filled:** The Board should be fully informed on how well the company is securing talent for leadership and other essential jobs as well as the pipeline for future needs.
- **Workforce analytics and planning:** CHROs can help review needed workforce capabilities to meet key strategic objectives, factors impacting those capabilities (such as retiring workforce

and automation), and plans to secure the needed skills ("build" and "buy").

CEOs usually have spent their career making people decisions and think they know a lot. Incorporate practices we offer for making talent decisions. **We're not doing voodoo**; we have established frameworks based on research and experience that will make talent decisions better.

—**CHRO survey respondent, U.S.-based $50–500M public company**

Reassess the Data   Research shows a disconnect between what workforce data is commonly shared with boards and what Board Directors most want to see: leading indicators of culture, capability, and workforce readiness.

See Figure 5.5 for metrics from the Institute for Corporative Productivity (i4cp).

If the culture isn't healthy, we see a lot of value destruction, and this is a fairly new phenomenon. Boeing and Wells Fargo are two standout examples, where boards were caught flat-footed—but we see examples every day with companies losing market share due to lack of innovation or responsiveness to market shifts.

Why is this happening now? Eighty-five percent of the value on the balance sheet of the S&P now comes from people, in the form of innovation, brand, intellectual property, and so on. In the last century, that share of value came from things boards could count on getting good data about, like factories, equipment, inventories, storefronts. But how to get their arms around the caliber of the workforce and the health of the culture? This is why there's increasing interest in adding an HR person to the board—to help them ask the right questions, and to drive the right conversations that will give boards the insights they need to do their job.

—**Diane Gherson, Board Director, Kraft Heinz, Centivo, and TechWolf, BCG Senior Advisor, CHRO Coach, and former CHRO IBM**

>>> Board directors seek **data and insights** on key leading indicators of **culture, capability, and overall workforce readiness** ...

Workforce data that boards would find highly valuable:

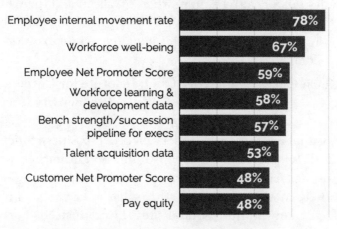

>>> ... yet two-thirds or more get **traditional HR metrics and high-level risk data**.

Workforce data most commonly shared with boards:

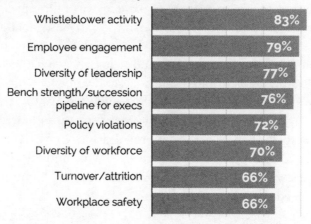

Figure 5.5   Boards Seek Higher Value Workforce Data

Source: Kevin Martin, "Human Capital Data Considerations for Corporate Board Directors" (Institute for Corporate Productivity [I4cp], 2021). Reproduced with permission from I4cp.

Open Your Inner Circle

> I can always tell a healthy culture when I walk in and the CEO
> and the CHRO are good friends, working in partnership, and the
> CHRO is in that inner circle of three, four, five senior executives
> inside the company.
>
> **—Kevin Oakes, Founder & CEO, Institute for Corporate**
> **Productivity (i4cp)**

Closely collaborating with leaders of other business functions
can help CHROs loosen a range of constraints on HR impact, which
benefits those leaders. Critically, strong relationships with C-level
peers and other senior leaders reduce the isolation keeping many HR
functions focused inwardly on administrative work instead of driving
strategic value.

It's only logical: CHROs who are better-informed about priorities
across the business can also spot opportunities to partner in support of
other functions' goals and company strategy overall, especially with
Workforce Analytics. Such partnerships can also facilitate all-
important collaboration around data and analytics, covered in Section 2, "Support Data Integration," and help colleagues outside HR to
better understand HR initiatives, impact, and value.

Returning to the Accenture CHRO study, we were not at all surprised that top-performing HR leaders are four times more likely to
have strong relationships across an organization, in particular among
C-level peers, and particularly likely to have mutually influential
relationships with the chief executive and finance, technology, and
operations leaders.[14]

***Strengthening CHRO Relationships Can Have Broader Bene-
fits***   Deloitte refers to **"symphonic C-suites,"** CXOs that practice
cross-functional vision, collaboration, and connectivity, both "playing" together as a team and managing their respective domains, in
harmony. This approach helps multiple leaders understand and coordinate responses to the many forces at work both outside and throughout an organization. Digital business models, integrating automation

and AI into the workforce, brand protection, and innovation are key areas for "symphonic" collaboration Deloitte identifies.[15]

And recent research from IBM shows that when C-suite leaders and CHROs are aligned on making data-driven people decisions, their organizations are more flexible, more innovative, and more profitable than their industry peers.[16]

The trend is moving in the right direction. Mercer's 2024 CHRO Survey reveals that 51% of CHROs increased their engagement with the C-level this year. Meeting weekly with the C-suite was reported by 56% of CHROs, and 65% of CHROs at companies that had significantly modified their HR operating model.[17]

Bottom line: If you are a business leader who wants great Workforce Analytics, advocate for deeper C-level relationships with your CHRO. It's one more (important) way to help HR become a true strategic partner in driving your most important business goals.

CHRO and CFO

Understand the History　This relationship needs some context to illuminate why many CFOs and CHROs don't (yet) work closely together. One contributing factor is an already-shifted power dynamic: HR once reported into Finance, a far less common arrangement today. And according to a 2023 CFO Insights Report from SAP Concur, 80% of CFOs admitted that they should "collaborate more effectively" with leaders in HR, in particular regarding business performance metrics and shared data sources.[18]

Workforce as Carpeting　While overlaps in data systems and reporting like payroll and headcount cause tension in the CFO/CHRO relationship, differing perspectives on workforce metrics—and accounting standards in the United States—contribute as well.

Peter Cappelli, author of the 2015 *Harvard Business Review* article, "Why We Love to Hate HR . . . and What HR Can Do About It,"[19] penned in February 2023 another *HBR* piece on this topic. Cappelli describes the impact of Generally Accepted Accounting Principles (GAAP), established by the U.S. Financial Accounting Standards Board (FASB), that public companies in the United States must use to guide their financial reporting. GAAP rules prevent employees from being counted as items with value, or assets, as the company cannot own them. Employees, and budgets dedicated to their development and retention, are considered costs.

"Despite all the rhetoric about 'investing in our people,'" Cappelli writes, "training and development [are] categorized as a current expense, a type of fixed cost—just as carpeting is." While further details on this topic would be beyond the scope of this book, we recommend reading the article in full to appreciate the extent to which financial accounting can lead to decisions that are, as Cappelli describes, "at odds with effectiveness and efficiency."[20]

Amit Mohindra, Founder and CEO of People Analytics Success, observed, "Finance and HR are two sides of the same coin in terms of dealing with workforce cost, with headcount, and with planning," he observed. "They're both data-driven. But they are vastly different paradigms, different world views, and different incentives. High attrition for HR is bad because they have to redo their work to hire and onboard a replacement. But for Finance, a high vacancy rate is welcome as it helps them balance the books."

Surely the corporate landscape is littered with the detritus of CFO/CHRO relationships gone awry. For one such story, *see* the "Penny Wise, Pound Foolish" case study in Section 1, "Let HR (Get Better) at Help(ing) You."

The CHRO and CFO Must Be Trusting Partners

The CHRO and the CFO have to be joined at the hip. There's human capital, and then there's working capital, and those two need to work in concert to inform the CEO on an integrated strategy across both facets.

—Melanie Tinto, Chief People Officer, WEX

Despite challenges, forging a productive partnership is worth the investment. In another seminal 2015 *Harvard Business Review* article on HR, management guru Ram Charan addresses the CFO/CHRO relationship head-on. He advises that CEOs form a triumvirate—a "G3"—with the CFO and CHRO, "the single best way to link financial numbers with the people who produce them" (*see* "CEO/CHRO/CFO Triumvirate").

Charan suggests the CFO and CHRO work together, for example, to determine novel approaches to financial incentives based on value delivered to the company. He also points out the potential to partner to evaluate the alignment between key performance indicators, current talent, and budgets and organizational priorities, developing new metrics as needed.[21]

SHRM also suggests metrics as a fertile opportunity for CHRO/CFO partnerships, to evaluate the impact on employee engagement and retention of a new benefits program or compensation adjustment.[22]

> Treat the CHRO as THE trusted advisor and their right hand (or left) with the CFO being the other hand.
>
> **—CHRO survey respondent,**
> **U.S.-based $500M+ public company**

Advance Strategy, Together   It seems eminently reasonable, too, for a CEO to ask that his CHRO and CFO develop joint strategies to align human capital and financial planning, then regularly review and adjust these strategies based on business performance and market conditions. Enhancing strategic decision-making overall can be achieved by building greater mutual understanding between HR and Finance teams, perhaps through exercises such as "synchronizing objectives, exchanging data, and hosting collaborative workshops."[23]

Another potential partnership realm is C-suite hires. One interviewee shared that her CFO and CHRO collaborated closely to recruit, vet, and hire a Chief Operations Officer who could become a CEO successor.

Grab the Benefits   A global EY study of 550 CFOs and CHROs found that higher levels of HR-Finance collaboration led to higher performance:

- EBITDA growth of more than 10% (41% among high collaborators vs. 14% of others)
- Marked increases in employee engagement (44% vs. 9%)
- Significant improvements in workforce productivity (44% vs. 10%).[24]

CEO/CHRO/CFO *Triumvirate*

The CHRO, CFO, and CEO are a trio in need of one another to optimize the business strategy through managing growth and labor costs. If the CFO and CHRO are not equals (same level, authority, decision-making, and organizational positioning), then the largest line item in your budget (salary and fringe) are not a priority to be managed and optimized in support of your business strategy.

**—CHRO survey respondent,
U.S.-based $500M+ private company**

The "G3" Ram Charan suggests can "shape the destiny" of a company by focusing on the big picture as others execute and troubleshooting as issues arise. He advises weekly "temperature taking" and monthly "looking forward" discussions. These meetings can also help CEOs get to know, and address any doubts regarding, their CHRO. It may take time to positively impact business outcomes, but Charan shares success stories that reflect a worthwhile wait.

- The G3 at Zaffino identified links between organizational design and potential impacts to business performance.
- Tata's G3 integrated financial and talent considerations to devise a workforce plan that reduced staff by 7%, freeing budget to fill strategically critical roles.

CEOs who form a G3 also convey that they are "lifting up HR into the inner sanctum and that the CHRO's contributions will be analogous to the CFO's."[25]

Others have singled out this CEO/CFO/CHRO grouping. Researchers at the Lancaster University Management School's Centre for Performance-led HR describe the "Golden Triangle" as a "mini think tank for the organization." They assert that it can help transform the CHRO role across four levels, for example from "Strategic Implementer" to "Strategic Progenitor" and "Performance Orchestrator" to "Performance Enabler."[26]

CEO.works founder Sandy Ogg saw the triumvirate as a way to understand patterns of rapid success at Blackstone portfolio companies. He advises filling the three roles with "the absolute best talent you are capable of attracting." According to Ogg, Blackstone invested significantly in putting together the right CEO/CFO/CHRO triangle for each portfolio company.[27]

Other C-Level Partnerships

CHRO and CIO   As technological advances reshape the workplace, CHRO/CIO collaboration can help align tech and human capital strategies to foster efficiency and innovation while also delivering a positive employee experience. Digital transformation, AI, remote work, implementation and configuration of HR systems, data security and privacy, and tech-related change management can all benefit from close, trusting partnerships.

The vast, mostly uncharted territory of human-machine collaboration merits an especially robust CHRO/CIO alliance. Chris Nardecchia, CIO for Rockwell Automation, reported working closely with his CHRO because he sees an "inherent link between leadership, culture, skills, and behaviors in achieving digital transformation outcomes." His collaboration helped achieve business process improvements that reduced total order cycle time by 75%.[28]

CHRO and COO   Here, too, human-machine collaboration offers fertile ground for deep thinking around workforce planning and logistical considerations impacting employee productivity and engagement, in addition to other areas of CHRO/COO partnership: aligning people strategy and culture with operational goals, driving efficiency and employee productivity, managing risk and compliance, and ensuring safety. A colleague shared with us that a close partnership between Operations and Learning & Development helped a global quick-service restaurant chain accelerate the training of more general managers, essential to achieving the company's expansion strategy.

CHRO and CMO   Collaboration between the CHRO and Chief Marketing Officer is crucial for aligning talent strategies with brand messaging and business goals including: employer brand and value proposition for attracting top talent, culture, employee and customer experience, and change management and transformation.

5.4 Integrate HR into the Business

A final area within the purview of the CEO (supported by other C-suite members) is helping HR stop feeling—and acting—like they are somehow not part of "the business." Do you want high-performing HR professionals who are true strategic partners and who deftly use Workforce Analytics to help you solve your thorniest challenges and achieve your most important goals?

Great. Two very straightforward actions you can take:

1. **Eliminate any daylight between your strategic priorities and HR's.** Throughout the book, we have talked about the importance of strategic alignment. You, dear CEO, are the final frontier.
2. **Treat them like high-performing professionals who deliver high value.** Empower your CHRO to re-engineer their team's DNA. It is their expertise, after all.

Really Know the Benefits of Alignment

It seems *prima facie* logic that aligning the function that oversees the workforce with a company's strategies and priorities would be a smart way to run a business. Alignment would mean both that HR participates in planning corporate strategy, and that HR strategy is seamlessly aligned with it. Yet we know from experience that these things are not happening universally, and research confirms it.

According to the HR Research Institute, 25% of organizations are not involved in any way in the strategic planning process, and in 31%, strategic planning is the ONLY time HR is asked for "talent-related input." Even among "high-performing HR departments," only 60% say HR is "an equal partner, involved early in the process, and key to designing the strategy of the organization."[29]

The 2024 HR Trends Report from McLean & Company paints a slightly rosier picture, with 50% of HR organizations involved in helping to develop and executing company strategy in 2024, although notably that's an increase from just 36% in 2021. We found these numbers both dismaying and unsurprising.

The under-utilization of HR (i.e., your workforce experts) happens despite the benefits documented in McLean's report: companies that do involve HR in planning and executing strategy were found to be 1.8 times better at changing quickly to scale and 2.7 times better at generating and implementing innovative ideas.[30]

Involving HR in strategic planning also significantly increases the likelihood that HR priorities will mirror those of your organization. The McLean report found that 85% of HR functions that are "strategic partners in planning and executing strategy" prioritize their own plans to line up with the organization at large. This, too, offers many benefits. HR functions with business-aligned priorities are more likely to provide a "great employee experience" (2.8 times), have a "strong organizational culture" (3.3 times), and be perceived as highly effective (3.3 times).

Empower HR to Support Your Priorities

It's a necessity to have a strategic people plan. But if that people plan is not aligned with a company's strategic plan, then your team should ask itself, what are we really doing here?

—Pamay Bassey, Chief Learning and Diversity Officer, The Kraft-Heinz Company

If HR alignment is not already happening as part of your standard operating model, CEOs will again need to shift expectations and partner with their CHRO to drive the change. Other business leaders can help by advocating for these shifts: greater HR alignment on strategy will benefit them, too, as more oars in the water steer the ship in the right direction.

Integrate HR into Planning Cycles Bringing HR to the planning table as an equal partner is nonnegotiable if you want your Workforce Insights dreams to come true. The CEO is THE essential player here.

Involve HR in Annual Corporate Planning   While Jenny was in Sales at SuccessFactors, it was widely known as a red flag if a CHRO client was NOT involved in annual planning. If the CEO has followed the advice in "Be a True Partner, Get a True Partner," mentioned previously, and ensured that the CHRO is an active member of the C-suite, this pitfall will be avoided naturally. As an indispensable annual planning team member, equal to other C-level executives, the CHRO can both respond to business needs and proactively raise concerns based on workforce trends, such as the availability of key talent.

Require a Multi-Year People Strategy Roadmap   This roadmap, which would be updated as part of the annual cycle, would include prioritized initiatives and—critically important—success metrics by which the CEO and CHRO will regularly, and jointly, evaluate progress. The HR road map should show how its activities link to the overall long-term business goals, outcomes, and key milestones to drive accountability.

Look for Other Alignment Opportunities   CEOs: use this transition time to bring in any other functions whose annual plans don't yet fully align with the company's. HR could be a key partner in helping to connect the dots with other functions to coordinate and drive workforce performance.

Have HR Focus on Areas of Highest Strategic Importance

Consider the parts of your business that have a disproportionate impact on your most critical business measures. The [HR] team should focus its initiatives and success measures on the key pivot points where improving people capabilities would make the biggest impact on strategy execution. Rather than scaling HR programs company-wide, differentiate and focus initiatives on those pivot points.

—John Boudreau, PhD, Emeritus Professor and Senior Research Scientist, Center for Effective Organizations, University of Southern California

Not All HR Initiatives Should Be Created Equal Your CHRO should shape a strategy and vision that creates the highest possible return on investment. Many HR programs impact the entire company, such as performance evaluations and other talent management processes. Yet just as business leaders fund projects according to where the funds will do the most good, HR must tailor its programs for maximum strategic impact. Help HR "do less, better" by focusing on the initiatives that provide the most value. If the question, "what's the business problem we are trying to solve?" can't be answered, de-prioritize.

Prioritize Workforce Planning

> A CHRO boosts a company's capacity to hit its most critical business metrics by acting as a bridge between the organization's strategic goals and its workforce capabilities.
>
> **—CEO survey respondent, Europe-based private company (<$1M)**

Workforce planning requires understanding both internal and external talent landscapes and aligning them with your organization's strategic goals, so you have the skills you need when you need them. After all, says Sandy Ogg, Founder at CEO.works, "Not having enough of the right talent where it matters is like trying to run a Ferrari with cheap gas in the tank. It's a formula for frustration and poor performance."[31]

Being able to anticipate, plan for, and effectively respond to workforce needs has become even more critical in every industry due to factors including increased competition, shifts toward task- and skill-based work

> *Workforce planning requires understanding both internal and external talent landscapes and aligning them with your organization's strategic goals, so you have the skills you need, when you need them. After all, says Sandy Ogg, Founder at CEO.works, "Not having enough of the right talent where it matters is like trying to run a Ferrari with cheap gas in the tank. It's a formula for frustration and poor performance."*

versus work defined by job descriptions, and demographic changes tightening the labor market.

The most significant pressure and uncertainty on workforce planning is, of course, the rapid pace of technological advancements and the skills required to keep up with them, not to mention maximizing their potential—including, and especially, the availability of machines that will work with, augment, and train human employees.

"Workforce Planning 2.0," in the words of analytics expert Max Blumberg, requires that HR "evolve workforce planning to encompass all productivity resources, assessing the optimal mix of human and non-human resources to achieve business goals."[32]

One of our CEO survey respondents, James Harvey, Chief Executive Officer and Board Member at QLess, Inc., reflected on this. "We are only hiring folks that are AI-enabled at their position. During interviews, every candidate is expected to articulate how they utilize AI (Gen or Machine Learning) to improve their productivity. We are hyper focused on teaching our employees to think, 'how can I use AI to help me with this problem?' Ultimately this will result in a higher Revenue per Employee ratio, and we will be able to produce at higher levels without increasing headcount at the same rate." Harvey added, "A CHRO will be pivotal to this type of transformation."

And of course, having the right people in the right roles never goes out of style.

The Good News, and the Bad News   Fortunately, the rise of AI and advancement of data and analytics puts the highly complex task of effective workforce planning within closer reach than ever. Unfortunately, many business leaders, including CEOs, do not take workforce planning seriously enough or WANT to improve workforce planning but have not evolved their HR function to be able to do so.

Remember how we keep saying that helping HR evolve is about benefiting you and advancing your strategic agenda? We hope you see this increasingly clearly.

One of our CHRO survey respondents, from a U.S.-based privately held company ($50–500M), identified the lack of HR evolution as a key way CEOs can *diminish* an HR leader's effectiveness. It happens when the CEO "forces (intentionally or unintentionally) the CHRO to 'run an HR department' vs. a talent and culture mentality of optimizing the workforce. Operating a department and running a talent and culture organization are very different."

Deploying the New CEO/CFO/CHRO *Triumvirate* Workforce planning may be the most important "G3" function, Charan asserted in his 2015 *Harvard Business Review* article (*see* "Evolve the Power Structure," above). Working within this trio enables CHROs to more effectively develop integrated strategies that align human capital initiatives with business goals and link to financial outcomes and growth.[33]

Regularly Review and Adjust Like any other function, HR must consistently review and reevaluate its initiatives to support the company's evolving goals.

You will note that we occasionally offer advice that seems obvious. Some of that advice is to treat HR the way you do other functions.

Reward a Business-First Mindset for HR

I'm a businessperson first and an HR person second. The most important thing is to deeply understand and connect with the business, see the enterprise in terms of what is a net-add and what is a net-detractor to business value, and adjust efforts in the People function accordingly.

—**Tamar Elkeles, PhD, Chief People Officer &
Board Director**

HR professionals must evolve their self-perception, as business contributors first and HR specialists second, and as true strategic partners integral to the company's success—not administrative functionaries whose work does not drive important outcomes.

Certainly, any business leader can help achieve this mindset shift: set new expectations for HR Business Partners, encourage them to develop new skills and request deeper reliance on Workforce Analytics to proactively achieve priority goals. Conditions may even allow for establishing stretch goals for an HRBP, with concomitant rewards.

Yet as with any other major corporate shift, the CEO is uniquely positioned to green-light change.

Update Job Descriptions

Where to Start?   CEOs: Task your CHRO with changing how HR work is defined and described, and reframing daily tasks to reflect the strategic outcomes they drive and not just the activity they generate. Connecting daily operations to company strategy will go a long way in shifting the HR professional's mindset to a workforce productivity problem-solver.

Prioritize Tech   Similarly, the CHRO should ensure that every HR role encompasses embracing and driving the success of next-generation technologies: from HR tech modernizing their work, to AI and automation and, of course, the tools enabling them to leverage Workforce Analytics in alignment with business priorities.

Assign KPIs   All HR professionals also need defined objectives to aim for. This should be part of tying annual HR planning to corporate priorities, brought down to the individual level.

Each area of HR, too, needs meaningful metrics aligned to organizational strategy and goals. For example, measure Talent Acquisition on how well they hire for key roles linked to a corporate expansion, examining these new employees' productivity, engagement, and retention (not just "time to hire"). Learning & Development would be evaluated on performance impact in areas of strategic priority (vs. training volume or learner satisfaction scores).

Update Incentives (i.e., Accept Human Nature)   You are surely aware of the 1975 classic management article, "On the Folly of Rewarding A, While Hoping for B."[34] To incent any specific behavior, from anyone, for any reason, you must reward that behavior. Up the chain of command, from entry level to CHRO, ensure that each

HR professional is properly motivated to be a strategic contributor to your company.

It's especially important to eliminate incentives that reward the wrong behavior. For example, companies who use an "agency" model reward recruiters for the volume of hires instead of quality.

Support New Skills

Transforming HR from an administrative function to a strategic partner in the business requires HR professionals who deeply understand both the business and the many factors that impact workforce performance and business performance. That requires CEO support, not just for funding and prioritizing time spent but also aligning internal resources to help HR along their journey to high performance.

First: Create the Conditions

> Adopt a growth mindset. Show some humility, curiosity, and vulnerability and we all can learn together to get better. It may feel uncomfortable but it is one of the best attributes a leader at any level can show his/her people. Repeat after me, "I don't know it all so teach me."
>
> **—CHRO survey respondent,**
> **U.S.-based $50–500M private company**

Many factors will contribute to the success of your efforts to uplevel your HR team, and the most important ones are within your control as CEO. You can shape an environment in which the team is inspired and empowered to grow into their full potential.

- **Set an example to strengthen your culture of learning:** CEOs can powerfully model lifelong learning. According to Deloitte, companies that invest in a culture of learning are 92% more likely to innovate, 17% more likely to lead their market, 37% more productive, and 34% more effective in response to their customers' needs.
- **Personally commit to learning.** In the words of Bill Gates, "You don't really start getting old until you stop learning."[35]

- **Share your learning.** This can inspire others to learn and authentically reveal who you are. Recommend go-to sources for news and insights. Divulge new knowledge that has recently influenced your thinking.
- **Champion curiosity.** Encourage your people to tap into their inner curiosity, which can generate innovation.
- **Be a leader who teaches and encourages other leaders to do the same.** If you aren't already playing an active role in developing your employees, now is an exciting time to start.

We consistently see that leaders teaching leaders in a safe simulated business context is the best way to build a strong leadership pipeline and drive transformative business success. This sharing of knowledge and expertise through personal story telling fosters continuous learning, empowers ownership, and ensures the company has well-prepared leaders ready to adapt to changing needs.

—Jessica Skon, CEO, BTS Group, Inc.

Join the Investment Trend

Investing in your latest marketing initiative may increase customer loyalty for a few weeks; but what will be the impact of not knowing where your workforce is, whether they have the skills to do their jobs, or how they behold your customers? Without the right investment, you are flying blind! The good news, however, is that you are in a unique position to drive the requirement to bring these data together to inform your decisions for the coming decade.

—Mark Lawrence, Founder and Executive Consultant,
Data Driven HR

HR upskilling in data and analytics is on the rise. According to Insight222 (*see* Figure 5.6), just more than half of companies surveyed (55%) increased their investment in "upskilling HR to be data-driven" in the past 12 months, but 70% plan to do so in the next 18–24 months.[36]

Past 12 months, investment was …

42% Same   55% Increased

3% Decreased

Next 18–24 months, investment will be …

29% Same   70% Increased

1% Decreased

Figure 5.6   **Companies' Investment in Upskilling Their HR to Be Data-Driven**

Source: Adapted from Naomi Verghese and Jonathan Ferrar, Verghese, "Upskilling the HR Profession: Building Data Literacy at Scale" (Insight222, 2023), https://publications.insight222.com/upskillinghrreport2023, 6.

Advocate for Budgets You already know that when money gets tight, HR's budgets are among the first cut. But if you want to see Workforce Analytics succeed, investing in HR upskilling is nonnegotiable. Fighting for that funding is self-serving in the best possible way.

> *If you want to see Workforce Analytics succeed, investing in HR upskilling is nonnegotiable. Fighting for that funding is self-serving in the best possible way.*

Workforce Analytics functions are growing in size—by 43% from mid-2020 to mid-2023, according to one source, reflecting a commitment to "build data-driven cultures in HR and use data to make better-informed people decisions."[37]

Yet according to Gartner, the average spend on the HR function as a percentage of revenue is, relative to other support groups, measly:

just 0.76%, versus Finance (1.30%), IT (3.25%), Sales (4.37%) and Marketing (7.5%). HR accounts, on average, for a mere 1.47% of operating expenses.[38]

The shoemaker's children go barefoot far too often. A 2024 study conducted by Josh Bersin found that only 18% of HR departments have a development initiative for their employees, just 19% have job rotations between HR and other departments, and only 55% have a "culture of professional development."[39] This must change.

Protect HR Learning Time   In some ways, protecting learning hours is even harder than budget. As CEO, only you can set the expectation that this investment is essential and will deliver strong ROI. Dispatch your CHRO to:

- **Prioritize** learning for every HR employee.
- **Identify** key players needing specialized skills in target areas, such as extra analytics training for HR Business Partners to help them uncover and communicate insights.
- **Develop and stick to** a timeline and schedule.
- **Set** measurement goals with specific metrics.
- **Hold accountable** the HR leadership team for learning completion and impact tracking.
- **Reward and recognize** HR for their commitment to learning and use as a role model for other functions.

Enlist Other Functions   You have a company full of subject matter experts (SMEs) who can help. Assign capable, articulate, interested SMEs from different domains to spend time with the HR team. Encourage leaders across the business to do the same. SMEs can educate HR not just on their function but also how HR can better partner with and support them. A monthly rotating series could cover a range of topics.

Import Skills, Export Skills

It's best to have HR leaders who have a hybrid combination of experiences in their careers—some time in HR and some meaningful time and accomplishments in the business. I know that can be upsetting to people who have grown up in HR and are trying to climb that traditional HR ladder, but I think that one of the goals of HR is to create an organization that works well together cross-functionally, so having that experience working in different functions really matters.

**—Laura Shubert, Vice President,
People Planning & Insights**

Encouraging bi-directional, cross-functional development between HR and other functions is an effective way to accelerate business acumen gain, networking, and collaboration.

Rotate HR *into Other Functions*   Giving HR practitioners experience in business units improves their ability to drive business results by better understanding operational challenges and fostering stronger relationships with business leaders. Firsthand experience elsewhere in the company also helps HR professionals broaden their horizons, deepen their insights, extend their network, and focus their thinking on strategic impact.

For Bill Conaty, who served as Senior Vice President of HR at General Electric under Jack Welch, these rotations helped create a sea change for the function and its relationship with the famously hard-charging CEO, who reportedly referred to HR's leadership program as the "picnics and benefits crowd." Conaty modified the program to include three eight-month rotations through various groups, including corporate audit, a change that he said, "bred internal credibility."

These rotations also helped Welch, previously skeptical of HR's value, see the function differently, eventually coming to regard it as "GE's most important department for the role it plays in anticipating business needs, attracting and developing talent, and building a leadership pipeline for long-term success."[40]

Rotations can be helpful for any HR professional, but may be reserved for high-performing talent and succession planning. HR rising stars, for example, would significantly increase their value to the function by gaining experience in Finance, Marketing, and/or Operations. Prior to taking on a senior leadership role, more tenured HR professionals could complete a rotation in Analytics, Strategy, and/or IT.

Cross-domain C-suite Expertise Needed   In a stark break from decades of rising through the ranks to CHRO, the top seat may now be occupied by someone from outside HR. The path to the CHRO is no longer linear, indicating that diverse employment experience is becoming more important for leadership roles. This trend actually holds true across the C-suite. The percentage of top executives with experience in only one domain decreased from 86.9% in 2018 to 59.4% in 2023.[41]

Rotate Other Functions into HR   Similarly, integrating professionals from other functions into HR can broaden appreciation of what HR actually does and how it contributes to business success while also offering the potential to seed ideas and innovation. This integration is increasingly seen as a way to elevate HR's strategic impact. Cross-pollinating functional expertise within HR benefits both the outsiders who become temporary insiders and HR overall.

A rotation in HR would be eye-opening for a rising star in any function or business unit, helping them to better understand the factors that can impact workforce performance. They may appreciate their HR colleagues in new ways as well as discover ways they can contribute their domain expertise. Two examples of fairly clear synergies: a Customer Service Support Manager spending time in HR Operations, and a Marketing leader rotating into HR Communications.

In fact, at SAP, the head of partnerships at an acquired company made a lateral move and became the HR Business Partner for the office of the CEO, helping make major workforce decisions. And we learned from an interviewee about a senior Finance leader at an e-commerce retailer who spent a few years as CHRO, then returned to Finance as the Chief Financial Officer.

Involve HR *in Cross-Functional Initiatives*   Gaining exposure to various parts of the business can also help HR professionals build business acumen, understand broader contexts for corporate projects, and align HR initiatives with business goals. For CHROs, involvement in cross-functional programs can also help them communicate and partner more effectively with other C-suite leaders.

Last Thoughts   "Teach a person to fish," we are told, to create a self-sufficient human rather than an ongoing burden. Teaching HR to fish, as it were, may seem like a burden, but business leaders who help do so will reap rich rewards in the form of newly empowered strategic partners whose work, and even whose lives, will be transformed. As learning professionals, we are a little envious of the opportunities to make this kind of impact that await you.

5.5 Key Takeaways

Major changes at any company require CEO backing and guidance. Same for advancing WFA, WFI, and HR.

- **All About the CHRO:** Like the function they lead, CHROs can be instrumental in driving positive organizational change but only if embraced and enabled to achieve their full strategic potential, not confined to back-office tasks. Know and nurture the traits of high-performing CHROs: they are elemental to companies making WFI a reality.
- **CEO: Be a True Partner, Get a True Partner:** The CEO/CHRO relationship strongly predicts whether HR is empowered as a strategic business partner. CEOs wanting a CHRO who will meaningfully contribute to business success can take concrete steps, including: hire according to expectations, make the CHRO a direct report, actively engage in people and culture, and authentically champion HR.
- **Evolve the Power Structure:** CHROs must have visibility and real influence at the top: in the CEO's inner circle and boardroom and through a CEO/CFO/CHRO "triumvirate." Benefits include better use of data to drive informed, effective decisions and greater cross-functional alignment, innovation, and efficiencies through other C-level collaborations.

- **Integrate HR into the Business:** The final, critical paradigm shift is C-level leaders consistently engaging HR in strategic planning and all critical decision-making. It's perhaps the most logical path to increasing workforce alignment with organizational priorities. It also requires that HR professionals be equipped, experienced, and incented to consistently think and act like business-first, HR-second partners.

Bottom line: Becoming an insight-driven leader requires vision and commitment at the C-level to drive a range of complex, difficult changes. We never said it would be easy. But CEOs (and aspiring CEOs) who want to truly transform their workforce, culture, and business performance will create these new paradigms and expectations for their HR function and its leader.

Conclusion

WE OPENED THE book referencing "The Rime of the Ancient Mariner," comparing the thirsty sailors gazing upon an ocean of salt water to business leaders surrounded by terabytes of data that offer no wisdom. Just as the Mariner's salvation began with a shift in perspective—recognizing the beauty and interconnectedness of life—your transformation starts with seeing the untapped potential in your workforce and, yes, in HR.

It's not about embracing data to be cool (although that would also be an outcome). It's about turning those terabytes into insights, those insights into decisions, and those decisions into tangible results. The tools are here: Workforce Analytics, automation, and AI. And the partner to help you unlock their full potential is sitting right in front of you—the HR team that's ready to evolve, if only you'll empower them.

This book isn't a call to blow everything up or start from scratch. It's an invitation to lead differently. To shed the albatross of missed opportunities and inefficiencies and step fully into the role of **The Insight-Driven Leader**—a leader who turns data into a competitive advantage through the power of Workforce Insights. You have the chance to unlock the kind of agility, resilience, and innovation that others will envy. The choice is yours.

As the Mariner says at the end of Samuel Taylor Coleridge's poem, those who embrace connection and act with intention will find their way forward. The leaders who tap into the power of Workforce Analytics and turn HR into a true business ally will be the ones who thrive—not just in the next quarter, but for years to come.

So, what's your next move?

Notes

Foreword

1. Dave Ketchen and Jeremy Short, "4.2 Resource-Based Theory," In *Mastering Strategic Management* (Minneapolis, MN: University of Minnesota, 2014), https://biz.libretexts.org/Bookshelves/Management/Mastering_Strategic_Management/04%3A_Managing_Firm_Resources/4.02%3A_Resource-Based_Theory.
2. John W. Boudreau and Peter M. Ramstad, *Beyond HR: The New Science of Human Capital* (Boston, MA: Harvard Business School Press, 2007).

Introduction

1. Samuel Taylor Coleridge, "The Rime of the Ancient Mariner, Part II," Poetry Foundation, accessed December 20, 2024, https://www.poetryfoundation.org/poems/43997/the-rime-of-the-ancient-mariner-text-of-1834.
2. Ram Charan, Dominic Barton, and Dennis Carey, "People Before Strategy: A New Role for the CHRO," *Harvard Business Review* (July-August 2015), https://hbr.org/2015/07/people-before-strategy-a-new-role-for-the-chro; John Boudreau and Steven Rice, "Bright, Shiny Objects and the Future of HR," *Harvard Business Review* (July-August 2015), https://hbr.org/2015/07/bright-shiny-objects-and-the-future-of-hr; and Peter Cappelli, "Why We Love to Hate HR . . . and What HR Can Do About It," *Harvard Business Review* (July-August 2015), https://hbr.org/2015/07/why-we-love-to-hate-hr-and-what-hr-can-do-about-it.

Section 1

1. Jenny Dearborn and David Swanson, *The Data Driven Leader: A Powerful Approach to Delivering Measurable Business Impact Through People Analytics* (Hoboken, NJ: Wiley, 2018), xvii, original emphasis.
2. MSys Marketing, "What Is Cognitive Analytics: A Comprehensive Guide," *MSys Technologies* (blog), July 25, 2024, https://www.msystechnol ogies.com/blog/what-is-cognitive-analytics-a-comprehensive-guide/.
3. Fortune Business Insights, "Cognitive Analytics Market Size, Share & Industry Analysis, 2024–2032: By Deployment (Cloud and On-premises), By Enterprise Type (Large Enterprises and Small & Medium Enterprises), By Application (Customer Management, Fraud Detection & Security, Supply Chain Management, Sales & Marketing Management, and Others), By End-user (BFSI, IT & Telecom, Government, Retail, Healthcare, Education, and Others), and Regional Forecast," Fortune Business Insights, 2024, https://www.fortunebusinessinsights .com/cognitive-analytics-market-108564.
4. Ciao-Wei Chen and Laura Yue Li, "Is Hiring Fast a Good Sign? The Informativeness of Job Vacancy Duration for Future Firm Profitability," *Review of Accounting Studies*, April 2023, https://papers.ssrn.com/sol3/ papers.cfm?abstract_id=4445683.
5. Peter Burnham, "Are You a People First Leader? What CEOs Should Be Asking of Their CHROs," *Visier Leadership* (blog), accessed December 2, 2024, https://www.visier.com/blog/people-first-leader-what-ceos-should-be-asking-their-chros/.
6. Peter Cappelli and Ranya Nehmeh, "HR's New Role: In this tight labor market, cost cutting is out. Championing employee concerns is in," *Harvard Business Review* (May–June 2024), https://hbr.org/2024/05/ hrs-new-role.
7. Cappelli and Nehmeh, "HR's New Role."
8. US Bureau of Labor Statistics' "Job Openings and Labor Turnover Survey," as cited in Jefferson Hansen, "Understanding Industry Employee Turnover Rates (And How to Improve Them)," *Awardco WorkLife* (blog), August 15, 2024, https://www.award.co/blog/employee-turnover-rates.
9. Cappelli and Nehmeh. "HR's New Role."
10. Academy to Innovate HR (AIHR), "The Balanced Scorecard Guide," *AIHR*, accessed December 2, 2024, https://resources.aihr.com/resources/ Balanced_Scorecard_Guide_RESOURCE_LIBRARY.pdf.
11. Erik Van Vulpen, "HR KPIs: All You Need to Know [+ 17 Examples]," *AIHR* (blog), February 19, 2024, https://www.aihr.com/blog/human-resources-key-performance-indicators-hr-kpis/.

12. Jonathan Ferrar and David Green, *Excellence in People Analytics: How to Use Workforce Data to Create Business Value* (London & New York: Kogan Page, 2021), 278.

13. HR Research Institute, "HR.com's State of People Analytics 2023–2024," Report, HR.com, 2023, https://www.crunchr.com/app/uploads/2023/10/HRdotcom-Crunchr-State-of-HR-Report.pdf.

14. Jasmine Panayides, "Partnering with Finance to Drive Greater Business Impact with People Analytics," *myHRfuture* (blog), May 23, 2024, https://www.myhrfuture.com/blog/partnering-with-finance-to-drive-greater-business-impact-with-people-analytics.

15. Elizabeth Ledet, Keith McNulty, Daniel Morales, and Marissa Shandell, "How to Be Great at People Analytics," McKinsey & Company, October 2, 2020, https://www.mckinsey.com/capabilities/people-and-organizational-performance/our-insights/how-to-be-great-at-people-analytics.

16. Insights2Action, "2023 High-Impact Analytics Research," Deloitte (US), 2024, https://www2.deloitte.com/content/dam/Deloitte/us/Documents/human-capital/us-high-impact-people-analytics-report.pdf, 2.

17. HR Insight Institute, "HR.com's State of People Analytics 2024-25: Commit to Data-driven Growth in Your Workforce." HR.com, 2024, https://www.hr.com/en/resources/free_research_white_papers/hrcoms-state-of-people-analytics-2024-25_m1g4f7he.html.

18. Insight222 Team, "What Are the Five Trends Shaping People Analytics in 2024?" *myHRfuture* (blog), September 25, 2024, https://www.myhrfuture.com/blog/what-are-the-five-trends-shaping-people-analytics-in-2024.

19. Insights222, "People Analytics Trends 2023 Report," Insight222.com, 2023, https://publications.insight222.com/peopleanalyticstrends2023.

20. HR Insight Institute, "HR.com's State of People Analytics 2024-25," 10.

21. Max Blumberg, Alec Levenson, and Dave Millner, "A Strategically Aligned HR Operating Model." G23-02701. USC Marshal Center for Effective Organizations, 2023, https://ceo.usc.edu/wp-content/uploads/2023/11/G23-02701.pdf, 3.

22. Deloitte United States, "US Manufacturing Could Need as Many as 3.8 Million New Employees by 2033, According to Deloitte and the Manufacturing Institute." Press release, April 3, 2024, https://www2.deloitte.com/us/en/pages/about-deloitte/articles/press-releases/us-manufacturing-could-need-new-employees-by-2033.html.

23. Graham Kenny, "Don't Make This Common M&A Mistake," *Harvard Business Review*, March 17, 2020, https://hbr.org/2020/03/dont-make-this-common-ma-mistake.

24. Andy West, "HR Leaders' Role in M&A: An Interview with Lisa Blair Davis," *McKinsey & Company*, September 6, 2024, https://www.mckinsey .com/capabilities/people-and-organizational-performance/our-insights/ hr-leaders-role-in-m-and-a-an-interview-with-lisa-blair-davis.

25. As quoted in Stacia Garr and Priyanka Mehrotra, "Unlocking the Hidden C-Suite Superpower: People Analytics," RedThread Research & Visier, https://www.visier.com/lp/dm-redthread-research-report-unlocking-hidden-csuite-superpower/.

26. Visier, "Delivering People Insights at Scale: How to Automate Foundational People Analytics to Drive More Impact," 2024, 4–9, https://assets. ctfassets.net/lbgy40h4xfb7/5TkzpBGmB8bxukqPcGP0Oe/0981f442a4 50a58aa1bbee85c2b153ad/delivering-people-insights-at-scale-visier.pdf.

27. HR Insight Institute, "HR.com's State of People Analytics 2024-25."

28. Josh Bersin Company, "The Definitive Guide to People Analytics: The Journey to Systemic Business Analytics," Josh Bersin.com, November 19, 2024, https://joshbersin.com/definitive-guide-to-people-analytics/, 13–14.

29. Josh Bersin Company, "The Definitive Guide to People Analytics," 14.

Section 2

1. Deloitte Global, "Beyond Productivity: The journey to the quantified organization," Deloitte Global, 2023, https://www2.deloitte.com/ content/dam/Deloitte/uy/Documents/human-capital/Deloitte_The %20Quantified%20Organization.pdf.

2. Josh Bersin, "People Analytics, a Complex Domain, Is About to Be Transformed by AI," *Josh Bersin* (blog), November 21, 2024, https://joshbersin .com/2024/11/people-analytics-a-complex-domain-is-about-to-be-transformed-by-ai/.

3. Alexander Locher, "How to Harness the Value of People Data and Operational HR Insights," *EY Insights* (blog), February 19, 2024, https://www .ey.com/en_ch/insights/workforce/how-to-harness-the-value-of-people-data-and-operational-hr-insights.

4. Jasmine Panayides, "Partnering with Finance to Drive Greater Business Impact with People Analytics," *myHRfuture* (blog). May 23, 2024. https://www.myhrfuture.com/blog/partnering-with-finance-to-drive-greater-business-impact-with-people-analytics.

5. Randy Bean, "2024 Data and AI Leadership Executive Survey," Wavestone, 2024, 5. https://www.wavestone.com/en/insight/data-ai-executive-leadership-survey-2024/

6. HR Research Institute, "HR.com's State of People Analytics 2023–2024," Report. HR.com, 2023, https://www.crunchr.com/app/uploads/2023/10/HRdotcom-Crunchr-State-of-HR-Report.pdf.

7. HR Research Institute, "HR.com's State of People Analytics 2023–2024."

8. Bersin, "People Analytics, a Complex Domain."

9. Gartner, "2024 HR Budget & High Efficiency Benchmarks," 2024, https://www.gartner.com/en/documents/5199863.

10. Bersin, "People Analytics, a Complex Domain."

11. Ellyn Shook, Eva Sage-Gavin, and Susan Cantrell, "How Companies Can Use Employee Data Responsibly," *Harvard Business Review*, February 15, 2019, https://hbr.org/2019/02/how-companies-can-use-employee-data-responsibly.

12. Sue Cantrell and Brad Kreit, "Navigating the Data Dilemma: Can Organizations Build Trust While Using Workforce Data to Improve Performance?" *Deloitte Insights* (blog). May 31, 2023, For the full report, *see* Sue Cantrell, Michael Griffiths, Robin Jones, and Julie Hiipakka, "Building Tomorrow's Skills-based Organization: Jobs Aren't Working Anymore," Deloitte Global, 2022, https://www2.deloitte.com/content/dam/Deloitte/global/Documents/Deloitte-Skills-Based-Organization.pdf.

13. Naomi Verghese and David Green, "The Importance of Ethics in People Analytics for Leading Companies," *myHRfuture* (blog), November 29, 2023, https://www.myhrfuture.com/blog/the-importance-of-ethics-in-people-analytics-for-leading-companies.

14. Bernard Marr, *Data-Driven HR: How to Use AI, Analytics and Data to Drive Performance* (2nd ed., London: Kogan Page, 2023), 61.

15. Dirk Petersen, "6 Steps to Ethically Sound People Analytics," *myHRfuture* (blog), April 29, 2018, https://www.myhrfuture.com/blog/2018/11/19/six-steps-to-ethically-sound-people-analytics.

16. As quoted in David Green, "How IBM Is Reinventing HR with AI and People Analytics," *myHRfuture* (blog), September 8, 2020.

17. Jonathan Ferrer, Naomi Verghese, and Heidi Binder-Matsuo, "Investing to Deliver Value: A New Model for People Analytics (People Analytics Trends 2023)," Insight222, 2023, https://publications.insight222.com/peopleanalyticstrends2023; *see* the Data Governance Committees.

18. Bean, "2024 Data and AI Leadership Executive Survey," 12.

19. Margaret Engel, "New Human Capital Disclosure Requirements," The Harvard Law School Forum on Corporate Governance, February 6, 2021, https://corpgov.law.harvard.edu/2021/02/06/new-human-capital-disclosure-requirements/.

20. "U.S. SEC Committee Recommends Additional 10-K Human Capital Disclosures," *Aon Insights* (blog), October 3, 2023, https://www.aon.com/en/insights/articles/us-sec-committee-recommends-additional-10-k-human-capital-disclosures.

21. Elizabeth Ledet, Keith McNulty, Daniel Morales, and Marissa Shandell, "How to Be Great at People Analytics," McKinsey & Company, October 2, 2020, https://www.mckinsey.com/capabilities/people-and-organizational-performance/our-insights/how-to-be-great-at-people-analytics.

22. Deloitte Consulting, "2023 High-Impact People Analytics Research," Deloitte, 2024, https://www2.deloitte.com/content/dam/Deloitte/us/Documents/human-capital/us-high-impact-people-analytics-report.pdf, 3.

23. PwC, "People Analytics Maturity Assessment Framework," *PwC*, 2021. https://www.pwc.com/m1/en/services/consulting/documents/people-analytics-maturirty-assessment-framework.pdf.

24. Insights222, "People Analytics Trends 2023 Report," Insight222.com, 2023, https://publications.insight222.com/peopleanalyticstrends2023, 20–21.

25. Insights222, "People Analytics Trends 2023 Report."

26. Verghese and Green, "The Importance of Ethics in People Analytics for Leading Companies."

27. Visier, "7 Steps to Becoming a Highly Effective HR Organization: Using people analytics to drive better business outcomes," Visier, 2023, https://www.visier.com/lp/people-analytics-data-driven-hr/.

28. Josh Bersin, Stella Ioannidou and Kathi Enderes, "The Definitive Guide to People Analytics: The Journey to Systemic Business Analytics," Josh Bersin Company, November 19, 2024, https://joshbersin.com/definitive-guide-to-people-analytics/.

29. Nitin Razdan and Japneet Kaur Sachdeva, "People Analytics Maturity Report: Unlocking the Value," Deloitte India, 2023, https://www2.deloitte.com/content/dam/Deloitte/in/Documents/Consulting/in-hc-people-analytics-16-10-noexp.pdf. *See also*: Deloitte Consulting, "High-Impact Workforce Research: In Brief," 2020, https://www2.deloitte.com/content/dam/Deloitte/us/Documents/human-capital/us-hc-high-impact-workforce-research-in-brief.pdf; and Deloitte Consulting, "2023 High-Impact People Analytics Research."

30. Deloitte Consulting, "2023 High-Impact People Analytics Research," 3.

31. HR Research Institute, "HR.com's State of People Analytics 2024-25: Commit to Data-driven Growth in Your Workforce," HR.com., 2024, https://www.hr.com/en/resources/free_research_white_papers/hrcoms-state-of-people-analytics-2024-25_m1g4f7he.html, 13 & 18.

32. Bersin, Ioannidou and Enderes, "The Definitive Guide to People Analytics," 16–17.

33. Nigel Guenole, Jonathan Ferrar and Sheri Feinzig, *The Power of People: Learn How Successful Organizations Use Workforce Analytics to Improve Business Performance* (Hoboken, NJ: Pearson FT Press, 2017), 170.

34. Guenole, Ferrar and Feinzig, *The Power of People*, 170.

35. Erik Van Vulpin, "What Is HR Analytics? All You Need to Know to Get Started," *AIHR* (blog), May 31, 2024, https://www.aihr.com/blog/what-is-hr-analytics/.

36. Richard Rosenow, "9/3 Edition - People Analytics Roles Review," LinkedIn, September 3, 2024, https://www.linkedin.com/pulse/93-edition-people-analytics-roles-review-richard-rosenow-kzl5c/. The database can be viewed here: https://www.onemodel.co/roles-in-people-analytics-hr-technology, accessed December 3, 2024.

Section 3

1. "Alfred P. Sloan Jr.," Alfred P. Sloan Foundation, accessed December 3, 2024. https://sloan.org/about/who-was-alfred-p-sloan-jr.; Paige McGlauflin, "How the C-Suite Has Transformed Over the Last Century—and Where It's Heading Next," *Fortune*, December 20, 2022, https://fortune.com/2022/12/20/c-suite-transformation-century-general-motors-corporate-leadership-alfred-sloan/.

2. Linda Tucci, "The Evolving CIO Role: From IT Operator to Business Strategist," *Search CIO* (blog), June 24, 2022, https://www.techtarget.com/searchcio/cio-role.

3. Gartner Executive Programs, "Insights from the 2016 Gartner CIO Agenda Report," *Gartner CIO Agenda Report*, 2016, https://www.gartner.com/imagesrv/cio/pdf/cio_agenda_insights_2016.pdf, 1.

4. McGlauflin, "How the C-Suite Has Transformed Over the Last Century."

5. Henri Steenkamp, "The Evolution of CFO Leadership: From Number-Crunchers to Strategic Partners," *Forbes Money* (blog), September 4, 2024, https://www.forbes.com/councils/forbesfinancecouncil/2024/09/06/the-evolution-of-cfo-leadership-from-number-crunchers-to-strategic-partners/.

6. Kelly Blum, "How The CMO Role Has Evolved—and What's Next," *Gartner Insights* (blog), March 28, 2022, https://www.gartner.com/en/articles/how-the-cmo-role-has-evolved-and-what-s-next.

7. Simone Grapini Goodman, "The Evolution of the CMO Role: Becoming the Chief Multipurpose Officer," *Forbes Leadership* (blog), March 27,

2024,   https://www.forbes.com/councils/forbescommunicationscouncil/ 2024/03/27/the-evolution-of-the-cmo-role-becoming-the-chief-multipurpose-officer.

8. Amy Wright, Josh Bersin, Diane Gherson, and Janet Mertens, "Accelerating the Journey to HR 3.0: Ten Ways to Transform in a Time of Upheaval," IBM Institute for Business Value, 2020, https://www.ibm.com/downloads/documents/us-en/107a02e97dc8fd47, 5.

9. Kraig Eaton, Cantrell Sue, Kim Eberbach, and Julie Duda, "From Function to Discipline: The Rise of Boundaryless HR," *Deloitte Insights* (blog), August 1, 2024, https://www2.deloitte.com/us/en/insights/focus/human-capital-trends/2024/human-capital-strategy-boundaryless-organization.html.

10. Deloitte, n.d., "Deloitte 2021 Global Human Capital Trends Report," Press release, Deloitte Ukraine, https://www2.deloitte.com/ua/en/pages/about-deloitte/press-releases/gx-2021-global-human-capital-trends-report .html, accessed December 3, 2024.

11. Jim Clifton, "Gallup Finds a Silver Bullet: Coach Me Once per Week," *Gallup.Com* (blog), November 8, 2023, https://www.gallup.com/workplace/350057/gallup-finds-silver-bullet-coach-once-per-week.aspx.

12. Institute for Corporate Productivity (i4cp), "Culture Fitness: Healthy Habits of High-Performance Organizations," 2023, 20, https://go.i4cp .com/culturefitness.

13. Institute for Corporate Productivity (i4cp), "Culture Fitness," 20.

14. Shane McFeely and Ben Wigert. 2019, "This Fixable Problem Costs U.S. Businesses $1 Trillion," *Gallup Workplace* (blog), March 13, 2019, https:// www.gallup.com/workplace/247391/fixable-problem-costs-businesses-trillion.aspx.

Section 4

1. As quoted in Tarek Elmasry, "Direct From Michael Dell: Leadership Lessons and the Future of AI," *McKinsey Quarterly*, September 16, 2024, https://www.mckinsey.com/capabilities/mckinsey-digital/our-insights/direct-from-michael-dell-leadership-lessons-and-the-future-of-ai.

2. Randy Bean, "2024 Data and AI Leadership Executive Survey," Wavestone, 2024, 16, https://www.wavestone.com/en/insight/data-ai-executive-leadership-survey-2024/

3. Harvard Business Review Analytic Services, "Transforming Data into Business Value through Analytics and AI," Harvard Business School

Publishing, 2023, 12, https://hbr.org/resources/pdfs/comm/google/TransformingData.pdf.

4. Alec Bokman, Lars Fiedler, Jesko Perrey, and Andrew Pickersgill, "Five Facts: How Customer Analytics Boosts Corporate Performance," *McKinsey & Company* (blog), July 1, 2014, https://www.mckinsey.com/capabilities/growth-marketing-and-sales/our-insights/five-facts-how-customer-analytics-boosts-corporate-performance.

5. Alex Camp, Arne Gast, Drew Goldstein, and Brooke Weddle, "Organizational Health Is (Still) the Key to Long-term Performance," *McKinsey & Company* (blog), February 12, 2024, https://www.mckinsey.com/capabilities/people-and-organizational-performance/our-insights/organizational-health-is-still-the-key-to-long-term-performance.

6. Bob Parr, "A Data-Driven Culture Will Differentiate the Winners from the Losers: What Businesses Should Do to Stay Ahead," *KPMG Insight* (blog), February 20, 2024, https://kpmg.com/us/en/media/news/data-driven-culture-kpmg-insight-2024.html.

7. Efe Ejofodomi, "What's the Value of Becoming a Data-Driven Business?" *Forbes Leadership* (blog), January 7, 2022, https://www.forbes.com/councils/forbesbusinessdevelopmentcouncil/2022/01/07/whats-the-value-of-becoming-a-data-driven-business/.

8. Deloitte Consulting, "2023 High-Impact People Analytics Research," Deloitte, 2024, 5, https://www2.deloitte.com/content/dam/Deloitte/us/Documents/human-capital/us-high-impact-people-analytics-report.pdf.

9. Jonathan Ferrar and David Green, *Excellence in People Analytics: How to Use Workforce Data to Create Business Value* (London & New York: Kogan Page, 2021).

10. As quoted in Polly Mosendz, "Microsoft's CEO Sent a 3,187-Word Memo and We Read It so You Don't Have To," *The Atlantic*, July 10, 2014, https://www.theatlantic.com/technology/archive/2014/07/microsofts-ceo-sent-a-3187-word-memo-and-we-read-it-so-you-dont-have-to/374230/.

11. As cited in Aon, "The Impact of Organizational Culture on Business Performance," *Aon Insights* (blog), accessed December 3, 2024, https://www.aon.com/apac/insights/blog/impact-of-organizational-culture-on-business-performance.

12. As quoted in "How T-Mobile's Culture Powered It to Become the World's Most Valuable Telecom Company," *Fortune Leadership* (podcast transcript), October 9, 2024, https://fortune.com/2024/10/09/t-mobiles-culture-ceo-mike-sievert/.

13. As cited in Brit Morse and Emma Burleigh, "Most managers think they have a great corporate culture. Their employees aren't so sure," *Fortune's*

CHRO Daily, November 13, 2024, https://fortune.com/2024/11/13/managers-think-they-have-great-corporate-culture-employees-arent-sure/.

14. As cited in Emma Burleigh, "Exclusive: AI fears and 4-day workweek dreams—here's what a survey of hundreds of interns reveals about Gen Z." *Fortune's CHRO Daily* (blog), October 10, 2024. https://fortune.com/2024/10/10/kpmg-interns-gen-z-ai-flexible-work-culture

15. Ellyn Shook, Eva Sage-Gavin, and Susan Cantrell, "How Companies Can Use Employee Data Responsibly," *Harvard Business Review,* February 15, 2019, https://hbr.org/2019/02/how-companies-can-use-employee-data-responsibly.

16. Bean, "2024 Data and AI Leadership Executive Survey," 17.

17. Peter Drucker, *Managing for the Future: The 1990s and Beyond* (New York: Penguin, 1992), 151.

18. Kai Hahn, "Market Study: AI & the Future of Work," Intelligent Enterprise Leaders Alliance, 2024, 5, https://eco-cdn.iqpc.com/eco/files/event_content/iela-market-study-093024liJS04fKuJ0s62T9AG2fniOVppxnqRCTdoognEhU.pdf.

19. As cited in Max Blumberg, "Slashing HR Costs: The Ultimate Blueprint for Implementing GenAI in HR," Blumberg Partnership, 2024, 4, 14 & 15, https://blumbergpartnership.com/.

20. As cited in Hahn, "Market Study: AI & the Future of Work," 5.

21. Bean, "2024 Data and AI Leadership Executive Survey," 12.

22. As cited by Burleigh, "How Microsoft HR Is Rolling Out AI Within Its Own Ranks."

23. As cited in "Chipotle Introduces New AI Hiring Platform to Support Its Accelerated Growth," Press release, October 22, 2024, https://newsroom.chipotle.com/2024-10-22-CHIPOTLE-INTRODUCES-NEW-AI-HIRING-PLATFORM-TO-SUPPORT-ITS-ACCELERATED-GROWTH.

24. As cited in Nick Otto, "How McDonald's reduced time-to-hire by 60 percent," *HR Executive,* April 19, 2023, https://hrexecutive.com/how-mcdonalds-reduced-time-to-hire-by-60/.

25. HR Research Institute, "HR.com's State of People Analytics 2023-2024," HR.com, 2023, 46-7, https://www.crunchr.com/app/uploads/2023/10/HRdotcom-Crunchr-State-of-HR-Report.pdf.

26. Stacia Garr and Priyanka Mehrotra, "Unlocking the Hidden C-Suite Superpower: People Analytics," RedThread Research & Visier, 2021, https://www.visier.com/lp/dm-redthread-research-report-unlocking-hidden-csuite-superpower/; Workforce Institute, "The Heard and the

Heard-Nots: Who feels heard at work and why giving employees a voice isgoodforbusiness,"UKG,2024, https://www.ukg.com/blog/workforce-institute/new-research-the-heard-and-the-heard-nots.

27. CNBC Events, "IBM's AI-backed 'employee Retention' Software Can Predict When You're Going to Quit With up to 95% Accuracy," *CNBC Events,* May 22, 2019, https://www.cnbcevents.com/news/ibms-ai-backed-employee-retention-software-can-predict-when-youre-going-to-quit-with-up-to-95-accuracy/.

28. David Green, "How IBM Is Reinventing HR with AI and People Analytics: An interview with Diane Gherson," *myHRfuture* (podcast transcript), September 8, 2020, https://www.myhrfuture.com/digital-hr-leaders-podcast/2020/9/8/how-ibm-is-reinventing-hr-with-ai-and-people-analytics.

29. Josh Bersin and Kathi Enderes, "Coca-Cola Europacific Partners Addresses Skills Gaps With Enterprise Talent Intelligence," Josh Bersin Company, 2024, 2–3, https://eightfold.ai/wp-content/uploads/Coca-Cola-Europacific-Partners-Addresses-Skills-Gaps-with-Enterprise-Talent-Intelligence-case-study.pdf.

30. David Green, "The Best HR & People Analytics Articles of October 2024," LinkedIn, November 3, 2024, https://www.linkedin.com/pulse/best-hr-people-analytics-articles-october-2024-david-green--kvape/.

31. Josh Bersin, Stella Ioannidou and Kathi Enderes, "Definitive Guide to People Analytics: The Journey to Systemic Business Analytics," Josh Bersin Company, November 19, 2024, https://joshbersin.com/definitive-guide-to-people-analytics/, 39–40.

32. Qliktech Data Literacy Project, "Data Literacy: The Upskilling Evolution," QlikTech International, 2022, 8 & 11, https://thedatalit eracyproject.org/wp-content/uploads/2022/11/Data-Literacy-The-Upskilling-Evolution-Report-1.pdf.

33. Ferrar and Green, *Excellence in People Analytics,* 278.

34. Naomi Verghese and Jonathan Ferrar, "Upskilling the HR Profession: Building Data Literacy at Scale," Insight222, 2023, https://publications .insight222.com/upskillinghrreport2023.

35. Verghese and Ferrar, "Upskilling the HR Profession," 5.

36. Verghese and Ferrar, "Upskilling the HR Profession," 17.

37. Verghese and Ferrar, "Upskilling the HR Profession," 8.

38. Josh Bersin, "People Analytics, a Complex Domain, Is About to Be Transformed by AI," *Josh Bersin* (blog), November 21, 2024, https://joshbersin.com/2024/11/people-analytics-a-complex-domain-is-about-to-be-transformed-by-ai/.

39. Bersin, Ioannidou and Enderes, "The Definitive Guide to People Analytics," 17.
40. Deloitte India, "People Analytics Maturity in India – 2022," 2022, 30, https://www2.deloitte.com/content/dam/Deloitte/in/Documents/Consulting/in-hc-people-analytics-maturity-in-India-2022-noexp.pdf.
41. Qliktech Data Literacy Project, "Data Literacy," 8–9.
42. This case study integrates information gathered in our interview process along with material from this previously-published case study: BTS, "Salesforce.com Accelerates a Cultural Transformation: Security Starts with Workforce Alignment," BTS, 2015, https://bts.com/wp-content/uploads/2015/06/Salesforce.com-Accelerates-a-Cultural-Transformation.pdf.
43. Qliktech Data Literacy Project, "Data Literacy," 8.
44. Garr and Mehrotra, "Unlocking the Hidden C-Suite Superpower."
45. As quoted in Emma Loxton, "Rolls-Royce in Transformation: An Interview with Nikki Grady-Smith," McKinsey & Company, September 17, 2024, https://www.mckinsey.com/industries/aerospace-and-defense/our-insights/rolls-royce-in-transformation-an-interview-with-nikki-grady-smith.
46. Josh Howard, "Data Democratization: Embracing Trusted Data to Transform Your Business," Databricks (blog), April 24, 2024, https://www.databricks.com/blog/data-democratization-embracing-trusted-data-transform-your-business.
47. As cited in Businesswire.com, "Nearly 90% of Organizations Say Success Depends on Data-Driven Decisions Made by Frontline Employees, According to New Report," Press release, May 5, 2020, https://www.businesswire.com/news/home/20200505005195/en/Nearly-90-of-Organizations-Say-Success-Depends-on-Data-Driven-Decisions-Made-by-Frontline-Employees-According-to-New-Report.
48. McKinsey's Organizational Health Index (OHI) data as cited in Camp, et al. "Organizational Health Is (Still) the Key to Long-term Performance."
49. Bersin, Ioannidou and Enderes, "The Definitive Guide to People Analytics," 33-7.
50. Bersin, Ioannidou and Enderes, "The Definitive Guide to People Analytics," 37.
51. Richard Branson, 2023, "Train people well enough so they can leave, treat them well enough so they don't want to," LinkedIn, https://www.linkedin.com/posts/rbranson_train-people-well-enough-so-they-can-leave-activity-7094663480783327232-WDuo/.
52. As cited in Workforce Institute, "The Heard and the Heard-Nots."
53. Workforce Institute, "The Heard and the Heard-Nots."

54. Camp et al., "Organizational Health Is (Still) the Key to Long-term Performance."

55. Talia Varley and John Glaser, "Using Data to Improve Employee Health and Wellness," *Harvard Business Review*, November 10, 2023, https://hbr .org/2023/11/using-data-to-improve-employee-health-and-wellness.

56. As cited in Sara Brown, "How to build a data-driven company," *Ideas Made to Matter* (blog), MIT Sloan School of Management, September 24, 2020, https://mitsloan.mit.edu/ideas-made-to-matter/how-to-build-a-data-driven-company.

57. As quoted in Loxton, "Rolls-Royce in Transformation."

58. Ranil Boteju, "How we're building a data-driven culture," *Lloyd Banking Group Insights* (blog), May 23, 2023, https://www.lloydsbankinggroup .com/insights/building-a-data-driven-culture.html. More generally, *see* "Putting Analytics Practitioners at the Heart of Value Creation, Lloyds Banking Group, Ranil Boteju," 2023 Interview by Kyle Winterbottom, .https://www.youtube.com/watch?v=eAFw86wh540&t=6s.

59. Ranil Boteju, "Building a Data-driven Culture." *Lloyds Banking Group Insight* (blog). May 25, 2023. https://www.lloydsbankinggroup.com/ insights/building-a-data-driven-culture.html; Josh Cunningham, "Josh Cunningham – Articles by Josh," LinkedIn, accessed December 3, 2024. https://uk.linkedin.com/in/josh-cunningham-a2293050; Orbition Group, "Putting Analytics Practitioners at the Heart of Value Creation at Lloyds Banking Group," *Driven by Data Magazine*, August 7, 2024. https://orbitiongroup.com/putting-analytics-practitioners-at-the-heart-of-value-creation-at-lloyds-banking-group/; "Putting Analytics Practitioners at the Heart of Value Creation, Lloyds Banking Group."; Catherine King, "Ranil Boteju, Featured Driven by Data Magazine Leader Interview," Orbition Group. November 15, 2023, https://orbitiongroup .com/ranil-boteju/.

60. Lucy Adams, *HR Disrupted: It's Time for Something Different* (2nd Ed.; Norwich, UK: Practical Inspiration Publishing, 2021).

Section 5

1. Jack Welch Management Institute, "How to Get a Seat at the Table," *Winning*(blog),May 4, 2023,https://jackwelch.strayer.edu/winning/how-to-get-a-seat-at-the-table/.

2. Vince Molinaro, "The Most Important Hire a CEO Will Make: The CHRO," *Forbes*, April 28, 2023, https://www.forbes.com/councils/

forbesbusinesscouncil/2023/08/28/the-most-important-hire-a-ceo-will-make-the-chro/

3. Ellyn Shook and Yusuf Tayob, "The CHRO as a Growth Executive," Report, Accenture, 2023, https://www.accenture.com/content/dam/accenture/final/capabilities/strategy-and-consulting/talent-and-organization/document/Accenture-CHRO-Growth-Executive.pdf, 6–8.

4. Shook and Tayob, "The CHRO as a Growth Executive," 7.

5. Johnny C. Taylor, Jr., "What Are the 3 Key Qualities CEOs Look for in a CHRO?: Message from the President," *People + Strategy Journal (SHRM)*, January 9, 2024, https://www.shrm.org/executive-network/insights/people-strategy/key-qualities-ceo-look-for-in-chro-johnny-taylor.

6. Alan Guarino, "Why CHROs Really Are CEOs." *Korn Ferry Insights* (blog), April 2, 2021, https://www.kornferry.com/insights/this-week-in-leadership/why-chros-really-are-ceos.

7. As cited in Lindsey Gallow, "Why CHROs Are the New C-Suite Power Players," *Leading Through Disruptions*, *Chief.com* (blog). January 6, 2024, https://chief.com/articles/why-chros-are-the-new-c-suite-power-player.

8. Shana Lebowitz, "Microsoft's HR Chief Reveals How CEO Satya Nadella Is Pushing to Make Company Culture a Priority, the Mindset She Looks for in Job Candidates, and Why Individual Success Doesn't Matter as Much as It Used To," *Business Insider*, March 17, 2020, https://www.businessinsider.com/microsoft-hr-chief-kathleen-hogan-company-culture-change-satya-nadella-2019-8.

9. Shook and Tayob, "The CHRO as a Growth Executive." 18.

10. As quoted in Amit Batish, "CHRO Content Series: CHRO Presence in the Boardroom Offers Organization-Wide Impacts," *Equilar CHRO Navigator* (blog). September 23, 2022, https://www.equilar.com/blogs/546-board-members-with-chro-experience.html.

11. Sharon Sutherland and Lay Keng Tan, "The Board Imperative: Further Unlock the Strategic Value of CHROs," *EY (Ernst & Young Global)*, April 8, 2022, https://www.ey.com/en_gl/board-matters/the-board-imperative-unlock-the-strategic-value-of-chros.

12. Coco Brown, "Why a CHRO Will Be the Next Must-Have Role in the Boardroom," LinkedIn, March 7, 2018, https://www.linkedin.com/pulse/why-chro-next-must-have-role-boardroom-coco-brown/.

13. As cited in Batish, "CHRO Content Series: CHRO Presence in the Boardroom Offers Organization-Wide Impacts."

14. Shook and Tayob, "The CHRO as a Growth Executive."

15. Dimple Agarwal, Josh Bersin and Gaurav Lahiri, "The Rise of the Social Enterprise: 2018 Deloitte Global Human Capital Trends," *Deloitte Insights*, 2018, 17–21, https://www2.deloitte.com/content/dam/insights/

us/articles/HCTrends2018/2018-HCtrends_Rise-of-the-social-enterprise.pdf.

16. Institute for Business Value, "The Human Side of Data: Chief Human Resources Officer Insights from the Global C-Suite Study," IBM, 2020, https://www.ibm.com/downloads/documents/us-en/10a99803fd2fdd99.

17. Mercer, "2024 Voice of the CHRO: Maximizing HR Effectiveness," 2024, https://www.mercer.com/assets/us/en_us/shared-assets/local/attachments/2024-pdf-chro-survey-report.pdf.

18. SAP Concur, "CFO Insights Report: A New Role in Managing Uncertainty." SAP, 2023, 5, https://hrinterests.com/wp-content/uploads/2024/07/CFO-Insights-Report-A-New-Role-in-Managing-Uncertainty.pdf.

19. Peter Cappelli, "Why We Love to Hate HR . . . and What HR Can Do About It." *Harvard Business Review* (July/August 2015), https://hbr.org/2015/07/why-we-love-to-hate-hr-and-what-hr-can-do-about-it.

20. Peter Cappelli, "How Financial Accounting Screws up HR." *Harvard Business Review* (January/February 2023), https://hbr.org/2023/01/how-financial-accounting-screws-up-hr.

21. Ram Charan, Dominic Barton, and Dennis Carey. "People Before Strategy: A New Role for the CHRO." *Harvard Business Review* (July/August 2015), https://hbr.org/2015/07/people-before-strategy-a-new-role-for-the-chro.

22. Joanne Sammer, "Building an HR/CFO Partnership." *HR Magazine*, March10,2022.https://www.shrm.org/topics-tools/news/hr-magazine/building-hr-cfo-partnership.

23. Jasmine Panayides, "Partnering with Finance to Drive Greater Business Impact with People Analytics," *myHRfuture* (blog). May 23, 2024. https://www.myhrfuture.com/blog/partnering-with-finance-to-drive-greater-business-impact-with-people-analytics.

24. As cited in Michele Lerner, "How to Foster CFO-CHRO Collaboration and Improve Your Bottom Line," *Forbes Workday Brandvoice*, September 1, 2016, https://www.forbes.com/sites/workday/2016/09/01/how-to-foster-cfo-chro-collaboration-and-improve-your-bottom-line/; PR Newswire and EY, "Greater Collaboration Among CFOs and HR Leaders Drives Stronger Business Performance," Press release, May 12, 2014, https://www.prnewswire.com/news-releases/greater-collaboration-among-cfos-and-hr-leaders-drives-stronger-business-performance-258892031.html.

25. Charan, Barton, and Carey, "People Before Strategy."

26. Anthony Hesketh and Martin Hird, "The Golden Triangle: How Relationships Between Leaders Can Leverage More Value From People," CPHR White Paper 09/03, Centre for Performance-Led HR (CPHR),

2016, 8, https://www.thehrdirector.com/wp-content/uploads/2016/10/CPHR_Golden_Triangle_WP.pdf.

27. Sandy Ogg, "Identify the Critical Roles - Part 2," *CEO Works* (blog), March 27, 2019, https://www.ceoworks.com/blog/connecting-talent-to-value-part-2.

28. As quoted in Kraig Eaton, Sue Cantrell, Kim Eberbach, and Julie Duda, "From Function to Discipline: The Rise of Boundaryless HR," *Deloitte Insights* (blog), August 1, 2024, https://www2.deloitte.com/us/en/insights/focus/human-capital-trends/2024/human-capital-strategy-boundaryless-organization.html.

29. HR Research Institute, "HR.com's Future of the HR Function 2024," HR Research Institute, 2024, 4 & 21, https://www.hr.com/en/resources/free_research_white_papers/hrcoms-future-of-the-hr-function-2024_lvulv6e9.html.

30. McLean & Company, "HR Trends Report 2024." McLean & Company, 2023, https://hr.mcleanco.com/research/ss/hr-trends-report-2024.

31. Sandy Ogg, "Connecting Talent to Value," LinkedIn, November 8, 2018, https://www.linkedin.com/pulse/connecting-talent-value-sandy-ogg/.

32. Max Blumberg, "Future Fit: Reimaging HR," Unpublished manuscript, August 15, 2024, typescript.

33. Charan, Barton, and Carey, "People Before Strategy."

34. Steven Kerr, "On the Folly of Rewarding A, While Hoping for B." Academy of Management Journal 18, no. 4 (1975): 769–71, https://web.mit.edu/curhan/www/docs/Articles/15341_Readings/Motivation/Kerr_Folly_of_rewarding_A_while_hoping_for_B.pdf.

35. As quoted in Claire Howorth and Sam Jacobs, "Bill Gates discusses his lifelong love for books and reading," *TIME*, May 22, 2017, https://time.com/4786837/bill-gates-books-reading/.

36. Naomi Verghese and Jonathan Ferrar, "Upskilling the HR Profession: Building Data Literacy at Scale," Insight222, July 2023, 6–7, https://publications.insight222.com/upskillinghrreport2023.

37. Insights222, "People Analytics Trends 2023 Report," July 2023, 7, https://publications.insight222.com/peopleanalyticstrends2023.

38. As cited in Gartner, "2024 HR Budget & High Efficiency Benchmarks," Gartner, Inc., 2024, https://www.gartner.com/en/documents/5199863.

39. Josh Bersin, "Why is it so hard to be a Chief HR officer (CHRO)?" *Josh Bersin* (blog), July 12, 2024, https://joshbersin.com/2024/06/the-expanding-role-of-the-chief-hr-officer-chro/.

40. Tom Starner, "Ex-GE CHRO on how (and why) Jack Welch came to respect the HR department," *HR Dive*, June 15, 2015, https://www.hrdive.com/news/ex-ge-chro-on-how-and-why-jack-welch-came-to-respect-the-hr-department/400712/.

41. Caroline Liongosari, Silvia Lara, and Sharat Raghavan, "State of the C-Suite and Executives Report," LinkedIn, 2024, 3. https://economicgraph.linkedin.com/content/dam/me/economicgraph/en-us/PDF/state-of-the-c-suite.pdf.

Guide to Workforce Data

THE FOLLOWING INFORMATION is reproduced with permission from "Data Types for HRBPs," a guide from the Academy to Innovate HR (AIHR) that we feel anyone seeking to generate Workforce Insights will find valuable. Knowing the different data types, how they add value, and where they can typically be found is key to Workforce Analytics. Each section provides an overview of data types, sources of the data, and questions the data can answer.

Compensation Data

Compensation data covers information about employee salaries, bonuses, and benefits. HRBPs use this data to maintain competitive and fair compensation structures, design benefits packages, ensure internal equity, gauge employee satisfaction with benefits, and address any pay-related issues.

Application: You can use compensation data to conduct salary benchmarking, ensure internal pay equity, design bonus and incentive programs, and create competitive benefits packages.

Data in this category:	Data sources:	Questions this data can answer:
• Base salary • Bonuses • Pay ranges • Employee benefits participation • Internal pay equity • Pay gap analysis • Pay changes over time • Compa-ratios	• Payroll systems • HRIS • Compensation committees • Industry compensation benchmarks • Employee feedback	• Is compensation competitive and equitable? • How does compensation vary across different roles or departments? • What benefits are most valued by employees? • Are there potential flight risks of critical and scarce talent? (looking at pay vs. benchmark vs. tenure)

Figure A.1   Compensation Data

Source: Adapted with permission from the Academy to Innovate HR (AIHR), "Data Types for HRBPs Guide" (n.d.), 6.

Employee Data

Employee data includes information about individual employees in an organization. This includes details like demographics, job roles, tenure, salary, performance records, and other personal or professional information. Analyzing this data helps you understand your workforce, monitor demographic trends, and devise development strategies.

Application: Use employee data to perform workforce planning, identify opportunities for diversity and inclusion initiatives, track employee tenure, create succession plans based on employee demographics, and map out organizational structure and roles. You can also use this type of data to create employee personas based on shared characteristics, which can inform priorities in employer value proposition (EVP) and benefit design.

Data in this category:

- Demographics (e.g., age, gender, tenure, educational background, and departmental segmentation)
- Turnover rates: The rates and reasons behind employee turnover help identify patterns and underlying issues that may require attention.
- Attendance: Patterns and trends in absenteeism can indicate employee engagement or operational issues.
- The span of control data (i.e., number of employees reporting to each line manager within a given structure): Ensure optimal team management and organizational design.
- Headcount over time: Inform workforce planning and talent demand projections.

Data sources:

- Employee records from the Human Resources Information System (HRIS)
- Exit interview data
- Payroll systems

Questions this data can answer:

- What are the characteristics of employees who stay with the company long-term versus those who leave within the first year?
- What is the diversity profile of the workforce?
- Are there disparities in employee demographics at different levels?
- How does the workforce distribution vary by department or location?
- What can be inferred about the needs of employees based on shared characteristics?

Figure A.2   Employee Data

Source: Adapted with permission from the Academy to Innovate HR (AIHR), "Data Types for HRBPs Guide" (n.d.), 3.

Employee Engagement Data

Employee engagement data encompasses employee morale, satisfaction, and engagement information. HRBPs use this data to assess employee morale, determine engagement drivers, and develop strategies to improve workplace satisfaction.

Application: Use employee engagement data to analyze employee engagement survey results, design initiatives to boost engagement, address areas of low morale, and evaluate the impact of HR programs on employee satisfaction.

Data in this category:	Data sources:	Questions this data can answer:
• Employee engagement survey result	• Employee surveys	• What is the overall level of employee engagement?
• Feedback from focus groups	• HR databases	• What factors contribute to or hinder employee morale?
• Absenteeism rates	• Focus groups	• How can employee engagement be improved?
• Employee participation in company events	• Feedback from managers and team leaders	
• Experience feedback	• Recognition systems	
• eNPS scores	• Disciplinary records	
• Recognition data	• External employer reviews, e.g., Glassdoor	
• Grievances and complaints		

Figure A.3   Employee Engagement Data

Source: Adapted with permission from the Academy to Innovate HR (AIHR), "Data Types for HRBPs Guide" (n.d.), 7.

Performance Metrics

Performance metrics include data related to individual and collective employee performance and productivity at one point in time or over time. This information helps you evaluate employee performance, identify high-performing employees, and measure overall productivity.

Application: You can use performance metrics to conduct performance reviews, identify future leaders and manage talent, identify potential gaps, develop employee recognition programs, and make decisions about promotions. They can also inform development initiatives applicable to individuals or groups (i.e., gaps that are identified across a group), as well as remuneration and reward decisions.

Data in this category:	Data sources:	Questions this data can answer:
• Performance ratings	• Performance management systems	• Who are the top-performing employees?
• 360-degree feedback		• What performance trends are observed across teams?
• Self-ratings	• HRIS	
• Productivity measures (e.g., for service and call center staff, you could look at calls resolved and lost call rates)	• Feedback from managers	• What factors influence employee performance?
	• Employee files	• Where are the biggest development gaps?
• Promotion rates	• Production systems (e.g., query logging platforms, call center systems)	• How do performance ratings compare across different areas of the business?
• Performance improvement plans	• Business financials	
• Career development plans		
• Peer review		

Figure A.4   Performance Metrics

Source: Adapted with permission from the Academy to Innovate HR (AIHR), "Data Types for HRBPs Guide" (n.d.), 4.

Recruitment and Hiring Data

Recruitment and hiring data comprise information about the recruitment process, including metrics related to hiring and sourcing candidates. This data helps HRBPs assess the efficiency of recruitment, identify effective sourcing channels, and enhance candidate quality.

Application: Use recruitment and hiring data to streamline recruitment processes, reduce time to fill for open positions, evaluate candidate sources, and candidate experience.

Data in this category:
- Time to fill
- Cost per hire
- Candidate sources
- Offer acceptance rates
- Diversity in the hiring pipeline
- Conversation rates within the funnel
- Number of applicants
- Referrals
- Application source
- Experience feedback
- Candidate NPS scores
- Social media conversation data (e.g., how many people view adverts and apply)
- SLA tracking (at each point of the process)

Data sources:
- Applicant Tracking Systems (ATS)
- Social media engagement dashboard
- HR databases
- Feedback from recruitment teams
- Onboarding data

Questions this data can answer:
- How effective are recruitment strategies?
- What are the best sources for high-quality candidates?
- What is the diversity profile of the recruitment pipeline?
- Which sources produce the best quality applicants?
- What experience does the recruitment process deliver?
- How effective is the process?

Figure A.5   Recruitment and Hiring Data

Source: Adapted with permission from the Academy to Innovate HR (AIHR), "Data Types for HRBPs Guide" (n.d.), 5.

Risk and Compliance Data

Risk and compliance data focus on ensuring that HR practices comply with legal requirements and managing associated risks. HRBPs use this data to ensure that HR policies align with laws and regulations, while also maintaining a safe and compliant workplace.

....

Application: With risk and compliance data, you can conduct compliance audits to ensure adherence to laws, address workplace safety concerns, implement diversity and inclusion policies, and manage legal risks related to HR practices.

Data in this category:	Data sources:	Questions this data can answer:
• Compliance audits	• Legal and compliance teams	• Are HR policies compliant with regulations and laws?
• Workplace safety records	• Safety records	
• Diversity metrics	• HR policy documents	• What risks exist in terms of compliance or workplace safety?
• Employee relations issues	• Employee relations records	
• HR policies		• What corrective actions are needed to address compliance issues?
• Incident reports (e.g., for drivers or miners)		
• Safety and compliance training completion		

Figure A.6   Risk and Compliance Data

Source: Adapted with permission from the Academy to Innovate HR (AIHR), "Data Types for HRBPs Guide" (n.d.), 9.

Strategic Business Data

Strategic business data is essential for HRBPs to align HR initiatives with business objectives and understand the broader context in which HR operates. This data covers business strategy, organizational goals, and overall performance.

....

Application: Use strategic business data to develop HR strategies that support business goals, participate in strategic planning meetings, ensure HR objectives support the broader organizational objectives, and measure the impact of HR activities on business performance.

Data in this category:	Data sources:	Questions this data can answer:
• Business goals and strategies	• Business strategy documents	• How does HR align with business objectives?
• Financial performance	• Organizational charts	• What are the strategic goals of the organization?
• Business unit structures	• Financial reports	• How does HR contribute to achieving business success?
• Market trends	• Feedback from business leaders	
• Industry analysis and insights		

Figure A.7   Strategic Business Data

Source: Adapted with permission from the Academy to Innovate HR (AIHR), "Data Types for HRBPs Guide" (n.d.), 10.

Technology Use Data

Technology use data allows HRBPs to evaluate the effectiveness of HR technologies and identify opportunities for automation and greater efficiency. HRBPs need to understand how technology is used in the workplace, including software, hardware, and cybersecurity risks and awareness.

Application: Use technology data to assess the adoption rates of HR technologies, identify technology-related training needs, enhance HR processes with the right technology, and explore new tools to streamline HR operations. You can also use this data to mitigate cybersecurity risks through awareness and training.

Data in this category:
- Usage of collaboration tools
- Software adoption rates
- Remote work technology
- IT support requests
- Awareness training completion rates (compliance)
- Manager self-service use
- Employee self-service use

Data sources:
- IT departments
- Technology usage logs
- Employee feedback
- Software analytics

Questions this data can answer:
- How are employees using technology to perform their jobs?
- What technology trends are affecting workplace productivity?
- Are employees satisfied with the technology provided?

Figure A.8   Technology Use Data

Source: Adapted with permission from the Academy to Innovate HR (AIHR), "Data Types for HRBPs Guide" (n.d.), 8.

B

CEO+CHRO Survey Results

WE SURVEYED CEOs and CHROs in Spring 2024, asking a few simple, open-ended questions to better understand how each group views and wants support from the other. We used Generative AI to identify key themes from our 32 CEO and 71 CHRO respondents. It was helpful validation that most topics were already slated for inclusion and interesting to see what emerged. We hand-selected excerpts that we found especially insightful.

About the global respondents: CHROs were mostly U.S.-based, with 9 from Latin America; CEOs were about half U.S. and half Europe; both groups included a few respondents from Asia. Most represented companies with $50M+ or $500M+ in annual revenue. Public/private companies were about evenly split.

CEO Survey Results

Ways CHROs Contribute to Business Success

As detailed in Higher Math, key CEO themes:

1. Attracting and Developing Top Talent
2. Building a High-Performance Culture
3. Driving Revenue and Growth Through People Strategies
4. Using Workforce Analytics for Strategic Decisions
5. Leading Change and Promoting Agility
6. Serving as a Trusted Advisor

Ways that CHROs Diminish Business Outcomes

Transactional or Administrative Focus
There's hope yet for that top right quadrant of the CEO/CHRO Alignment Matrix.

Lack of Flexibility and Innovation
Being too process-driven can slow down progress.

Failure to Align with Business Objectives
Limits HR effectiveness.

Not Speaking Up or Challenging Leaders
Being too consensus-driven diminishes the CHRO's role as a strategic partner.

CHRO Survey Results

Key Ways CEOs Support CHROs to Deliver Key Business Metrics

Early Inclusion in Strategic Discussions
And not just in talent-related issues.

Role Clarity and Authority
On par with other C-level leaders, with accountability for results.

Commitment to People Strategy
Talent and culture prioritized alongside revenue and customer metrics.

Transparent Communication
For strategic insights and mutual trust.

Resource and Investment Support
For HR initiatives, technology, and tools.

Key Ways CEOs Diminish CHRO Effectiveness

Micromanagement and Lack of Trust Reduces trust and credibility.	**Excluding HR from Business Strategy** Precludes CHRO impact.
Short-Term Focus on Financials Risks damaging culture and engagement.	**Undervaluing People Metrics** Prioritize, and have leaders share accountability.

CHRO Quotable Quotes

We're taking the opportunity to highlight important points from CHRO respondents.

With country of operations, company type, and annual revenue

Only in the past 10–15 years are we seeing strategic, professionalized CHROs at scale in most geo markets, and often CEOs are experiencing this for the first time.
U.S./Public/$50–500M

When the CEO leverages the science of data and the art of great leadership, the partnership with HR is optimized.
Europe/Private/$10–50M

Listen to your CHRO and hold them responsible for driving the strategic workforce strategy; designing L&D that supports development of the right skills; and appropriately resourcing the team to support the extremely diverse and challenging remit of the function.
U.S./Private/$50–500M

Talent is the #1 driver of a company's success (or failure) and also the top cost. CEOs that understand this fully benefit from the CHRO partnership at a strategic level.

Take full ownership that HR metrics are business metrics. Know that anything on the people agenda needs to be your agenda.
U.S./Public/$500M+

Commit to accepting truth telling . . . even when the truth telling gets hard to hear.
U.S./Public/$500M+

Proactively discuss and share where your head is on company strategy, areas of strength, weak spots. The best CEOs use their CHRO to organize their own thinking.
U.S./Public/$500M+

Knowledge is power! The more the CEO tells the CHRO about their world (from thought process to goals to fears), the more effective the CHRO can be at seeing around the corner.
U.S./Private/$50–500M

HR is not the company party planner or the police. When the CEO directs those tasks or sentiments to the CHRO, it diminishes the strategic partnership needed to deliver business results.
U.S./Private/$500M+

The best CEO I worked for partnered with HR at the same level (time and energy) as they did the CFO. We met every week to review key talent decisions and manage an operating rhythm/ governance we had set to drive rigor and excellence. The expectation was that all function leaders were business leaders first and expected to lean in outside their discipline. When a CEO places value in, and understands, how HR is a lever for business execution, it makes our work more impactful.
U.S./Public/$1–10M

Pay, voice, and board access on par with other C-suite. Inclusion in key decision-making discussions about the business. High expectations and demands, as well as performance-based goals just like any other C-suite. The CHRO is playing the game, not watching from the sidelines.
U.S./Public/$50–500M

Spend as much time and energy on people-related topics as you do Finance, IT, Sales, etc. That will better inform the CEO and send a clear message to all about the importance of people.
U.S./Private/$1–10M

Instill support into the executive team—create a level playing field at the C-suite level.
Asia/Private/$50–500M

Support the CHRO when the going gets tough (and the going WILL get tough).
U.S./Public/$500M+

When a CEO is talking about the priorities, results, and importance of the organization's culture, diversity, retention, or engagement, it demonstrates how all leaders are accountable for the results—not the HR team.
Private/Over $500M/U.S.

Make sure to bring in the CHRO prior to big decisions—understanding that we can help influence and get to the optimal outcome.
U.S./Public/$10–50M

C

Interviewees

As MENTIONED IN the Acknowledgments, we are indebted to the more than 100 Workforce Analytics practitioners, senior HR professionals, business executives, consultants, academics, researchers, and thought leaders for revealing, insightful conversations that helped inform this book. Interviews took place between February and December 2024.

Lucy Adams, CEO, Disruptive HR, UNITED KINGDOM

Matt Allen, PhD, Professor, Kellogg Graduate School of Management, Northwestern University, USA

Philios Andreou, Deputy CEO, BTS, SPAIN

Tony Ashton, Chief Product Officer, One Model – People Analytics, AUSTRALIA

Andy Atkins, Executive & Team Performance, Global Practice Leader, BTS Inc., USA

Pamay Bassey, Chief Learning and Diversity Officer, The Kraft Heinz Company, USA

Josh Bersin, Founder and CEO, The Josh Bersin Company, USA

Gargi Bhattacharya, PhD, Behavioral Scientist, USA

Max Blumberg, PhD, Founder, Blumberg Partnership, UNITED KINGDOM

Paul Bohne, Managing Partner, WittKieffer, USA

John Boudreau, PhD, Emeritus Professor and Senior Research Scientist, Center for Effective Organizations, University of Southern California, USA

Hallie Bregman, PhD, CEO, The Bregman Group, USA

Robert O. Brinkerhoff, Professor Emeritus Western Michigan University, Director of Research & Evaluation, Promote International, USA

Kevin Bronk, Vice President, Change & Transformation, BTS, USA

Coco Brown, Founder & CEO, The Athena Alliance, Corporate Board Director, USA

Andrew Burns, Head of Learning & Development, Guardant Health, USA

Matt Burns, Founder, Atlas Copilot, CANADA

Ram Charan, PhD, Professor Emeritus, Harvard University, INDIA

Sanjala Chitnis, Director of Talent, UNITED KINGDOM

Kathryn Clubb, CEO, BTS North America, BTS, USA

Phil Cognetta Jr, SVP IT Enterprise Technologies, PTC, Inc., USA

Lynn Collins, Head of North America Assessment, BTS Inc., USA

Ian Cook, VP Product Management, Visier, CANADA

Patrick Coolen, Partner, KennedyFitch, NETHERLANDS

Josh Cunningham, Group Head of Data Culture, Lloyds Banking Group, UNITED KINGDOM

Dr. Laura P. Dannels, Chief Talent Officer, Wellstar Health System, USA

Michelle Deneau, Sr Director, People Experiences and Analytics, Cloudflare, USA

Gianfranco Di Maira, Partner, SVP, Managing Director BTS Southeast Asia, BTS, SINGAPORE

Brynna Donn, Product Leader, Udemy, Mountain View, USA

Sergio Dosda, Senior Director, BTS, SPAIN

Tamar Elkeles, PhD, Chief People Officer & Board Director, USA

Ben Eubanks, Chief Research Officer, Lighthouse Research & Advisory, USA

Barrett Evans, Chief Learning Officer, Ford Motor Company, USA

John Fiore, Chief Data & Analytics Office, Senior Manager, Lloyds Banking Group, UNITED KINGDOM

Charlie Galunic, PhD, Professor, INSEAD, FRANCE

Diane Gherson, Board Director – Kraft Heinz, Centivo, and TechWolf, BCG Senior Advisor, CHRO Coach, and former CHRO IBM, USA

Francesca Gino, PhD, Professor, Harvard Business School, USA

Rochana Golani, VP Learning & Enablement, Databricks, USA

Sergey Gorbatov, Managing Partner, Intalensight, SPAIN

Heather Goudey, Head of GTM Enablement, North America & Global SMB, Talent Solutions, LinkedIn, USA

David Green, Managing Partner, Insight222, UNITED KINGDOM

Matthew Guss, Russell Reynolds, USA

Greg Hessel, Partner, Korn Ferry, USA

Shelly Holt, VP Talent Development, USA

Steve Hunt, PhD, Founder, i3 Talent, LLC, USA

Judy Kopa, CEO, Arroo, Inc., USA

Glen Lally, Global Director of Sales Enablement, Amazon Web Services (AWS), USA

Meg Langan, Founder, ML Consulting & Advisory, Previously, Chief People Officer, Turbonomic, USA

Mark Lawrence, Founder and Executive Consultant, Data Driven HR, UNITED KINGDOM

Dillion Lee, Senior Vice President, BTS, USA

Preeti Lokam, AI Skills Lead, Microsoft, USA

Sean Luitjens, General Manager, Visier, USA

Suku Mariappan, Workforce Analytics Leader, USA

Caitlin MacGregor, CEO & Co-founder, Plum, CANADA

Brigette McInnis-Day, CHRO & COO, Former UiPath, Google, SAP, USA

RJ Milnor, Chief Human Resources Officer, Valuetainment, LLC, USA

Amit Mohindra, Founder & CEO, People Analytics Success, USA

Peter Mulford, EVP & Chief Innovation Officer, BTS Inc., USA

Cole Napper, Principal Owner, Directionally Correct, USA

Ian O'Keefe, Founder & CEO, Ikona Analytics, USA

Kevin Oakes, CEO, Institute for Corporate Productivity (i4cp), USA

Kelly Palmer, Author, Advisor, Speaker, ITALY

Dan Parisi, Executive Vice President, BTS, USA

Peggy Parskey, Owner Parskey Consulting, Co-author of *Measurement Demystified, Measurement Demystified: Field Guide, and Learning Analytics*, USA

Mauricio Pena, Head of Sales & Marketing Practice, LATAM & Iberia, BTS, MEXICO

Andrea Pisani, Chief Financial Officer, USA

Rebecca Port, Chief People Officer, 10x Genomics, USA

Ben Putterman, Vice President, Learning and Talent Development, HubSpot, USA

Noah Rabinowitz, Chief Learning Officer, USA

Doug Randall, Partner, The Trium Group, USA

Huggy Rao, PhD, Atholl McBean Professor of Organizational Behavior, Graduate School of Business, Stanford University, USA

Andre Ribeiro, Senior Vice President, Partner and Head of Iberia, BTS, SPAIN

Tim Richmond, Chief Human Resources Officer, AbbVie, USA

Laura Rizzo, Employer Branding Expert, USA

Brandon Sammut, Chief People Officer, Zapier, USA

Maider Santos, Vice President, BTS, MEXICO

Steve Scott, Global Head, Workforce Management, People Insight & Analytics, Standard Chartered Bank, SINGAPORE

Fleur Segal, HR Practice Consultant, Spencer Stuart, USA

Jeremy Shapiro, AVP, Workforce Analytics, Merck & Co., USA

Laura Shubert, Vice President, People, Planning & Insights, USA

Jessica Skon, CEO, BTS Group, Inc., USA

Stan Slap, Chief Executive Officer, SLAP, USA

Keith Sonderling, Former Commissioner, United States Equal Employment Opportunity Commission, USA

Kady Srinivasan, Chief Marketing Officer, Lightspeed, CANADA

Craig Starbuck, Co-founder & CEO, OrgAcuity, USA

Dan Strauss, Client Partner & Practice Lead, KleinHersh, USA

Kelley Steven-Waiss, Chief Transformation Officer, ServiceNow, USA

Julia Stiglitz, CEO & Co-founder, UpLimit, USA

Sanchita Sur, CEO, Emplay, USA

Jack Tarlton, MBA Candidate, Class of 2026, Anderson School of Management, UCLA, USA

Annette Templeton, Partner, Trium Group, USA

Melanie Tinto, Chief People Officer, WEX, USA

Matt Tonken, Assessment Practice, BTS, USA

Dave Ulrich, Co-founder & Principal, The RBL Group, USA

Eric Van Iersel, Vice President, SuccessFactors, CANADA

Bennet Voorhees, People Data Science Leader, USA

Brad Warga, Global Managing Partner, Heidrick & Struggles, USA

Karie Willyerd, Chief Customer Strategy Officer, Learning Technologies Group, plc, USA

Anne Wilson, Strategy & Leadership Consultant, BTS, USA

Liz Wiseman, Author and CEO, The Wiseman Group, USA

Emma Woodthorpe, Chief People Officer, Brooks Automation, USA

Lydia Wu, VP of Products, MeBeBot, USA

Marta Zaragosa, Executive Vice President, BTS, SPAIN

About the Authors

JENNY DEARBORN IS the author of the business best-sellers *Data Driven: How Performance Analytics Delivers Extraordinary Sales Results* in 2015 and with David Swanson *The Data Driven Leader: A Powerful Approach to Deliver Measurable Business Impact Through People Analytics* in 2017. She is recognized as one of the 50 most powerful women in technology and is an industry thought leader and authority on applying data and analytics to workforce development and human capital transformation. She has been a C-level executive in Sales, Professional Services, and Human Resources at companies including Hewlett-Packard, Inc, Sun Microsystems/Oracle, Hewlett-Packard Enterprise, SumTotal Systems, SuccessFactors, Actionable Analytics Group, SAP, Klaviyo, and BTS.

Jenny earned an MBA from San Jose State University, M.Ed. from Stanford University, BA from University of California, Berkeley, and an AD from American River College. She is an investor, advisor, and board director.

Jenny lives with her family in Palo Alto, California, where she is a painter, beekeeper, and is learning to fly a helicopter. She can be reached at https://www.linkedin.com/in/jdearborn/.

KELLY RIDER is an accomplished Learning & Development professional with extensive experience shaping organizational learning strategies. Beginning her career in instructional design, Kelly advanced through the L&D functions in both Sales and Human Resources, ultimately spearheading initiatives to transform learning strategies into impactful experiences. She has worked at HP, SuccessFactors, SAP, PTC, and AAG. An active L&D thought leader, Kelly authors articles for leading industry publications and speaks at conferences.

As a consultant, Kelly partners with organizations to reimagine learning strategies, optimize technology investments, and elevate learning programs to meet the demands of a rapidly evolving workforce.

Kelly earned her M.Ed. in Information and Learning Technologies from the University of Colorado, Denver, and a BA in English from the University of Tennessee in Knoxville.

She lives with her sons in Lakewood, CO. Kelly used to play roller derby under the alias, Floora Goodtime. She can be reached at https://www.linkedin.com/in/kelly-rider/.

Index

257